Freedom, Justice and
Christian Counter-Culture

D0129997

Michael C. Elliott

FREEDOM, JUSTICE & CHRISTIAN COUNTER-CULTURE

SCM PRESS
London

TRINITY PRESS INTERNATIONAL
Philadelphia

First published 1990

SCM Press
26–30 Tottenham Road
London N1 4BZ

Trinity Press International
3725 Chestnut Street
Philadelphia Pa. 19104

British Library Cataloguing in Publication Data

Elliott, Michael C.
    Freedom, justice and Christian counter-culture.
    1. Justice – Christian viewpoints
    I. Title
    261.7
    ISBN 334–02452–8

Library of Congress Cataloging in Publication Data

Elliott, Michael C.
    Freedom, justice, and Christian counter-culture/Michael C.
    Elliott.
        p.   cm.
    Includes bibliographical references.
    ISBN 0–334–02452–8
    1. Christianity and culture.   2. Christianity and justice.
    3. Christianity and politics.   4. Christianity–20th century.
    5. Elliott, Michael C.   I. Title.
    BR115.C8E44   1990
    261–dc20   90–33252

Photoset at The Spartan Press Ltd, Lymington, Hants
and printed in Great Britain by
Richard Clay Ltd, Bungay, Suffolk

If Caesar is Right, Christ is Wrong both in Politics and Religion.

William Blake

The real question is whether the 'brighter future' is really always so distant. What if, on the contrary, it has been here for a long time already, and only our own blindness and weakness has prevented us from seeing it around us and within us, and kept us from developing it?

Vaclav Havel

CONTENTS

INTRODUCTION

They tell me that theology is autobiography. I can't argue with that. There was no way that I could have foreseen, growing up in a quiet, conservative, provincial New Zealand town, that I would one day be negotiating funding for a Black Marxist bookshop in Brixton, become caught up in a war in the Middle-East, have my telephone tapped in the course of an indigenous land rights struggle, be thrown out of a right-wing political meeting in a Baptist Church while giving a Christian testimony, or awarded an Oscar for Imbecility by a white South African newspaper. Yet these are but some of the unexpected consequences which have flowed from my decision to become an Anglican priest.

In the late 1950s when I was in the midst of my theological training, the world was undergoing one of those profound changes which can only be appreciated with hindsight. The era of old soldiers, the war heroes who had governed our lives, was passing. In America, Jack Kerouac's road novels were chronicling the lives of those trying to break free from the militaristic, consumerist, conformist and competitive values of the past. They called themselves the Beat Generation. James Dean's films, riddled with teenaged angst and androgynous sexuality, fomented rebellion against patriarchal authority and conventional values. Bob Dylan's plaintive folk songs warned us that the old way was changing so rapidly that we had better get with it before it was too late. Jack Kennedy was elected President. There was a feeling of springtime abroad and people were saying that the Christian faith would have to adapt to these daring visions of a new world, or be forever left on the sidelines.

In many ways we were babes in the woods. We were completely oblivious to the way in which the media and the political machinery had combined to create an image of Kennedy for popular consumption which was little more than an illusion. We pereceived him as young, as a peace-bringer, as the harbinger of a new set of values for our tired world. It would be twenty years before we discovered the extent to which we had been deceived and the manner in which the President had in his personal life betrayed most of the principles he espoused, forfeiting any claim to moral leadership. It was rather summed up for me recently when I saw JFK's photograph on an advertising hoarding for a certain permanent exhibition of world records in London. 'JFK fast talked his way in. You can just walk in.'

Nevertheless Kennedy did act as a catalyst, engineering the space in which new ideas could be examined and our generation inherited something of the optimism, the vision of freedom and the promise of new possibilities for humanity which his dream encouraged. To a great many of us, America was where it was all at. We felt ourselves called on a pilgrimage to the shrine of the new liberalism. For those who lived on the far side of the world, getting there became an adventure in itself. In a complete reversal of today's economics, then only the rich could afford to fly, while the poor travelled by ship! Transported beyond the borders of our South Pacific paradise, we saw for the first time the world as it really is. My awakening began the morning when, in an Asian port of call, I had to step over the bodies of those who had died of starvation in the streets overnight. It is no exaggeration to say that from that moment on, my life would be forever changed.

America was bristling with theological energy. Tillich was still teaching at Chicago. The Death of God school ruled the roost. In the postgraduate theological studies I pursued in Boston, I had rare mentors. Harvey Cox introduced us to the creative possibilities of the secular city; Joseph Fletcher to the dynamic of situation ethics; Harvey Guthrie to studies in the prophets; John Coburn to the search for a spirituality which would sustain us in action. And action there was aplenty. Breakfast meetings with the Berrigan brothers to discuss strategies for opposing the war in Viet Nam. Protest marches from Cambridge Common to Boston Common. The burning of draft cards in Arlington Street Church. The enrolling of American Black communities on to voting lists in the Southern States, an enterprise which tragically claimed the life of one student in our seminary. A People's March on Washington. My theological programme regarded involvement in these activities as integral to the curriculum.

The Viet Nam war in fact provided the crucible and training ground for a whole generation of Christian activists, not just in the

United States, but throughout Western democracies. In listening to the testimonies of people involved today in many different kinds of social activism, I've frequently heard it said that their first action was to participate in a demonstration against the Viet Nam War in Los Angeles or London, Paris or Perth, Auckland or Amsterdam. It was as if Christians who had failed to act with sufficient conviction to stop people dying in their thousands in the gas chambers of Europe were doubly determined to prevent a napalm holocaust in Asia.

From the street marches of Boston I made my way to the heady atmosphere of 'South Bank Theology' in riverside London where Bishop John Robinson was being honest to God and Canon Douglas Rhymes promulgating a new morality. John Robinson invited me to test whether the Saul Alinsky inspired community organization techniques being used effectively by some churches in the United States could be translated into new forms of inner city ministry in South London. He placed me in one of the most run-down areas of his oversight, one which was embarking upon a programme of urban renewal. This called for wholesale demolition of the old and the construction of vast housing blocks designed to free people from their past, but which today are experienced as even more of a prison than those they replaced. These were nonstop days: establishing local community work projects; working on a new system of parish organization for the Diocesan Pastoral Committee; learning from models like the French worker-priests and the Taizé Community; participating in John's christology forum held, in fine weather, in his back garden.

I had already learnt in my early parish experience in New Zealand that the fact that one could fill a church building with people was no reliable indicator of a response to the gospel. In South London the church had become so marginal to people's lives that many were questioning the point of it remaining there. This was particularly apposite when one considered the failure of traditional methods of mission and evangelism. Those of us from middle-class backgrounds, for all our good intentions and contemporary theology, found it impossible in terms of preaching and liturgy, to make the gospel relevant to a community characterized by the apparent contradictions of debilitating apathy and intense violence. As one priest colleague humorously put it, 'I spent years learning Greek and Hebrew, only to discover that people in

Camberwell spoke neither language.' If the community didn't profit from the experience, we professional clergy certainly did in the sense of learning hard lessons. It was here that I began to understand from the witness of the poor, the way that in a capitalist economy resources are distributed on the basis of class, and the way that the structures of society violate people's lives. I had taken the first step in a process of analysis.

My next appointment was to be in the Middle East, working with the Church Missionary Society and the local church to establish social service and development projects in a tradition which had very little experience of these. The Evangelical Episcopal Church of the Middle East, as the Anglican Church is known there, was in those days (though thankfully not so today) little more than a tiny outpost of English culture and tradition, whose members looked back to the golden days of the British Mandate. Its Archbishop had warned us of the partisan nature of life in Palestine, advising us that we could be 'pro' anyone we liked but that we must avoid at all costs being perceived as 'anti' anybody. So in the course of establishing community development programmes amongst some of the most oppressed people in the world, we tried to walk the narrow line of personal neutrality. It was when war broke out in 1973 that the truth was brought home to us as Arab groups with whom we had worked declared that, as we had stood alongside them in various community struggles, so they knew we stood with them in the armed struggle. In the course of our work we had made many decisions, most of them unconsciously, which had in fact located us firmly on one side. Again, we learnt the hard way that in struggles for justice the church cannot be neutral. Or as Paulo Freire put it: to wash one's hands of the struggle between the powerful and the oppressed is not to remain neutral but to side with the oppressor.

There followed a return to England to work in the field of race relations for the British Council of Churches. My task as Development Officer was to travel the country evaluating multi-racial projects and programmes which had applied for funding. We saw ourselves responding to the sufferings of the Third World in the midst of the affluence of the First World. We seldom used the word 'racism'. Its overtones were considered too negative for an era which believed that establishing a consensus between races would lead towards integration. But it was in the course of this work, and again learning from people suffering the most vicious kinds of discrimination, that I came to understand that racism is not primarily a question of personal prejudice, but a question of power, and is a deeply entrenched oppression in all of our society's institutions, including the church.

I subsequently spent twelve years back in New Zealand, working ecumenically in what was in its genesis called 'development education', but which is perhaps better described as 'training for transformation'. This involved campaigning in support of groups on a wide range of issues: unemployment, the national development plan, the ordination of women, homelessness, racism, land rights, poverty, and the Christian Right's attempts to hinder the passage of homosexual law reform and the United Nations' Convention on Women, to name but a few. I quickly learnt that its liberating gospel notwithstanding, the church is almost universally perceived as an integral part of the structure of oppression by the victims of our society. Resourcing groups committed to justice and liberation meant having to break the gospel out of its colonial shackles so that its radicalizing message could be heard afresh. It meant developing an analysis of global and local society which reflected biblical principles. It meant having to work at strategies which were consistent with the ethics of the Kingdom of God. It meant helping people develop a spirituality which, rather than cosset them in a private and anonymous world, urged them to publicly proclaim their pain in a creative act.

These experiences, and the fundamental lessons I had learnt in each of them, had all contributed to my analysis of society. By this time I was employing those elements of Marxian analysis without which it is impossible to develop an adequate critique of capitalism. I was consequently excited by the opportunity in 1979 to visit Cuba, to view first hand a Latin American Marxist state, and to learn of the role of the churches in post-revolutionary reconstruction. I remain to this day deeply impressed with the achievements of the Cuban revolution and the vision for humanity which it fosters. But I found myself, to the exasperation of some Marxist ideologues, having almost as many questions to ask about the structures through which the revolution is institutionalized as I had to pose to the oppressive structures of capitalism. One of them declared: 'You want to question every structure. You are an anarchist and as such, an obstacle to the Marxist–Leninist revolution.' Despite my negative initial response to this description of myself, I felt that it was incumbent upon me to explore what he meant.

This book tries to share something of those learnings and that exploration. A few years ago an invitation came to write a small 'handbook for Christian activists': something which would indicate the issues which needed to be addressed and the strategies which might be tested in relation to them. Very early on in the task I became aware that the strategies didn't make sense unless the analysis of society underlying them was spelt out, and that for Christians, the relationship of that analysis to biblical insights had to be established. It seemed to me that a great deal of foundation work was required before a simple handbook could be attempted.

Those foundations developed as I worked with a group of student activists in a provincial university town. At a time when many conservative Christian groups were organizing *against* issues, they simply referred to themselves as Christians *for* Jesus. Unusually from the context of my work, almost all came from charismatic or pentecostal backgrounds associated with conservative rather than radical attitudes. Yet in the life-style they lived, the actions they initiated and the projects they supported they demonstrated that, if through the intervention of the Spirit one's life has been radically changed, if one genuinely attempts to live out the radical demands of the gospel, one is called to right wrongs as an integral part of Christian mission and witness. I learnt from them something of the anarchic nature of the Holy Spirit which breaks through all that would constrain humanity. This book is a testimony to the ideas we discussed in the formal setting of the lecture room, over meals in their various community houses, at national gatherings for workers for justice, but above all in our planning of, and reflection upon particular pieces of social action. They urged that this book be titled *Christianarchy*.

The work lays no claims to being either exhaustive or original. It delves into those issues which either I have had to face personally or which were raised by activists in the course of their work. It draws heavily upon, and freely acknowledges, the studies of a great many other people. Because it relates to my own experience in an 'activist' ministry, it employs examples drawn primarily from settings with which I have a degree of familiarity: New Zealand, Great Britain, the United States, Palestine and Cuba.

This book was completed as the Berlin Wall was being dismantled and popular revolutions taking place in Hungary, Czechoslovakia, Romania, Bulgaria and other Eastern European countries, and as pressure for democratization and national independence increased in the Soviet Union. Some have rushed to hail these developments as the final triumph of capitalism over communism. That is not only a typical Western propagandist judgment; it ignores what the architects of these revolutions have declared to be their objectives. For example, Vaclav Havel, once a dissident playwright and guiding spirit behind Charter 77, now interim President of Czechoslovakia, has made it clear in all his political writing that he is not interested in reproducing the failings of the West. He regards those living in Western democracies as just as manipulated as people in totalitarian regimes, albeit in more subtle and refined and less brutal ways. They also stand in need of a liberating revolution.

These events, rather than vindicating capitalism, point to the need for a new way of politics, rooted in the human condition. Economists, social scientists and theologians alike, critical of the failures of both socialist and capitalist modes of development, have long urged consideration of 'a third way'. The problem with Third Way thinking in the past is that in Latin America it has manifested itself as capitalism under another guise, and in the West as socialism wearing a new mantle. This book tries to carry that debate further, not only by offering critiques of the two dominant models, but by suggesting a different and until now largely unconsidered path which a growing number of Christians feel to be entirely consistent with biblical witness and truth.

Those like myself who are advantaged by the present social and economic arrangements are generally protected from the realities of poverty and oppression. After years of writing learned articles on unemployment, and campaigning alongside unions of the unemployed, I unexpectedly found myself in the dole queue. The Camden Office (Initials A to G) of the Department of Employment confessed bewilderment. 'Surely the church looks after its clergy?', the clerk said. I quickly disabused him of that idea, replying that I was as much an embarrassment to the church as I was to his Department. A bishop in whom I confided my predicament responded with laughter saying: 'That's what Christian vocation means: it doesn't ultimately matter whether we're employed or unemployed.' It certainly didn't matter to him as he motored back to his palace. With hindsight, I'm now grateful for the experience as it enabled me, for one of the rare occasions in my life, to view systems from the perspective of their victims. And even more grateful to the City of London Polytechnic who rescued me from unemployment and encouraged me to complete this piece of writing.

While expressing gratitude, I'd particularly like to thank Father Filip Fanchette who, while working with the Ecumenical Institute for the Development of Peoples (INODEP) shared a method of social analysis with groups in the Pacific. That process was like a long missing piece of a jigsaw puzzle for me. When discovered, it made sense of an otherwise bewildering picture.

I am not, however, thanking 'my' secretary, 'my' typist or 'my' research assistant, as many authors do on these occasions. The dominant consciousness lulls us into the belief that it is part of the natural order to have people undertake the more dull and boring tasks for one. As this book is an attack upon everything which that consciousness represents, and furthermore argues that we have to embody the kind of society we are working for, it would have been a betrayal of my vision to have accepted such a model of working. I therefore have only my wordprocessor to thank, and there is only myself to accept the blame!

Readers will have to cope with some sexist language in this book. I try to employ inclusive language, but where I have used direct quotations I have not attempted to alter the male dominated language which is a feature of most theological writing and nearly all church documents. Perhaps the negative reaction of readers will serve to underscore the point that we are only very slowly moving on from a past which shackles us to discriminatory and oppressive modes of expression.

If this work were to have a special dedication, it would have to be to the particular expressions of Christian community in which I have, with others, tried to embody the vision and which have sustained me in my struggles. The Pembroke community in South London, where we tried to combine Bonhoeffer's suggestion of a religious community of radically secular people, Cardinal Suhard's notion of Christians creating a mystery in the world, and St Francis's sense of identification with the dispossessed, provided the ground in which many ideas were to germinate. I still remember the excitement generated by those who dared to be different and who risked much in the testing of those principles.

Then there was the team alongside whom I worked at St Luke's Centre in Haifa. In that most unjust of situations, which sadly seems to have advanced no further towards resolution today than it was twenty years ago, we shared hopes and friendships. To the team: Ray, Alice, Malone, Rusty, and Marc; and to Cedar, Khalil and Omar who sustained us, this book is offered at the time of the *intifada*, as a dream of what may yet be.

Finally, for the last twelve years I've been a member of a small community which draws its inspiration from the nature of the extended family: friends wrestling with ideas of justice, peace and liberation, and trying to embody them both in our personal relationships and in our relationship to the world. So my heartfelt thanks for their nurture, support, solidarity, understanding and frequent challenging go to Freda and Ron, to Madame Glenise, and especially to Mark, whose determination to make me live what I believe acknowledges no limits.

CHAPTER ONE

Looking Through Scripture
Gospel and Ideology

Jesus promised that being a Christian would be neither comfortable nor easy. He warned that his followers would very quickly
find themselves up against the principalities and powers of the day,
accused of promoting views which would be considered destructive of the good order and sound values of society. What was true
for those first followers, remains generally true today. Christians
who have developed a critique of contemporary society and who
commit themselves to working for fundamental social change find
themselves out of tune with these conservative times. They are
charged with a great many things: stirring up trouble for trouble's
sake; acting as naive agents of foreign ideologies; and biting the
hand that feeds them, to mention but three.

When these Christians seek to explain their activities by
reference to the Bible they are charged with abusing scripture. It is
said that they manipulate scripture to their own advantage; or that
they conveniently overlook those elements which contradict their
position. And naturally, they always read scripture through
ideologically tinted spectacles!

That such allegations invariably come from those whose own
use of scripture is suspect in the first place; from biblical
fundamentalists and literalists who brook no interpretation other
than their own; and from that vast array of text droppers who can
match each of life's situations with a scriptural gem, should
immediately arouse suspicion.

The truth of the matter is that Christians generally read out of
scripture what they bring into it. They often talk about 'New
Testament principles' as if these were a commonly agreed set of
guidelines upon which all Christians base their activity, and which

point in a common direction. But this is clearly not the case. For capitalists claim to construct their morality upon New Testament principles; communists claim them as their basis for the new society; militarists weave them into the doctrine of national security; and pacifists establish their case upon them.

The editor of a major New Zealand Christian newspaper commenting on the radio about the passage in Luke's Gospel where Jesus is accused by some of casting out evil through the power of Beelzebub, the prince of demons, applied the passage as a justification for nuclear deterrence. If we examine the passage closely, we can see that Jesus was employing that confrontation to suggest that this manifestation of power over evil is a sign that the Kingdom is already here. He calls on an illustration which in all probability refers to a contemporary event which would be well known to his hearers: 'When a strong man fully armed guards his own palace, his goods are undisturbed; but when someone stronger than he is attacks and defeats him, the stronger man takes away all the weapons he relied on and shares out his spoil' (11.21f.).

The broadcaster maintained that Jesus was teaching the population the importance of a strong and secure defence against outside aggression. He developed this theme further by arguing that the most effective defence is nuclear deterrence, and that being the case, Christians should fall in behind President Reagan's defence objectives for the Free World. So a real life event which Jesus employed to talk about the presence of the Kingdom, a latter day commentator interprets as a piece of Gospel advice for the nuclear age!

The speaker in this case was approaching scripture already ideologically committed to the politics of Reaganomics and nuclear deterrence. With this perspective in mind, it is not too difficult to determine from scripture that Jesus supports militarism. This same process enables capitalists to take heart from the Parable of the Talents, and socialists to exhort us to sell all that we have and give to the poor.

It is argued in some quarters that we should not tax ourselves too greatly with this issue, for the gospel has always demanded an ideological framework in order to mediate its principles. The word 'ideology' itself poses difficulties to begin with. The powerful in society use the word in a negative sense to suggest that any theory which contradicts their understanding of reality is 'revolutionary': the victims of oppression employ the term to describe the process by which the powerful mystify reality. And in between are people who think of ideology simply as that framework of values and perceptions which enable a person to give meaning to the world.

The World Council of Churches' working definition of ideology is: 'a system of thought or blueprint used to interpret society and man's (sic) place in society, the function of which is either to legitimate the existing structures of society or to change them'.[1] On this basis, the World Council acknowledges the ideological character of many of its own statements, but adds the important rider that all ideologies need to be held up to a critique of the gospel. It also draws attention to the way in which Christians, working for human solidarity within particular social contexts, and sharing the hopes and tensions of those to whom they are committed, become subject to the dominant political forces of a society, and always run the risk of being 'ideologized'.

Whatever we understand by ideology, and whether or not we believe that the gospel was written from an ideological standpoint, we would be hard pressed to avoid the conclusion that the gospel is invariably interpreted ideologically. So let us begin by looking at how this is happening today.

Reading the gospel in a socialist context

My first experience of a socialist reading of scripture came in the course of a visit to Cuba to learn something of the churches' contribution to post-revolutionary reconstruction there. In sermons, liturgies and statements of faith, as well as in personal conversations, the Cuban Christians I met appeared to express the gospel entirely within Marxist constructs which sounded very strange to my untutored ears. For them, the revolution had become, along with the exodus and the incarnation, one of the central tenets of salvation history. Every event, structure and process was referred to either as being part of the dark age 'before the Revolution', in which the church had been co-opted as an instrument of popular repression; or as an element of the new order 'after the triumph of the Revolution', which is seen as a moment of liberation, purifying all society's institutions including the church, so releasing it to fulfil its true vocation.

There is no contesting the fact that in pre-revolutionary Cuba the churches were firmly aligned with the oppressive ruling establishment. The Roman Catholic Archbishop of Havana, I was told, would bless the dictator Batista's troops before they went about their brutal and destructive business. The churches also served as one of the major instruments of American ideology and as a consequence, played an important role in furthering American imperialism. Many Cuban Protestants can give testimony to the way in which they had been taught by their churches in pre-revolutionary days to honour and promote The American Way.

Dominating the old harbour of Havana is a magnificent white statue of Christ, his hands outstretched in blessing. I was interested to know why the Revolution was maintaining it in perfect condition and wondered whether it might not reflect a deep-seated respect for Christian values on the part of the Marxist–Leninist government. A government official explained that the statue had been a gift to the nation from the Batista family, built with the profits of the greed and exploitation of that regime, at the expense of its peasant population. 'We keep it', she said, 'to remind us of what the Revolution has delivered us from.' This Christ stands as a permanent statement to the nation not of liberation, justice and peace, but of repression and death.

In Cuba as elsewhere, the manipulation of scripture by the colonial church became a critical factor in its alienation from the people. In the course of a visit to an inland sugar plantation, once in multi-national ownership but now run as a co-operative, I noticed that the village church was preserved in immaculate condition, with neat flower beds and manicured lawns. It prompted me to ask whether the church still had an important role to play in that community.

My question was answered by a woman, one of the oldest people in the village. 'When we went to church,' she told me, 'we were living in misery. We had houses only if we were working for the sugar company. There was no school, no doctor, no hope for our children. The parish priest would read the Bible to us, and tell us not to worry about our poverty and misery, because God was storing up rewards for us in heaven. And then', she said pointing to a dusty road which ran straight up to the mountains, 'one day Fidel came down that road, and he gave us all this.' She gestured around her, pointing to the modern homes, the medical clinic, the school, healthy children playing in the shade. 'What need do we have of the church?' It was a powerful testimony from a woman who had endured fifty years of Christian exhortation to be content with her lot but who, in the twilight of her days, is experiencing what must seem to her very much like the Kingdom of God on earth!

There are obviously as many pressures on the Cuban churches to recognize and support the new order as there are pressures on the churches in the West to support their particular governments. But that process in Cuba has been facilitated by the emphasis within revolutionary thought on a new, liberated humanity, a concept which closely parallels elements of Christian theology. It is therefore not surprising to find other traditional areas of Christian doctrine being re-shaped within that context of a Marxist–Leninist Revolution.[2]

The Confession of Faith of the Presbyterian Reformed Church in Cuba treats the traditional doctrines of creation, sin, salvation, atonement, crucifixion, resurrection, death and judgment in precisely this way. It may sometimes run the risk of confusing the achievements of the Revolution with the Kingdom of God, but in the process provides us with a powerful critique of what happens to both scripture and gospel when they are delivered within a capitalist ideological framework. Take these passages for example:

> The 'creation' of a 'new man' means the establishment of a new community life in the new society, where there is no place for the exploitation of the work of another, nor for racial discrimination, nor the subjection of women as objects of mercantile, commercial or sexual consumption; nor will there be tolerance for the self-interested use of the legitimate values of family life in benefit of the false interests of the classist and discriminatory society.

> The Church teaches that, when our people chose the Marxist–Leninist way of development through a social-political revolution, a more human relationship with Nature has been brought about as well as a primary concern for the health of the people. The Marxist–Leninist revolution has proved to be the only way which makes the technological and ecological development possible and which successfully puts an end to underdevelopment. This phenomenon of underdevelopment has pro-

duced infra-human beings, victims of exploitation and oppression with the World Capitalist and Imperialistic System.

The Church joyfully lives in the midst of the Socialist Revolution since the Revolution has concretely and historically inaugurated a series of values in human relations that makes it possible for the whole modern technical-scientific development to be at the service of the full dignity of the human being.

The Church teaches that the 'atheism' of the ideology sustained by the Socialist Revolution, makes more clearly evident the atheism of the 'believers' who are not capable of 'discerning' 'the signs of the times' in the midst of the new society being constructed, in which the radical transformations of the unjust structures make possible the creation of a more integrally reconstructed human being. The most important thing, in this case, is that the atheist-communists serve as an inspiration to us because of their readiness and willingness to live sacrificial, solidary and effective love.[3]

One finds it hard to imagine any church in the West producing a statement which addresses as integral to faith the core issues of contemporary society: economics, work, sexism, racism, the family, technology and human development. This Presbyterian Church, historically emphasizing reliance on scripture rather than tradition as a basis for doctrine, prefixes almost every section of its document with the words 'the Bible teaches'. There can be no doubting that for this Christian community the scriptures are the 'norm of its faith, the paradigm for its action'. Biblical principles are identified, then elaborated in terms of the concrete realities of people's lives. So 'sin', 'death' and 'resurrection' are treated not as theories which are manipulated in order to give 'spiritual' significance to life, but as manifestations of the social, cultural, economic and political processes through which the Revolution discards the corrupt structures of the old life and creates both a new social reality and a new person restored in God's image.

There can be no question, in this case, of the Christian's commitment to socio-political and economic action. Rather, this Christian community regards as a heresy, contrary to scriptural truth, that 'aberration' of faith which refers to itself as 'apolitical'. Participation in the economic, political or social life of the nation is not something the Christian 'can choose to add or not to add to his condition of believer . . . but is an integral and inseparable part of the loving practice of the Christian faith'.[4]

I am amongst those who have been deeply impressed by the immense achievements of the Cuban Revolution in terms of its provision of basic needs – housing, food, education, health, employment; in terms of the building of structures which enable people to take control of their lives and participate more fully in political and economic decision-making; and in terms of the emphasis it places on people rediscovering their culture and re-establishing their cultural values. No other Third World country that I have visited has achieved this level of development, which mirrors in so many of its aspects the principles to which I'm committed as a Christian. That is not to suggest that the socialist option of development has no difficulties or contradictions, or is beyond criticism, as we shall see, but it certainly offers a model with a clear vision for society which energizes people for change.

Reading the gospel in a capitalist society

Although I was not particularly conscious of it at the time, what the Cuban experience encouraged in me was a capacity to listen more carefully to the way the gospel is being communicated, and to become more aware of the ideological elements in its proclamation. Having been jolted out of my complacency by those who read scripture from a Marxist–Leninist perspective, I returned to the West to become equally conscious of the ideological captivity of scripture within my own traditions.

As we might expect, a good deal of this ideologized gospel emanates from the guardian of the free world, the United States of America. It is probably most easily identified amongst the countless televangelists whose programmes bombard the American television screen. But it is also present amongst the more mainstream evangelists, people like Billy Graham, who are regarded as a safe bet by the churches. Kenneth Leech[5] has noted the way that Graham, far from being an apolitical preacher, has always faithfully reflected the major shifts within American society, moving from a vigorously anti-communist stance to affirming communist regimes; from acceptance of nuclear deterrence to a critique of nuclear warfare. In all cases this has happened when it became ideologically fashionable and safe for him to do so.

Graham's Christianity, Leech argues, is tailored to the values of American capitalism and individualism. Jesus is seen in personal and individualistic terms as coming to redeem 'my life' rather than to transform both the dominant culture and my life.

The popular evangelist Luis Palau conducts evangelistic campaigns all over the world. He is another evangelist to have won wide acceptance in the churches, not that church leaders accept his views, but because they believe that evangelism is a good thing. In New Zealand his campaign was supported by a coalition of the major churches including the Roman Catholic Church whose members Palau is bent on proselytizing. In Britain, the Anglican Archbishop of Wales declared Palau's message to be 'marvellous news for Wales' at the conclusion of his 1989 'Tell Wales' campaign. Palau preaches an individualistic gospel, divorced from both issues of justice and critical dimensions of faith. In his record of involvements with political organizations and governments, he forfeits any claim to being 'non political'. He was one of the founding supporters of the Latin American Evangelical Fraternity (CONELA) in 1982, which was established in direct opposition to the Latin American Council of Churches, the World Council of Churches and the Roman Catholic Church, all of which have made strong stands for human rights, justice and peace in a continent largely ruled by oppressive military regimes. The leadership of those mainline churches who support Palau's evangelistic crusades seem oblivious to the fact that, in their enthusiasm, they lend credence to a person who actually rejects the fundamental doctrinal positions their churches espouse.

Palau also provides us with a good example of the way that a communicator of the gospel, however unwittingly, may become the ideological agent of American capitalism and its economic and foreign policy objectives. Bolivia is a country with a history of destabilizing military coups. Following one of these coups, Palau was chosen as the evangelist to play a primary role in a programme known as the 'moralization of Bolivia'. He was awarded a week of prime-time exposure on national television for this purpose. The evangelist thus became one element in a strategy for maintaining the new regime in power and extending its control over the people. In particular he helped undermine the influence of the Roman Catholic Church's theology of liberation which was speaking out in terms of justice for the poor.

In this process the political and economic interests of the United States were enhanced. Despite its poverty, Bolivia is one of the three producers of tin in the world, and a major exporter of cocaine. The United States had an interest in seizing control of the tin industry and in reducing the trade in cocaine. The programme of moralization helped make people more sympathetic to United States ideas and objectives. Given this United States' propensity for exploiting evangelistic campaigns for ideological purposes, it seemed no accident that, following the New Zealand government's decision not to participate any longer in the nuclear dimensions of the ANZUS alliance, Luis Palau should appear on the scene. Defence Secretary Caspar Weinburger had declared that if the United States could not convince the New Zealand government of the error of its ways, America would have to 'go over the top of government and direct to the New Zealand people'. In so far as the 'non political' Palau's addresses espouse the importance of competition, the ability of people to make it to the top, the legitimacy of profit making, the preservation of the democratic way of life and the necessity of nuclear deterrence, he was the ideal vehicle for appealing directly to the New Zealand public.

The capitalist ideology is packaged in a less aggressive way for home consumption by televangelists like Dr Robert Schuller whose 'Hour of Power' is beamed around the world from his Crystal Cathedral in Anaheim. This organization claims, I'm sure correctly, that millions of people see the weekly broadcast. This now includes people in Britain as Rupert Murdoch's Sky Channel selected the Schuller organization as the most appropriate form of American televangelism for the British viewer. Schuller's sermons focus on the values of individual self-esteem, hard work and financial reward. An integral part of his ministry outreach is a training programme to enable people to become successful salespersons for socially acceptable products. His sermons are generally success stories about individuals who made it from the bottom of the heap to the top. He quotes models like Walt Disney, who was apparently so poor at twenty-one that he had to eat cold beans out of a can but who pulled himself together and went on to create Disneyland, which brought pleasure to millions and millions to his pocket. Then again, there was the young impoverished Korean pastor who so marvelled at Dr Schuller's thirteen- storeyed tower, that he went home to Korea and built a fourteen-storeyed one! Anyone can succeed in this capitalist paradise.

> You have the freedom today to set any goal you want to set. That's right. You have the freedom to pick any dream you want to pick. I know people who are considered by many to be great, but I've learned one thing: There are no great people. There are only ordinary people, who have made bigger decisions and picked bigger dreams. When you choose your dream, you choose your future. And if you're unemployed today, you're lucky. I mean, you're absolutely free to start something new. That's right. It takes guts to leave the ruts, and chances are you would never have had the courage to quit and start something new. The me I see is the me I'll be.[6]

In contrast to the Marxist–Leninist interpretation of scripture, which appears so blatantly political, the capitalist interpretation often appears in the guise of folksy common sense! These same capitalist values in a more sophisticated form have so permeated the institutions of society, including the church, that they appear to be part of the way things are. Those who want to question them identify themselves as 'leftists', opposed to the natural order of society. So far have these values been absorbed into the Western church's theory and practice, that they rarely need to be publicly defended. Indeed, the less they need to be debated and defended, the more they can be regarded as the norm. It is really only at moments of crisis when, for example, a counter-ideology appears to be gathering momentum, that defence of capitalist values on the basis of Christian teaching becomes a rather unfortunate necessity.

One person who readily leaps to the defence of capitalism is Edward Norman, formerly Dean of Peterhouse and Lecturer in History at Cambridge University. In his 1978 BBC Reith Lectures,[7] he attacked what he regards as the politicization of religion in general, and the work of the World Council of Churches in particular. He argues that the derivation of Christian political and social ideas from society's values was legitimate when those values were distinctively Christian. But it is not so today when those values have become distinctly secular. Christians need to wake up to the *relative* nature of human values before the

Christian faith is absorbed by a single historical interpretation, which he obviously feels is Marxism!

Norman says that although we can discern in scripture God and humanity interacting in concrete historical situations, God is always depicted as being separated from human values. His actions are predominantly those of delivering judgment upon and offering forgiveness to those who confuse the changing values of society with his eternally established principles. Christianity ought not therefore to be associated with *any* set of political values.

His argument implies that we are about to be offered a detached view of Christian political and social action, based only on a traditional understanding of the gospel, and certainly free from the kind of secular values which socialists and Marxists employ to subvert the historic gospel.

In some of his other writing, however, Norman reveals considerably more about his own value-base. In a lecture commissioned by the United Kingdom's Standing Conference of Employers of Graduates,[8] he offers a classic defence of capitalism. He regards the advance of collectivist principles in Britain as having eroded the workers' ability to produce, and having painted capitalism as a friend of élites but an enemy of society.

Norman contends that those who blame the proliferation of social ills upon capitalism generally make the error of assuming that a particular example of social injustice is so widespread as to be universal. He considers the claim that capitalism exploits people unsubstantiated and asserts that the idea that the Victorian slums exploited downtrodden workers is exaggerated. In view of the squalor of rural communities, cities offered people liberation and improved the wealth and health of the whole community. Similarly, the capitalism of wealthy Western nations should not be depicted as exploiting developing nations. The West is not to be blamed if Third World countries have thus far been unable to make their economies productive enough to satisfy their aspirations.

One hundred and fifty years ago, the author says, capitalism was being vigorously promoted on the basis of its moral qualities. Subsequent critiques have attacked and discredited that moral basis, to the extent that many of the values now need to be rehabilitated.

What are these values? Firstly, capitalism gives people freedom of choice. It enables individuals to choose how they will participate in the economy, to have control over their labour, and to maintain a livelihood independently of the provisions of the state. Secondly, the competition which capitalism fosters is character forming; encouraging people to accept responsibility for their actions; and instils a sense of moral duty in them. Thirdly, capitalism is realistic about human nature, recognizing that people do not by nature act in the interests of other human beings. Capitalism modifies the destructive consequences of self-interest by directing human energy into the creation of wealth which benefits the entire community. In this regard, the sanctions of religion are along with the prospect of self-improvement and the coercion of economic subsistence, important elements of control.

The moral collectivism of socialism in general and Marxism in particular is thus seen as destructive both of essential human values and the natural social order. All societies, proclaims Norman, are run by élites and the guarantee of personal freedom in a society run by a small group of capitalists is infinitely preferable to the 'legal compulsion of moral order' characteristic of 'totalitarian collectivisms and social democracies' which fail because they have an over-optimistic view of human nature which lacks capitalism's realism.

Very few references are made to scripture to substantiate the supposed moral base of capitalism. The only major reference in the lecture is to the Christian understanding of 'original sin' which he interprets as evidence that human nature is intrinsically evil and self-seeking. Whereas the Cuban Presbyterians were concerned to establish a compatibility between political commitment and biblical concepts, capitalists strive for a separation of faith from politics. In their view, faith transports the believer into a spiritual and eternal dimension in which individual morality and conscience is developed. The individual can subsequently bring that personal morality to bear upon the world of politics whose concepts are not derived directly from scripture, but from the philosophical deliberations of wise men. The deliberations of wise women have traditionally counted for very little in this scheme of things!

The capitalist reading of the gospel is frequently presented in the guise of common sense, with any alternative reading of scripture, because of the threat it poses to the established order, being dismissed as barefaced propaganda. A good example of this is a book by Professor Brian Griffiths, which claims to be concerned with Christian alternatives to capitalism and socialism.[9] Professor Griffiths is a Director of the Bank of England and Head of the Prime Minister's Policy Unit at No. 10 Downing Street! Writing from an evangelical perspective, he is critical of people who talk of a social gospel or liberation theology. He is unhappy with the latter because, he charges, liberation theology accepts uncritically an economic and political ideology which is Marxist, and then proceeds to interpret holy scripture from within that framework.

By way of contrast, Griffiths presents his approach to scripture as being free of ideological permeation. His social ethics are those which scripture reveals in creation order and which have been codified in the Old Testament Law. From this basis he argues that the Bible indicates that wealth creation is legitimate, that private ownership of property is a necessity, that the norm of ownership is the ability of each family to retain a stake in the economy, that Christians must be concerned with the relief of poverty rather than the pursuit of equality, that there is a mandate for government to remedy injustice, that materialism carries great dangers, and that accountability and judgment are important elements in human life. Like other dominant ideology commentators, his obsession with the Marxist mote in other people's eyes blinds him to the reality of the Thatcherite timber in his own. It does not occur to him to ask the same searching questions of his own framework of interpretation that he demands of liberation theologians. If he were to closely examine the tools he employs to examine scripture and to acknowledge the market economy mindset through which he instinctively interprets reality, he might perceive that he is not being 'neutral' at all but, like those he criticizes, viewing scripture from within an ideological framework.

His advocacy for capitalism on the one hand, and denigration of Marxism on the other, confronts the reader at every turn and at points becomes overt propaganda. To illustrate communism's evils, he quotes a table called 'The Human Cost of Communism' which estimates the worldwide number of victims of its political terror since 1917 as 143 million. When dealing with capitalism, on the other hand, it does not occur to him to quote the numbers who have died as a direct result of the policies of market economy governments, or as the result of interventions by powers like the United States to establish or maintain those governments in power. Thus the victims of 'communist aggression' in Cuba are accounted for; the victims of the dictator Batista's United States supported campaigns of terror do not brook mention.

A study of Griffiths' thinking is illuminating inasmuch as he can be seen as the 'theologian' who informs and helps drafts Margaret Thatcher's sermons on the market economy. In his book, Griffiths reflects that John Wesley's themes expressed in a sermon on the use of money: 'Gain all you can, save all you can, give all you can',[10] demonstrate the ideal of individual Christian responsibility. Margaret Thatcher some years later seizes on the words as Christian justification for the Conservative values of free enterprise, thrift and philanthropy. Furthermore, her famous 'Sermon on the Mound' delivered to a somewhat surprised General Assembly of the Church of Scotland in May 1988 which has been called 'the single most important ideological document to come out of the Thatcher era'[11] echoes Griffiths faithfully. The Bible indicates that people must work and use their talents to create wealth. This is legitimated by Creation itself. The spiritual questions are to do with how one handles wealth: what Griffiths enunciates as the principles of justice which must moderate selfishness. The Thatcher sermon goes on to seek biblical and theological justification for the policies of tax cuts (for the rich) and control of benefits (for the poor). Seizing on the Pauline text 'If a man will not work, he shall not eat' she develops the argument that if we give the poor too much help they won't want to work, but if we give the rich too little help, they won't want to work either!

This thinking easily trickles down into the church. One of the features of church life today is that nobody can ignore the gospel mandate to work for greater justice in the community and the world at large. Even those sectors of the church which were once concerned only with individual salvation are now using the language of justice and liberation. One of the problems which emerges is that while Christians employ that rhetoric very successfully, when it comes to action, the capitalist prognosis takes over and dictates the run of play. Take, for example, this extract from the vicar's letter in an Oxfordshire parish magazine.

We seem to be living in a world and in a country in which the rich are getting richer and the poor poorer. As Christians we need to be concerned with those in need at home and abroad.

That is why Christian Aid and the Church Urban Fund deserve our generous support. It is not right that in many Third World countries people do not have a permanent home, basic health care and education, and clean water and land on which to grow food. It is not right that in our own country in one part of the North-East there is terrible unemployment and poverty whilst the rich South-East knows little of these ills. The rich must help the poor. The weak must be lifted up by the strong. This is God's command to his people.

This month we shall begin our great parish celebration of returning our bells to the tower, thanks to the great generosity and help of many people both within and outside the parish. Is it right to spend so much money on a project inside the parish when there are so many needs outside it? I believe that it is, provided that we are doing it to the glory of God. The bells have had to be rehung or else they would have gone silent. Church bells proclaim the Gospel of God's love for the whole world and His presence amongst us. They must never fall silent.

The extract demonstrates the insidious way in which dominant ideology values can permeate the gospel. The vicar is no doubt a good man, doing his best, but blissfully unaware of what it is that he is communicating. While the analysis of poverty in Britain is admirable and the call to right injustices acknowledged, the strategies recommended are those of charity (the rich giving to the poor), and firm leadership (the strong raising up the weak). These strategies have a religious basis claimed for them. The vicar assures us that this is what God has commanded his people to do. If challenged to provide the biblical evidence for this command, he would be extremely hard pressed, for the sentiments in fact smack far more of what Margaret Thatcher would have us do!

When it comes to justifying the expenditure of a great sum of money on rehanging the bells, the vicar is on even shakier ground. He appeals to the principle that it is all right if we are doing it for God's glory. As an ethical principle, this leaves a great deal to be desired, for it is hard to think of any act, no matter how unjust or abhorrent, that could not be justified on these grounds. When the principle is combined with the mystical belief that the ringing of church bells somehow conveys the gospel to people (rather than being perceived as an important cultural relic on the one hand, or a damned nuisance on the other) we move into an area in which the gospel imperative to strive for justice sinks without trace in a sea of religiosity.

In response to this kind of ideological captivity of the gospel, Christians have to develop the capacity to discern that so many of the things communicated to them in homilies – the value of competition in promoting individual and community development; material acquisitions as God-given rewards for moral rectitude and hard work; patriarchies as the appropriate mediators of knowledge and authority in society; the legitimacy of profit-making in personal and business life; the designation of religion's role as that of moral education and character-formation; the contemporary nuclear family as the God-given basis of society; and the solving of personal, national and global crises by reconciliation at any price – are not gospel teachings at all. Instead they reflect the values of the advanced capitalist state.

One of the problems facing Christians today is how to counteract this deception, how to penetrate beyond this ideological blanket. One step in this is to understand the process through which the institutional church, just as much as the media and the educational system and indeed, in partnership with them, has come to act in our kind of society as a servant of the dominant ideology.

The church as ideological agent

Bearing in mind then, that the gospel is already expressed within ideological frameworks, be they socialist or capitalist, let us try to identify more precisely how the relationship between ideology and the church as institution functions.

How is the capitalist ideology mediated? We have already seen that that those promulgating the ideology keep referring to 'the natural order'. In religious terms this embraces the world created by God which now runs according to laws of nature which God instigated. The purpose of this natural order is to further the 'general interest' or establish the 'common good' of the community, and so maintain and consolidate human unity. A basic concept in this view is that of a natural social order.

The satisfaction of human needs – food, shelter, clothing, work, education, and so on – demands an ordered system of economic production. This economic system embraces two distinct groups of people. These are described simply as those who own capital (or the means of production) who are free to invest it wherever they wish, and those who own labour, who are free to sell it to whomsoever they wish. These groups have sprung out of the natural social order. Some people are best fitted by nature to give orders; others to carry them out. Because of the inherent self-interest of people, however, there needs to be a contract established between the owners of capital and the owners of labour, so that the economic system can function smoothly.

It is the state's task to see that the owners of capital and labour respect this contract. The state is comprised of wise people, normally men, who act as neutral referees, and who mediate through laws based on the concepts of freedom and equality, which they believe to be derived from the natural order.

Another group of people, quite autonomous from the state, also play an important role. This group embraces those whose interest is in the areas of philosophy and science, art and culture, religion and education. Their task is to reflect on the natural order, in order to explain to people various aspects of its operation. These people, being separated from the political order, have no particular axe to grind. Their work is therefore held to be neutral, scientific and objective.

The church is one of the important institutions represented in this latter group. It is a neutral body separated from the political realm, whose principal task is to explain the natural order. It undertakes this by teaching a body of revealed and eternal truth. Those who possess this truth impart it to those who need to receive it. This systematized body of knowledge is known as theology.

Among the ideas that theology should reinforce are these. When the natural order in society is adhered to, there is stability. Disruption occurs when people tamper with the natural order. People should be content with whatever role they have been assigned in the natural order: God has given each person his or her own talents and called each one to a specific vocation. The major moral virtues are those which are in harmony with the natural order: individual freedom, personal responsibility, the fulfilment of duty, the preservation of the family, rewards for good behaviour and punishment for bad, respect for those in authority, obedience to the state. The church should also emphasize the need of people to place their trust in experts, whose fields of science and technology are objective and value-free; and seek to make people conform to the divinely instituted roles within marriage, with the man the decision-making head of the household, the woman subservient, and children obeying their elders.

Furthermore, there are two elements of the ideology which the church needs to especially affirm. The first is the fundamental importance of the *individual* conscience as contrasted with notions of *social* conscience. This sense of conscience and moral worth is to be developed within the individual through acceptance of and adherence to a code of personal holiness. On the basis of this code, the individual is then able to make judgments about other areas of life: politics, education, sexuality, economics, and so on.

Thus to take politics as an example, it is asserted that the church must maintain its autonomy and declare that neither scripture nor tradition provide any direct teaching on political matters. What scripture identifies is a series of eternal moral principles which the individual can apply to the world of politics in order to reach a personal conclusion and judgment. But on the whole, it is best that the weighty matters of politics and government are left to those best fitted by the natural order to fulfil them.

The second element follows from this. It is not the church's task to take sides in controversial matters. It should maintain a strict neutrality, and present the community with both or, as occasion demands, all sides of an issue, encouraging individuals to formulate their own response in accordance with eternal principles. Religion and politics – God's domain and Caesar's – being autonomous realms within the natural order, the church can make no authoritative or binding statement on any political issue. There is no biblical mandate for using its authority to support one political view in opposition to another.

In contrast to this position, those who regard themselves as the victims of this ideology naturally depict it in an altogether different light. Where people are having to struggle for survival, for food in their stomachs, their immediate reality is not that of some 'natural order' which cannot be altered, but a humanly designed, implemented and maintained economic order which exploits them and which can be changed. That, for millions of people living in poverty, is the bottom line.

The poor analysing their own situation generally identify three groups of people relating to the economy in different ways. The first group is relatively small and comprises those who own or control the means of production, distribution and exchange. That is, they either *own* the natural resources of the country, its forests, farmlands, crops and minerals; the factories, the machinery and the methods used to process these resources; the means of storing, transporting and selling the processed goods; and the merchant and trading banks which sustain the entire system; or they effectively *control* these elements.

In the advanced capitalist state the question of control is as important as that of ownership. While many large enterprises like to promote the myth that their public shareholding effectively prevents an elite from exercising control, it is clear that where public shareholding is widely spread, as little as a fifteen per cent interest held in the hands of an elite can effectively control the company. This control is enhanced by the interlocking nature of company directorships. Research quickly indicates the way in which 'professional' Board members serve on a number of enterprises, and thus can ensure harmony of interests between them. In most economies this controlling class is relatively small and quite easily identified. In New Zealand, for example, an economy of three and a half million persons, effective control of the economy rests in the hands of less than three hundred people. Needless to say, almost all of them are men.

The second group in the economy is the labour force. Like the rest of the community they participate in the economy as consumers of the goods produced and the services offered, but their fundamental relationship is that of selling their labour, their energy and skills to the productive and distributive systems. We can see this group as exploited by the controlling class in the interests of maintaining or increasing profits. This group is a relatively large one. Again to take New Zealand as our example, when we add to the present labour force those who are unemployed and therefore not able to sell their labour for the time being, and those engaged in 'shadow work' – work like that of the home-maker, which is essential to the functioning of the economy but unpaid – this group comprises over fifty per cent of the population. It is sometimes referred to as the subordinate class.

The third group is traditionally referred to as the middle class.

They are also consumers, but they do not contribute directly to the production of goods. They tend to work in the service areas of society – health, welfare, education, the civil service, and so on. As the welfare state has developed, so this class has burgeoned. Some people feel that the service industry has grown too quickly at the expense of the productive economy which is having to sustain more and more people as consumers on the basis of a declining work force. Others regard the advent of the new technology which can increase production with a diminished labour content as compensating for this and ensuring the survival of the system.

It is suggested that this class is more accurately described today as the auxiliary class. In contrast to the controlling class which embraces the capitalist ideology, and to the labouring classes for whom socialist ideologies appear to provide the only means of challenging the exploitative capitalist system, the auxiliary class vacillates with no determined ideology of its own. Its basic tendency is to become auxiliary to the controlling class by aspiring towards its ideology and values. But it is also possible for this class, or at least some members of it, to become auxiliary to the interests of the exploited, and to throw its weight behind them. The auxiliary class therefore has a crucial role within the processes of social, economic and political change.

Furthermore, the controlling or dominant class exercises its power through two sets of institutions, both of which are for the most part staffed by members of the auxiliary class. In this way, through working for the service industries, the auxiliary class become agents of the controlling class. They are on the whole quite unaware of the degree to which they are participants in the processes of exploitation and oppression.

The first cluster of state institutions is made up of those which operate upon society primarily in an attempt to persuade. They are therefore predominantly ideological in character and include the media, the education system, civic and cultural organizations, service clubs and political parties. The church is also an important institution in this cluster. These institutions transmit, however unconsciously, the controlling class's culture, value system and explanation of reality. They are employed to both justify and legitimate that class's position and role.

The way in which the dominant class controls these instruments of persuasion, and through them the labouring and auxiliary classes, can be easily plotted. In most situations one can undertake a simple analysis of any one of the institutions to show how its financial basis and effective control through inter-linking Board directorships is in the hands of the dominant class.

Take as an example the media. Within the newspaper industry, the interests of the dominant class are represented as 'news': anything counter to their interests is referred to as 'comment' or 'propaganda'. In countries where the dominant class's interests are most threatened by 'socialism', the press is strongly anti-socialist. It is usually militantly anti-Soviet, regarding the Union in President Reagan's words as 'the evil Empire'. When *glasnost* and *peristroika* took the wind out of the West's sails, American and British interests and their respective media had to rally to present overwhelming evidence that the Russians should not be taken too seriously. There *had* to be an ulterior motive. President Gorbachev's offers must on no account be accepted at face value. When the Soviet Union wishes to express its viewpoint through our media and remain free from our editorial censoriousness, almost the only avenue open to it is to pay for newspaper space. Soviet perspectives invariably appear with the wording 'Advertisement' featured boldly, so that the reader will immediately be able to identify it as 'paid propaganda'. The capitalist ideology of 'freedom of the press' relates only to the freedom of capitalists to promote their views. It has very little to do with the free exchange of ideas or indeed, freedom of speech.

Furthermore, this example illustrates the way in which auxiliary class people, journalists, editors, advertising executives and so on, serve as agents of the controlling class, even though they may be unaware of that. And we can press the analysis deeper still to show that members of the labouring or subordinate class who work at the production end of the media, are in a sense participating in their own oppression. In both cases, the classes have in an uncritical way accepted the dominant class's explanations of reality. This illustrates how subtle and how powerful ideological manipulation has become.

But what of the situation where media like broadcasting is a public service and therefore 'owned' by the state? In those cases where television is dependent upon advertising for its survival, there is a very direct financial link to the dominant class. The same process of ideological domination which operates within the newspaper industry operates here as well. For example, the television coverage of one of the New Zealand's longest industrial strikes at a pulp and paper mill consistently portrayed the battle, both in terms of news items and documentaries, as between a modernizing, caring, progressive management, and a militant, wrecking, politically motivated union which had not emerged from the Dark Ages.

There is a second cluster of state institutions which operate by coercion rather than persuasion. These include the executive and the judiciary, the police and the armed forces, intelligence agencies and the prison service, any structure which can force people to behave or respond in a certain manner. Some of our institutions, of course, can be both persuasive and coercive. Those government departments which deal with welfare provision can have a strongly ideological thrust in so far as they try to persuade families to accept certain patterns of behaviour. But they also generally possess the legal power to enforce certain behaviours. They can remove, for example, children from their families and place them into state care if they decide that the family situation does not measure up to the ideologically and culturally determined standard.

The dominant class uses these institutions to protect the economic system and to maintain it as it is. We can illustrate this process by looking at any one of the institutions. Let's take the police force.

'Law and Order' is the popular cry of the dominant class. But who in the first instance determines what is good order and what is appropriate law? The notion of good order can be traced back to the Natural Order, and the need for the class structure to be recognized and natural freedoms, especially the freedom to possess one's properties and goods undisturbed, maintained. In so far as the legislative process is under the control of the dominant class, its members determine the nature of 'crime'. In capitalist societies the dominant class regards acts against property and possessions as equally important, if not more important than acts against persons. One only has to compare the seriousness with which theft has been regarded in comparison to say, rape.

While property is being safeguarded and attacks against it, generally by those from lower socio-economic groups, punished, the removal of property from those who are unable to meet mortgage or interest payments is sanctioned by law. And while a great deal of effort is made to trace and prosecute social welfare beneficiaries who are 'cheating' the system, so-called 'white collar crime' through which millions of dollars are embezzled each year is largely ignored. It falls into the category of smart business practice, and it, along with tax-avoidance and other activities, regarded as par for the course! In this way the interests of the dominant class are well served.

Moreover, the police force asserts that it serves 'community interests' and that it is accountable to the community. That this is a myth is revealed by the way in which whenever a person dies in police custody, or a member of public shot by mistake, the ensuing enquiry is almost invariably an internal one with the public entirely excluded. Where the public outrage cannot be ignored, an element of public accountability is introduced by appointing a member of the legal profession to conduct an enquiry. The legal profession is one of the instruments through which the dominant class maintains its control. The professed 'neutrality' of the police force is revealed the moment a society moves into crisis. One of the most clear examples of this in recent history was the 'neutral' role of the police in the British miners' strike of 1984–5.

When the ideological institutions in society are working effectively to persuade people to adopt the dominant class's interpretation of reality, and there is a high degree of consensus, the profile of the coercive institutions can be maintained at a low level. When consensus breaks down, however, and the dominant class's interest and expectations are being challenged by other groups in the community, the coercive elements need to be employed to encourage people to toe the line. The interests of the dominant class are best served by maintaining a high degree of consensus, for the oppressive use of coercive force can be counter-productive. 'Consensus politics' has become an articulated objective of the dominant class. It is a prominent feature, for example, of the Australian and New Zealand right-of-centre Labour governments of the mid-1980s, which are dominated by large economic interests, and have employed the strategy of 'summits' involving the 'whole community' on issues like economic policy and unemployment, in order to attempt to establish a national consensus.

This form of analysis suggests that there are only two ways in which changes to the power structure can come about. Members of the dominant class can take the initiative and make fundamental changes to the economic system. They are only likely to act in this way when they are under pressure, and in order to stave off more radical changes. And they will see to it that within the changes, their interests are as far as possible preserved.

The other possibility is that the subordinate classes, who are the victims of the system, may become instruments of change. The first stage in this process is the awareness creation or consciousness raising which has to take place in order that they perceive the reality of their oppression, and are able to organize themselves as a class. Over against the dominant ideology and its political system, they begin to create a counter-ideology and an alternative structure of political institutions, which can either through the democratic process, as in Allende's Chile, or through revolutionary action, as in Nicaragua, come to power.

The conscientized members of the auxiliary class – those who have made an option to serve the interests of the oppressed and marginalized in the community – have an important role to play in this process. They can contribute, in the first place, to the development of the counter ideology and commit themselves to the embryonic counter-structure. Moreover, because they work within the ideological institutions, like the media and education, and the political institutions, like the judiciary or the police force, they are able to actively promote the counter-ideology within their particular structure. Or if not actively promote it, at least employ its insights to reveal something of the contradictions which exist within it.

This brings us back to the institutional church again. It is to be clearly identified as one of the dominant class's instruments of persuasion. This is not to suggest that the church consciously places itself in that position, although my experience of church synods has provided numerous examples of individuals from the dominant class who see their task as aligning the church's teaching and practice with their own class interests. For example, in one diocese I've worked in, the cathedral's governing body is largely made up of people who represent those interests, and who redeveloped cathedral land to provide luxury town houses which would 'attract more cathedral-type people into the area'. But the process is generally a great deal less conscious than this.

We have already seen something of the way in which, in a capitalist society, the church begins to adopt and promote as 'gospel' the values of capitalism. This process is reinforced by the fact that the church is itself a member of the property-owning class, and in most cases has had to elaborate doctrines which justify this position. The Roman Catholic Church is the most noted exponent both of the right to individual ownership of property, and its basis in Natural Law. But other churches are equally committed to the principle, if perhaps less articulate about it. It is a logical step from this justification to support for policies of Law and Order which are going to protect one's property and economic interests.

It is for these reasons that revolutionary theories of social change generally regard the institutional power of the church as one of the first elements which needs to be overthrown. It is perceived both as an anachronism and a central element in dominant class oppression, which needs to be destroyed along with that class, and to be replaced by a more rational and scientific set of explanations about reality. The Cuban revolution is an example of that.

But it is also possible for the church to contribute to the process of radical social change, as the revolution in Nicaragua has demonstrated. There the church maintains an organizational unity, but was effectively divided into two camps: the hierarchy and the conservatives who continue to resist change; and the 'popular' church represented largely by the peasantry and their pastors, who became active in promoting revolutionary change.

The analysis from the underside of history suggests that it is possible for the church to cut its links with the dominant class and begin to serve the interests of social change. It can participate in the construction of a counter-ideology and counter-political apparatus. It is this aspect of involvement that Nicaragua illustrates well, for the implementation of participatory processes within the local church became one of the training and testing grounds for the new political structures. Furthermore, Christian intellectuals were able to make a contribution to the theory on which the new ideological and political institutions would be based. That contribution from a biblical basis and a gospel perspective is possible irrespective of the degree to which the revolutionary process has advanced.

Most Christians are unaware of the immense power that the church holds and exercises within the ideological realm. This always becomes clear, though, if the church does begin to challenge the dominant ideology. To the extent that the church supports that ideology, it is left relatively free to go about its business. When it becomes a critic of the present order, strategies from public ridicule to physical oppression may be employed against it.

In keeping with my desire to argue from the basis of experience, let's look at a couple of examples of the dominant ideology's denigration of the discussion of alternatives to it. The church agency I was working for in 1978, alarmed at the personal and community implications of the mounting crisis of unemployment, and concerned that the government's assessment of the situation excluded school leavers and part-time workers rendered unemployed and therefore concealed its true dimensions, decided to issue a public statement. We were determined to address the root causes rather than the symptoms of the problem, and we therefore focussed on the economic system itself.

Our statement was called *Time to Question the Free Enterprise System*, and highlighted some of the contradictions of that system: an excess of goods being produced but consumers unable to afford them; the potential contribution of the unemployed to the national economy; and the simultaneous evidence of falling profits, falling real wages and growing unemployment. The statement argued that we had reached a crisis in New Zealand's history where the free enterprise system should be re-examined, and pledged the agency's support both for the raising of key questions and for the search for just alternatives.

The dominant class's immediate reaction was issued through the Chambers of Commerce. 'It is hard to believe that a responsible body which takes to itself the role of leading opinion, could release such an ill-informed and unresearched statement.' It asked whether 'these church leaders accept that in throwing away an economic system called "free enterprise" we also throw away personal freedom? Freedom and free enterprise are intrinsically linked together. In the end, if one is destroyed, the other will inevitably cease to exist.' Unless the churches can come up with 'a just and acceptable and credible alternative' they are simply 'shouting in the wind'. The church would be better employed criticizing 'the results of excessive interference in a system of free choice, reward for initiative and consumer supremacy.' The nation has already strayed far enough away from free enterprise and is 'on the road to socialism or dictatorship'. The choice facing the churches is clear. They can add their voice to the mounting tide of criticism of free enterprise and 'wittingly play the game of the extremists of the left', or they can devote themselves to 'the freedom of worship and academic freedom to retain the qualities of "openness", "fairness" and "balance" which are essential to their intellectual significance'.[12]

I've quoted much of the response verbatim, lest readers should feel that I am deliberately caricaturing the capitalist position. What we have here is a classic defence of that system, employing all the elements of the Natural Order ideology: binding personal freedom to the economic system, insisting that there is no workable alternative, and taking the church to task for abandoning its neutral role, meddling in matters in which it has no competence, and allying itself not just with the left, but with the *extreme* left!

Three years later, we decided to make the focus of our national education programme, Christian Action Week, the government's national development plan. Labelled by government 'Think Big', the plan aimed to stimulate economic growth through the rapid development of giant industries in the petrochemical, mineral and forestry sectors. This development, we were assured, would create 400,000 new jobs within a decade. Our resource material for Christian Action Week questioned the wisdom of this plan, offered a Christian basis for developing a critique of it, and suggested alternatives more in keeping with a Christian vision of a just society.

On this occasion, the full weight of government was employed to try and publicly discredit the agency. At the ministerial level, the attack was quite carefully worded. The Minister of Labour publicly expressed his disappointment that the churches were showing so little understanding of the programme of economic development.[13] The Under-Secretary of National Development went further. He proclaimed this programme, supported by the thirteen major Christian churches in New Zealand as 'an exercise in mindless propaganda', with a 'predictable feminist contribution'. He particularly took the resource material to task for its use of the word 'struggle' which 'as usual in left-wing publications . . . is left undefined, being a concept well understood by readers of Marx, Lenin and Mao'.[14]

One Member of Parliament felt compelled to issue a personal statement. 'Christian Action Week', he said, 'is being used as a Marxist mouthpiece by a radical minority within the church.' The resource material is 'masquerading as a Christian publication' and 'preaches not love, but hatred, *even claiming biblical justification for working against this government'*. He found the material 'inflammatory, totally misleading and very unfair to those Christians who are unknowingly funding its publication'.[15]

The whole matter was raised in the legislature by another Member of Parliament who reiterated the charge that Christian Action Week was a Marxist programme. These people, he claimed, 'are isolating completely the part they should be taking in a caring society, which we have in New Zealand, and which is second to none in the world'. He regarded the programme as 'in keeping with a dirty tricks campaign' and appealed to 'the mainstream of New Zealand society, particularly the genuine Christian people, to isolate themselves from the extremists, for the good of democracy in New Zealand'.[16]

This orchestrated attack illustrates well the character of response at the political level. Any questioning of the dominant ideology – in this case its economic policy – is dismissed as 'mindless', 'feminist', 'Marxist' or 'extremist'. Any perspective critical of capitalism has to be less than honest and 'masquerading'. And an appeal is issued to the common sense of the 'real Christians' in the community who are blissfully unaware that their institutions have been infiltrated by the enemy intent on overthrowing freedom and democracy. This latter contention is particularly ironic in view of our programme's declared objective of encouraging people to become more active in decision-making processes to ensure that the important decisions about human life are not left to an élitist group of politicians, experts and industrialists. Perhaps the real threat was the spectre of too much democracy!

It is important for capitalism's survival that it is able to exert control over the churches and quickly call them home if they wander from its straight and narrow path. So subtle and yet so strong are the lines of control, that many church leaders are quite oblivious to the way in which they are being manipulated and co-opted into justifying the capitalist mode of existence.

The Pope's insistence that politics is the responsibility of lay people and that in no case should the clergy become politically involved is neither biblical nor born witness to within the long history of his church. It is a reflection of the capitalist separation of functions, and a strategy which effectively legitimates the politics of the Right while denigrating those of the Left.

The Bishop of Sheffield's contention during the British coal-miners' strike that the church had to remain neutral in that struggle meant in effect that he was siding with the employers. For as Freire and others have pointed out, there can be no neutrality in struggles for justice: to claim to remain neutral is in fact to take the side of the oppressor.

When the Headmaster of Ampleforth was challenged on television about the élitist nature of Britain's leading Roman Catholic public school, he insisted that 'God loves rich and poor equally.' This insight, used to justify the maintenance of that kind of institution, was not derived from scripture but from capitalist ideology.

Margaret Thatcher's determined efforts to dictate the contents of the Post-Malvinas invasion service of thanksgiving in St Paul's Cathedral had more to do with the sanctification of capitalism's aggressive patriotism than with any Christian sentiment.

The efforts of the Christian Right in New Zealand to prevent that country's government from ratifying the United Nations Convention on Women were based on the claim that the Convention undermines the Christian religion. What the Convention in reality undermines is the 'Natural Order' social organization of capitalism.

The same can be said for the arguments in church circles surrounding the ordination of women. It is generally admitted that there is no scriptural justification for withholding such ordination. What is really at stake is 'the tradition': the Natural Order's principle of organizing life on the basis of male hierarchies. In the Church of England's debates on this matter, one priest illustrated the break with the Natural Order which he believed the ordination of women involved by saying that one might equally well ordain a chimpanzee!

And so one could go on. The capitalist captivity of the church in the West can be illustrated at almost every point of its life. The first question that those Christians who want to work for justice and liberation have to address is that of the amount of energy which they will devote to the ideological task of opening Christians' eyes to that reality. The capitalists already have their strategies in place, and are using them to great effect. As Edward Norman sees it, the survival of capitalism depends on the degree to which the élite which defines the nature of public debate and sets the parameters of the morality to be instilled in the minds of the young, can promote the values of capitalism.

In view of its ideological framework, how can we best make use of scripture as a source of inspiration for Christian social action? Given the dominant ideology's determination to prevent scripture from being understood in any categories other than those of capitalism, how can we penetrate beyond ideology, to liberate scripture from this captivity?

CHAPTER TWO

Back to Basics

The Challenge of the Counter Culture

When St Paul speaks about the gospel as a treasure which is contained in earthen vessels (II Cor. 4.7), he is making a distinction between that which remains eternally pure and constant and that which cloaks, encloses or embodies it. Because the latter is subject to wear and tear, it can never be permanent. It may need to be changed like a worn or cracked clay pot. Whether by 'clay pots' St Paul was referring to human carriers of the gospel or to the more general ways in which the gospel is communicated is not clear in the text. Either way, the distinction remains important because it draws our attention to the tendency amongst some Christians to confuse the container with the treasure.

The question of whether the gospel necessarily demands an ideological framework is still being hotly debated by theologians today. On the basis of what we have already discussed, we must accept it is a fact that within capitalist societies the gospel is a mediator of capitalist ideas and values, just as within socialist countries it conveys socialist ideas and values. How are Christians concerned with social change to deal with this problem?

Walter Brueggemann argues very persuasively on the basis of his studies in the prophets that in every situation 'the task of prophetic ministry is to nurture, nourish and evoke a consciousness and perception alternative to the consciousness and perception of the dominant culture around us'.[1] He sees the crisis of the dominant culture as a resilient and permanent element which co-opts and domesticates all other visions which are proclaiming an alternative to it. The biblical prophets, unlike some of our contemporary liberal activists who dash around from issue to issue, were primarily concerned to address the ideology which underlies all issues. The counter-consciousness performs a double role. It exercises a critical function by delegitimatizing the present consciousness while at the same time energizing communities with its vision of a new state towards which they can move.

There is a fine line to be drawn here, for what is perceived as a critical and liberating counter-culture may itself develop imperialist ambitions. We can see this when we examine the great missionary era of the church in the nineteenth century. The missionaries were as much bringers of the good tidings of a counter-culture as they were bearers of the good news of the gospel. While perceiving some aspects of the critical function of the culture they represented, this was very often limited to disparaging indigenous cultures as primitive and uncivilized. More than this, there is plenty of evidence to show that they had in many instances confused this counter-culture and the imperial ambitions which attended it, with the gospel. Indeed, the Reports of such august bodies as the Church Missionary Society are often couched in the language of imperialism to such a degree that we have to deduce that officers of the Society were unaware of the distinction between missionary and cultural-imperial ambitions. This was graphically demonstrated by the Society's evangelist Samuel Marsden who, in New Zealand, insisted that the Maori people would first have to be introduced to English language, trades, manners, customs and dress before they would be able to understand the gospel. People had to be able to appreciate the beauty of the clay pot before being permitted to feast their eyes upon the treasure!

When missionaries claimed that the gospel spoke to native populations with freshness and power, this was generally because the ideological and cultural vehicles through which the gospel was being preached were, to the intellects of the hearers, a compellingly different way of understanding the universe and ordering human behaviour. The missionaries very naturally considered it to be a superior way, but this was not always the case. It certainly wasn't in New Zealand where the 'theology' developed by the indigenous Maori as a tool for understanding the relationship of humanity to creation and thus in turn for establishing the basis of social and economic life, was far more sophisticated than that being offered by the evangelical Christian colonizers. Indeed one CMS missionary, Thomas Kendall, was so attracted by it that he became the first missionary convert to Maori spirituality.

The end result of this style of missionary enterprise was, by deliberately and systematically destroying what it regarded as 'pagan' indigenous religion and theology, undermining as well the cultural, societal and economic structures which flowed from it. Maori culture became, in Paulo Freire's words, a culture of silence, driven underground, alienating a race from its meaning and value system. What began as a counter-culture, offering a liberating critique of the then dominant culture, when it asserted itself as the dominant culture became disabling, disruptive and oppressive.

The church's propensity for proclaiming the dominant culture's version of the gospel is not just a historical oddity. It persists to this day. Middle-class clergy will deliver a middle-class gospel. When I worked on the Old Kent Road, I very quickly discovered that the message the church conveyed bore no obvious relationship to, and made no meaningful connection with working people's lives. This failure to communicate occurred at a number of levels. It happened at the obvious level of values, where the church was talking from an auxiliary class value base assuming that these corresponded with working-class values. It happened at the deeper level of language, with the church attempting to communicate in conceptual language with people more familiar with non-conceptual expression. And it happened at the level of liturgy, with the church imposing a liturgy which embodies the history and heritage of one group of people, upon a local culture to whom that heritage was totally foreign. Evangelism in this situation was promoted in much the same way as it had been in the missionary era. It assumed that people needed to abandon their own history, culture and values in favour of an assured future (in the Kingdom), a better way of (spiritual) life, and more sophisticated (Christian) values.

This sad history alerts us to the danger of the imposition of foreign culture rather than the utilization of the critical functions of counter-culture. It also suggests that, instead of searching for a non-ideological reading of scripture, we should accept that scripture is generally mediated through a society's dominant ideology in a manner that will always compromise the radical nature of its message. On the other hand, the gospel will strike us with freshness and vigour and provide energy for action when it speaks out of a context which is essentially critical of our culture whatever it may be. The preaching of Jesus is certainly to be understood in this light: standing over against the dominant values of the society of his day and promoting an alternative set of values. It needs to stand in that relationship to every culture. This means that those of us who live within a capitalist culture in which the gospel, mediated through capitalist ideas, tends to support and affirm capitalist values uncritically, have to search for and be open to an alternative and critical reading.

The question then becomes 'where do we find this counter-consciousness'? It may be possible to find it in an external critical tradition such as those which have given rise to global political movements. It may be possible to discern it in the kind of cross-cultural witness that Partners in Mission and similar programmes have engendered through mission in reverse: the Third World sending missionaries to the First World. But it can also be identified in that presence within a culture of what is described as the Fourth World; those who are the dispossessed and the marginalized. In whatever situation people are in, the rich will hear the gospel speaking most powerfully from the situation of the poor, the powerful from amongst the powerless, members of the classes which shape history from the midst of those whom history shapes.

Most religious teachers and commentators studiously avoid the counter consciousness issue. A typical way of doing this is to locate the teaching of Jesus, and particularly his parables, within a modern day cultural rather than historic cultural context. Thus the significance of a person knocking on another's door at midnight as recounted in one of the parables (Luke 11.5–8) is explained as if this were happening in one's own community this evening. The question of whether door-knocking at that time of night meant the same thing within first-century Palestinian culture as it means in our advanced capitalist culture is made to appear irrelevant.

The majority of sermons I have listened to have been delivered in the context of Jesus having had a grammar school and university education, having undertaken post-graduate studies in English syntax, having lived in a well-to-do garden suburb, and having commuted to work in the City. We need to constantly remind ourselves that the man was a foreigner, that he spoke a language quite unintelligible to us, followed a life-style few of us would survive, and lived within a culture whose values most of us would reject!

We therefore need to develop a methodology which will help us locate this critical and energizing counter-consciousness. Several strands of scholarship developed over recent years can help us to do this. Firstly, there are sociological studies which enable us to build up an accurate picture of the structures of first-century Palestinian society and the dynamics at work within it. Secondly, there are studies which emphasize the cultural context of Jesus' words, and the particular nuances they carried for those who heard them at the time they were spoken. And thirdly, there are the testimonies from present-day communities which live if not in precisely the same situations as first-century Christians, in situations which closely parallel them. To these communities the gospel appears to speak more directly and with greater power.

The structure of society in Jesus' time

What were the social, political and economic realities facing the community in which Jesus lived? How was his society organized? How were the different groupings or classes of people identified? How did the power structure operate, and who held and exercised power? On what basis were laws enacted and enforced? What was the financial structure, and who controlled it? How did people support themselves in this society? What groups benefited most from these structures, and who were disadvantaged by them? Such questions appear totally irrelevant to some Christians, but we have to explore them if we are to determine the underlying significance and meaning of such things as the parable of the talents, or of Jesus' confrontations with the Scribes and Pharisees, or of his cleansing of the temple.

There are obvious dangers in this process. We could fall into the trap of reading back into the first-century Palestinian milieu the social, political and economic structures of the advanced capitalist state. I once saw amongst letters to a church newspaper one from a clergyman who was arguing that because Joseph and Jesus owned the means of production, in this case their carpenters' tools, they must have been members of the dominant class! Such an assertion not only misreads Palestinian society but also fundamentally misrepresents the socialist critique of capitalism.

One cannot do full justice to the task of presenting a sociological analysis of Palestine in a work such as this. That is a task which

Christian activists need to undertake in a disciplined way over a fairly long period of time. A great deal of help is to be had from contemporary scholars like Francois Houtart, Fernando Belo, Joachim Jeremias and George Pixley[2] who have undertaken major studies in this area. All we can do here is briefly outline the broad parameters of such an analysis.

To begin with, we need to be aware that there was a double system of exploitation operating in first-century Palestine. In the first place, there was the exploitation which emanated from the Roman empire and dominated all aspects of life. It was able to exert economic control through the exaction of a range of taxes, and political control through intermediaries and officials selected from the dominant classes in Israel. Then secondly, the Palestinian state itself was exploitative. Through the institution of the temple it demanded numerous economic contributions from the population including such things as tithes to support the clergy and funds to subsidize families attending religious festivals in Jerusalem.

The economy was divided into two sectors: urban and rural. The rural economy consisted in the main of small farms together along with which the village's common land could be used. This economy was largely self-sufficient and supported by a class of artisans who bartered their skills and services. There were also some large landholdings. Those in the Galilee raised cattle and produced corn, while those in Judaea were mainly olive groves and fruit orchards. The owners of these holdings generally chose to live in the towns and associate with the urban economy and lifestyle, leaving their properties to be managed by other people.

The urban economy produced textiles, perfumes, jewellery and food. There was a large construction industry, particularly at the time of the rebuilding of the temple, when it employed some 18,000 workers. This economy was dominated by merchants who traded in both agricultural products and raw materials, and who were generally slave owners.

As we might expect, there were distinct social groupings in the rural and urban sectors. In the countryside these were the largely absentee owners of the large estates, the small landholders, the artisans, the labourers and the slaves. In the urban setting there was an upper class embracing several groups: the priestly aristocracy which was confined to four families, the great merchants, and the leading officials. Then came a grouping of artisans, small tradespeople, lower ranking lay and priestly officials, and the Levites. The third grouping comprised labourers and slaves. Finally, there was a group of people marginalized by this society both socially and economically, on the religious and legalistic grounds that they were sinners, possessed by demons, or unclean lepers.

The political system operated somewhat differently in the urban and rural areas. In the countryside, power and authority were family based, and the eldest male member of a lineage sat on the Council of Elders which ordered local life. In the towns, the Councils of Elders had fallen under the control of the aristocratic and great landowning families, with others being excluded from power.

There were two institutions of state power. First, there was the Sanhedrin, which in Judaea at least operated as the supreme political power. In Galilee, on the other hand, King Herod governed on behalf of the Roman empire, and here, as with Jews living in other states, the Sanhedrin represented a Supreme Tribunal and dominated the ideological apparatus.

The Sanhedrin was composed of seventy-one persons who were drawn mainly from two parties, the Sadducees, and the Scribes/Pharisees. The authority of this body was rarely exercised in practice, day-to-day power in the political, economic and administrative spheres being exercised by the High Priest. In origin a hereditary office, the high priesthood had replaced the role of king following the Babylonian exile. Under Roman occupation however, the High Priest became an appointee of the Roman Procurator. The priestly community, based on the temple, had the functions of organizing worship, and policing the community through the Levites. A priest served as state treasurer.

There were three major political parties at this time. The Sadducees were drawn from the Jewish aristocracy and were linked through their economic interests to the Roman occupying power. The Pharisees were in the main artisans, small traders and scribes. The Zealots shared a similar ideology to the Pharisees – the restoration of a Jewish theocratic state – but were distinguished by their dedication to direct action in the form of guerilla warfare against the Romans.

The structure which most dominated people's lives was the religious and ideological system. In this society religion and ideology were almost completely identified with Israel's socio-political history being explained in terms of its unique relationship to God as his chosen people. Religion in that age went far beyond any definition we would offer of it today. It controlled literally all aspects of life, and the temple, the symbol and site of divine reality, was also site and symbol of economic and political power.

This is the particular context we need to assess whenever we wish to understand a particular word or action of Jesus. Houtart reminds us that the distinctions we make between different types of human activity, and the separation of functions did not exist in pre-capitalist societies. It would not have been possible, for example, for Jesus to have acted on the religious level without also being seen at the same time to be acting at other levels. To interpret Jesus' role simply as 'religious' is consequently erroneous.[3]

What this means for us is that the teaching parables of Jesus, his confrontation with different community groups, and his specific actions, cannot be taken as being exclusively or even necessarily religious in character. When he confronts the Sadducees, he is dealing with the most conservative of the political parties which represents aristocratic interests. The High Priest who summons him to appear before him is not so much an archbishop as the head of state. When Jesus cleanses the temple, he is attacking the state treasury. When he prophesies the destruction of the temple, he is speaking not just about the collapse of a building but the collapse of the whole political, economic and ideological fabric of the nation.

We shall return later, when we examine Jesus' strategies, to see how he set out to subvert the ideological system of his society. But we should note at this point the way in which he attacked the accepted codes of his time: what it meant to be pure or impure; who was rich and who was poor; who would be first and who last; who were blessed and who were judged. Events like his conversation with the Samaritan woman, his choice of apostles, his association with the outcast, are only to be fully understood in the context of his rejection of the dominant ideology.

The centres of power in the state, the Roman authority, the Jewish aristocracy and the Pharisees, were certainly aware of the danger that Jesus posed through his critique of religion and ideology. They very rapidly submerged their normally bitter differences in the common cause of putting an end to that threat. Their argument with him while appearing to be at the level of theological heresy was not ultimately at that level at all. The most threatening thing about Jesus was that he was calling for a complete, one is tempted to say Utopian, reconstruction of the social, political and economic orders.

The cultural significance of Jesus' teaching

Determining the cultural context and impact of Jesus' teaching is a more elusive task. Culture is a subtle phenomenon. Some of its basic elements are a common world view, the acceptance of common values and common goals, a common mode of thinking which provides consistency of meaning, a common environment, and common patterns of behaviour. A culture is transmitted by medium of such things as recognized symbols, through modes of behaviour, through etiquette, through common ceremonies, through artifacts, through the status and role systems in the community, and even through nuances of speech.

If we are to discover the fullest meaning of the gospel, we need to determine what those who first heard the words of Jesus took them to mean. They after all were the ones most likely to appreciate the nuances of cultural references and figures of speech. Yet very few New Testament commentaries treat this issue at all, let alone with a degree of seriousness. One colleague of mine has noted that of one hundred and twenty New Testament commentaries he has consulted, he can count on one hand those which locate the teaching of Jesus within first-century Palestinian culture. The works of Joachim Jeremias are the best known of this latter select group.

To those wishing to pursue the cultural approach to gospel teaching, the recent works of Kenneth Bailey[4] are indispensable. Bailey has worked for more than twenty years amongst peasant communities of the Middle East. For five years of that time he worked as a member of a village literacy team. It is his conviction that these peasant communities, emphasizing the supreme value of changelessness and continuity of culture, closely parallel today the communities of first-century Palestine. He has particularly focussed his work around the teaching parables of Jesus in the belief that, whereas Palestinian Christians would have employed their cultural elements to perceive the intent of the illustration, to those beyond Palestinian communities the parables had to be treated as stories about foreigners in a foreign culture.

The church has nevertheless, down through the centuries, recognized the problem posed by divorcing the parables from their cultural context. Origen, for example, allegorized the details of the parables. Some have used an indigenous approach and assumed that thinking has not changed all that much and that first-century people thought very much like we think. Others argue for universality, claiming that the human relationships portrayed in the parables are similar everywhere. Still others have adopted an existential approach by seeking the meaning of the parable for us today, without the need of considering what it meant to people back then. Then there are those who have despaired altogether and declared that the real meaning of the parables have been lost forever. Bailey rejects all these approaches.

It is his belief that we can understand the meaning of the parables in their cultural context through the methodology of Oriental exegesis which he has developed. There are three aspects to this methodology. First he discusses the cultural elements of the parables with contemporary Middle East peasant communities to see how they interpret them today within that culture. Secondly, he consults the relevant ancient literature which describes and comments upon the culture of the region at the time of Jesus. And thirdly, he consults Oriental rather than Western versions of the Gospels, making use of eighteen Syriac and Arabic texts. A great deal of his work addresses the literary form of the parables, itself a fascinating and revealing study, but we are here particularly interested in the cultural significance of the parables through which a great deal of Jesus' teaching was conveyed.

The process is best illustrated by way of example. The few years I spent as a church worker in Palestine introduced me to the way that scripture can be liberated by an Oriental perspective. One of the most popular parables in the West in terms of preaching and commentary is that of the Prodigal Son (Luke 15.11–32). This is interpreted within a Western cultural context as a story about a rebellious boy who squandered his inheritance in wild living, but who, when times became hard, had the good sense to return to the family home, where his father received him with great joy. The parable is used to teach Western and predominantly capitalist values: the futility of rebellion, the sinfulness of waste, the stress on individualism, and the dire results of rejecting family and society's values. In a religious sense it is exploited to illustrate the necessity of *individual* salvation; the demand that each individual experience a personal repentance and turning away from sin, a personal homecoming to a forgiving father.

When this parable came up for discussion in a Bible study group being led by an Arab Christian and I referred to it as 'the prodigal son', I was politely corrected. 'This is a parable about a forgiving father,' I was told, as the group proceeded to interpret it from within a commonly shared cultural experience. From that perspective, they regarded the father as breaking two of the community's most rigid cultural conventions. In the first place, the culture demands that a returning son must make the proper formal approaches to pay his respects to the seated head of the family. The fact that the father left his seat and went down the road to meet his son, and took him into his arms and kissed him tenderly, is in total defiance of accepted custom. But secondly, the parable recounts that the father *ran* to meet his son. No elderly man wishing to preserve his dignity in the community would be seen running anywhere! He would demean himself, his family and the community by doing so. The fact that the father turned his back on two of the important cultural conventions stresses the radical dimensions of God's forgiveness rather than the quality of the son's repentance.

Such was my introduction to an Oriental reading of scripture. Bailey's studies help us penetrate even more deeply into a story such as this, and illustrates the way in which some of its major implications completely elude the Westerner. For example, today as in those days, not even an elder son, let alone a younger son, would expect to receive his inheritance before his father's death. For a son to ask for his inheritance would be the equivalent of declaring to the father, 'I wish you were dead.' Both family and community would be outraged and seek retribution. In the case of such a dispute arising within a family, it is the role of the elder son to mediate between father and younger son and to reconcile them. In this story, however, the father abandons the demands of his culture, and gives not only the younger son, but both sons their inheritance before he dies. In such a case, the sons would be expected to guard their inheritance and to see that their father was

provided for until he died. The younger son behaves outrag-
eously at this point by selling his inheritance so that it is entirely
lost to the family. Village hostility over such a betrayal would
have forced the younger son to live elsewhere, had he himself not
chosen to do so.

We are being introduced here to an aspect of the parable
neglected by most commentators, but of immediate concern to
the Oriental reader: the behaviour of the elder son. He has been
irresponsible from the beginning. He failed in his duty of mediating between his father and brother and effecting their reconciliation. When the younger brother returns home, the elder begins to
behave in an even more insulting fashion. It was his role to act as
host to his brother's homecoming feast. Had he harboured any
criticisms of the event, he should have discussed these with the
family privately after the guests had left. But he refuses even to
attend the feast, let alone host it, and he airs his grievances in
public. This is an insult to the father, and involves just as radical
a break with him as that of the younger son.

As in the case of the younger son, however, the father is willing
to ignore convention, and approaches the elder son with an
unexpected offer of love and forgiveness. In contrast to his
brother, the elder son remains unmoved, and responds with a list
of complaints about his brother's behaviour and his father's
apparent favouritism. Although his integrity is really under
attack at this point, the father avoids the culturally anticipated
response of anger, and ignoring the distortions the elder son is
articulating, continues to offer love and conciliation.

The Jerusalem Bible's description of the elder son as 'the
dutiful son' is therefore misleading. He has patently *not* fulfilled
his duty to either his father, his family or the community. There
is no happy ending to this parable. Middle East communities are
invariably left reflecting not so much on the younger son who has
been reconciled with his father, but on the elder, who has
continued to behave in a culturally unacceptable way. The
question they're left with is whether the father will succeed in
bringing the elder son in from the cold!

Bailey sums up the meaning of the parable by saying that
Jesus is reflecting upon two types of person: one who is lawless without the law, and the other who is lawless within the
law. Both are rebellious; both end up in a distant place, one

geographically, the other spiritually; both break their father's heart but both are offered his unconditional acceptance and love.[5]

The Bible tells us that Jesus employed this parable, amongst others, to address the questions raised by Pharisees who had complained of his keeping company with sinners and even eating with them. From our structural analysis of Palestinian society we know that the Pharisees were predominantly artisans and small traders, roughly the equivalent of what we would today refer to as an urban lower middle class. As a class they were moving towards a lower rather than higher position on the social ladder. They therefore had a great deal to protect. They had little political clout, but were of great ideological significance in that they espoused those apocalyptic and eschatological traditions which stressed the return of the Messiah, the coming judgment and resurrection, and the inaguration of the Kingdom of God.

The parable would therefore constitute a threat to this class not simply on the religious level, but on other levels as well. For if it is possible to be 'lawless within the law', then those who regard themselves as being the most loyal upholders of the law may, in fact, be excluding themselves from the Kingdom. Such a suggestion undermines both the ideological control and the social position of the Pharisees. That they redoubled their efforts to entrap Jesus and construct a watertight criminal case against him indicates that these points were not lost on them.

We can thus see the importance of relating the teaching of Jesus to its cultural milieu, particularly if we concentrate not simply on the external manifestations of culture, but on the internal questions of responses, value judgments, relationships, attitudes, expectations, and aspirations. Once we understand the response a father ought to make to a son, the relationship between a master and a servant, the value judgment that is made about a guest who fails to turn up to a dinner party, the attitude the community exhibits towards foreign rule, the conclusion to be drawn from a certain series of events, we can, with a reasonable degree of accuracy, determine the impact of Jesus' words and actions upon those who heard and observed them, and therefore draw closer to their intended meaning.

The testimony of today's marginalized communities

Many of the processes which shaped Palestinian society remain in existence to this day, albeit in changed and more sophisticated forms. Foreign powers continue to colonize, extending their influence over smaller and more vulnerable countries. The powerful continue to organize themselves as a group and to devise ways of maintaining and extending their power against the interests of the poor. The rich still accumulate wealth through profit, violence and the exploitation of other people. Human relationships manifest elements of lust, coercion and manipulation. People are excluded from society on the basis of illness, or simply because they are 'different'. Religion is co-opted by the rich and powerful in defence of their status and life-styles.

A growing number of the world's people live in situations of poverty and oppression. Thousands of Africans die because there is not enough food. Thousands in Latin America die at the hands of ruthless political regimes. Thousands of migrant workers in Europe are exploited and socially outcast in industry's drive for increased profits. Thousands in Southern Africa are denied basic human rights on the basis of skin pigmentation. Thousands in the Middle East are oppressed because of their gender. Thousands in the Soviet Union are punished and given corrective treatment because they question the dominant ideology. Thousands of Aboriginal people in Australia have been alienated from their traditional land and forced to live within a culture which neither acknowledges nor respects their culture and values. Thousands live in abject poverty in the United States of America, the model of free enterprise, the champion of democracy.

To people in such situations of oppression, alienation and marginalization, the gospel speaks with freshness and with liberating power. This should come as no surprise when we recall that the gospel as Jesus preached it was good news to the poor, bad news to the rich. So when the poor read scripture they are able to identify very precisely those in their concrete historical situation who are the equivalent of the various actors in, for example, the story of the Exodus. Similarly, the poor immediately understand the significance of Jesus' words that the first shall be last, and the last first.

Those of us who benefit most from the present economic and social order, and who may unconsciously serve its interests and ensure its survival, do not experience the power of the gospel in the same way. Indeed, as we saw in the last chapter, because we are often auxiliary to the aspirations of the powerful in our society, we domesticate and emasculate the gospel. In our hands it becomes an instrument of oppression, and it is for this reason that so many of the world's oppressed people regard the institutional church not as an ally in their struggle for liberation, but as an obstacle to dignity and freedom. In a very real sense, we can never actually hear the gospel, until we have learnt to sit at the feet of the poor, and receive it from those to whom Jesus has entrusted it.

One of the best known attempts to document the way in which the gospel speaks to the contemporary poor is that undertaken by Father Ernesto Cardenal in Nicaragua. While a member of a religious order which was initially contemplative, but which began working with the peasant communities in the isolated region of Solentiname, he began encouraging the faithful to reflect openly on the meaning of the gospel after it had been read at Mass. This began at a time when the repression of the Somoza dictatorship was at its height.

Cardenal approached the 'proclamation of the Word' in a non-traditional way. Rather than the priest, who by birth, education and profession stands outside the peasant culture, declaring what the gospel means in his experience, the community of faith declares what the gospel means in terms of the concrete realities of their lives. The priest's professional theological training has a part to play in this process, but it is that of explaining and facilitating rather than making authoritative proclamations. So farmers and fishermen, husbands and wives, young and old, conservatives and revolutionaries, were given permission to apply the gospel to their own lives. With the aid of a piece of contemporary technology, the tape recorder, Cardenal documented their reflections, and later edited them into a four-volume work.[6]

The gospel as it is understood in Solentiname, is not a word of wisdom from a distant culture which needs to be interpreted and applied to situations within their own culture. The gospel is actually proclaimed anew in the conflicts, needs, processes, fears and aspirations of their social reality. Jesus came not to deliver the Jews from oppression, but to deliver the campesinos of Solentiname. They experience at the hands of the rich and powerful in their economy the same inequalities and injustices as the poor and powerless of Galilee. Herod and his troops behave in the same manner as Somoza and his National Guard. Jesus responds to injustice in the same way that they are eager to respond. His vision of the Kingdom of God is hauntingly similar to the objectives of the revolutionary movement. Every word of the gospel seems to speak with directness and clarity to their situation.

Traditionalists maintain that this is not an accurate way to read the gospel. I find their arguments unconvincing. And there are certain scriptural tests which can be applied. Wherever we see people's eyes being opened to the truth; wherever we see people identifying Christ's activity in the world and gathering as a worshipping community at those points of activity; wherever we see the barriers between people breaking down and those formerly at enmity with one another uniting in a common vision; wherever we see despair edged out by hope; and wherever we find Jesus acknowledged as Lord and Saviour, there we can determine that the Holy Spirit is at work. For all of these are the signs of the new humanity which, St Paul asserts, Jesus died to create (Eph. 2.11–22).

While we might expect the Christians of Solentiname to make immediate identifications with those of Jesus' parables which have an explicitly socio-economic content, what surprises is the degree to which they perceive as socio-economic those passages of teaching which our culture and ideology have designated 'spiritual' in content.

One example is the Parable of the Good Shepherd (John 10.7–16). From our Sunday School days onwards, most of us in the West have been raised on verbal and pictorial representations of Jesus as a somewhat effeminate man in a flowing robe, clutching a helpless and innocent lamb to his chest. We teach that this is an image of the way in which Jesus cares for each vulnerable individual. When we apply the image to the church, we say that it is the church's vocation to protect the faithful from the ravening wolves of false teaching, and work for that unity when all sheep from all flocks are gathered together in the care of the Chief Shepherd. The parable is also considered to serve as the model by which the shepherds of the institutional church, its paid clergy, are to exercise their pastoral responsibilities towards the community.

The campesinos understand the parable differently. For them it is the Parable of the Good Leader, and it highlights the differences in behaviour between power-hungry dictators, and power-sharing popular leaders. So when Jesus says in the parable, 'all who came before me are thieves and bandits', he is indicating the way in which governments impose themselves upon people and enact laws protecting private property and their own personal power, while slowly killing the people by not giving them what is due to them. Jesus is saying that in such cases, the people have no respect for the shepherds, and if they respond at all to them, it is because they are obliged to. They are not responding from the basis of spontaneous love. Jesus, like the contemporary revolutionary, condemns all previous political systems on the basis of their theft and violence. This demanded immense courage on his part, for the systems he was confronting were like ours, considered to be of divine origin and sanction. Jesus is telling his hearers, however, that his approach and style of leadership is radically different.

'The good shepherd gives his life for the sheep, while the one who works only for pay, runs off when the wolf comes; and the wolf seizes the sheep and scatters them.' There are people in power, in both government and church, who are only there for the money and the privilege which they can selfishly accumulate. They are wolves, who behave towards others on the basis of exploitation rather than love. Exploitation treats people violently and divides them from one another. The exploiting wolves are to be contrasted with those who give their lives to protect their brothers and sisters. The good leader behaves in the way that Jesus did, and in our time, according to the campesinos, is someone like Fidel Castro who loves his people and was willing to lay down his life for them.

'I am the good shepherd. I know my sheep and my sheep know me.' Good leadership is not exercised by people like dictators who stay in their offices and do not move among the people. The good leader is in touch with all aspects of his people's lives, and the people love and respect him for this reason.

'There are other sheep not of this fold . . . there will be a single flock and a single shepherd.' Jesus doesn't speak about uniting the sheep with the wolves, of bringing the exploited into unity with the exploited. The inference is that the wolves must cease exploiting, and become like the sheep. Jesus is not talking here only about the unity of the church. He is speaking of a human solidarity that goes beyond institutional religion and supersedes nationalism. Jesus has a global vision. Once we've perfected communism, the world will be able to live peacefully as a single flock under a single shepherd. Mao's China, which put an end to hunger, misery, ignorance and prostitution, and gave people food, clothing, health, education and dignity, provides a contemporary model of the church.

In the hands of this peasant community, a biblical passage which we have spiritualized to the point of banality, confirms the accuracy of their analysis of society, explains why exploitation and violence are occurring in the community, provides a concrete vision of the future, and sets out a model of leadership. Elements of their perception may surprise, challenge, even hurt us. But by doing so they help us uncover aspects of our own ideological conditioning. Our shock or pain may be due to the unrecognized degree of our enslavement, or to the compromises we've made which in reality ensure that injustice and violence continue. We ought to experience pain over that!

Having heard the gospel as it speaks to Solentiname, we need to develop the skill to discern its articulation within our own communities. For most of us, that voice can be most clearly heard amongst members of the Fourth World; those who exist on the margins of our society's life.

In New Zealand we can say that the voice emerges from the Maori population which provides a disproportionately high share of victims for the altars of Pakeha or European progress. Whether we examine the nation's health statistics in terms of disease, infant mortality and hospitalization on grounds of mental illness; or its prison population or its pool of unemployed people, the Maori proportion is by comparison to the Pakeha excessive.

The Maori experience matches that of all indigenous cultures when they are first infiltrated by, and eventually overwhelmed by a foreign culture. The indigenous economy which is dependent upon the natural resources of earth, forest, river and sea, is devastated and polluted by the new economy of industrial growth. The old belief system, based on concepts of co-operation and harmony between the community and the natural world, is submerged by a new ideology which sets out to tame the environment and profit from it. The agrarian and communitarian structures of life are subverted by urbanization and individualism. New laws and new politics are imposed, which do not acknowledge in any way the traditional culture, its moral judgments and its patterns of authority. Under constant pressure to conform and adapt to the new society, the indigenous culture becomes either of historic interest, or what Paulo Freire has called 'The Culture of Silence'[7] which may be lost for ever.

So the gospel's voice in New Zealand is being most clearly heard through the Maori renaissance; through demands for justice, cultural pluralism, and the return of illegally confiscated tribal lands. In the hands of white settlers and missionaries, the gospel became a tool for the establishment of Pakeha ideology and power. It was the missionaries who interpreted for the Maori people the nature of the treaty they were signing with the British Crown which was subsequently used to expropriate enormous tracts of land. It was not by accident that these same missionaries were establishing, far beyond the requirements for family subsistence, enormous personal landholdings. Today, on the other hand, the gospel is claimed as an ally by the Maori seeking to expose the fraudulent nature of the Treaty of Waitangi and to recover tribal land. There is an indigenous theology developing, over against the theology of the dominant culture. Few of its flowers have thus far been exposed to the view of the dominant culture. This is not surprising when one recalls the flower beds it has trampled across in the past. The Pakeha's history makes him blind to the Word.

One Maori writer has found new significance in the parable of Dives and Lazarus.[8] One man, the Pakeha, possesses so much that both his mind and his heart were closed to the recognition of the poor man at his gate. The poor man, the Maori, keeps knocking at the door of Pakeha society, asking to be allowed in. The Pakeha allows the Maori a few crumbs, some small concessions. But the Maori is not simply asking for employment, food, clothing, the freedom to use his own language, the return of his stolen land; he is seeking *mana motuhake*, independence, justice, opportunity, genuine human dignity, the chance to determine and to control his own life. All the rich Pakeha holds out are a few crumbs: the token use of Maori language in schools and newspapers, on radio and television; and the benefits of a few government housing programmes and job creation schemes.

Although the rich Pakeha may genuinely and earnestly wish to see his society redeemed, he does not know how to go about this. The gulf seems to him to be too great. He wishes to be reconciled with the poor Maori without giving up any of his possessions or privilege, without basically altering the relationship between them. But there can be no reconciliation of races or redemption of culture without such a change. It is the vocation of the poor to initiate this process. It is through the Maori struggle for justice that Pakeha society can gain its salvation.

In seeking the gospel through the voice of the poor in our communities, we should remember that the 'voice' may take many forms. It may be in the form of oral tradition, or drama, or music or street art. It may appear far more negative and destructive than a cogently argued positive contribution. It may well be a sob of despair or a howl of rage which draws our attention to human pain and its causes.

An example of this comes from the New Zealand Christian Action Week programme in 1983, which was organized around the theme of homelessness. We were trying to draw attention to the housing crisis in New Zealand, which had left families living in caravans, tents, sheds and cars, and had seen a dramatic upsurge in the street kids who had organized themselves into 'families' in the heart of the city, sheltering beneath motorway bridges, in disused warehouses and empty houses.

During the week, a street family took possession of a vacant house which belonged to one of the church's social service agencies. In doing so the family pointed to its urgent need and to the fact that this was Christian Action Week on homelessness. Their action infuriated the church authorities, who initiated negotiations with the street kids from which no workable compromise emerged. The church subsequently called on its allies in the political apparatus, the police, to have the squatters evicted.

A poster quickly appeared around the city, plastered on the cathedral notice board and on the walls of city churches. It depicted a wild-eyed bishop in full regalia egging on police dressed in riot gear as they evict the family from the house. Its wording was simple: Christian Action on Homelessness! It is a cry of anger, representing the reality which the street family experiences. For them, Christian Action Week was not the church putting its considerable resources into providing shelter for the homeless, but the church lending its authority to the use of force against those who are the poor and marginalized of the community. The poster came across to us as an authentic gospel voice. It may not contribute a great deal to our vision of the Kingdom of God, but it makes it abundantly clear that in the Kingdom of New Zealand the poor perceive the gospel as working against their interests.

Applying the methodology

These three elements constitute a methodology which enable us to understand scripture in a new way. Through undertaking a structural analysis of the society in which Jesus lived we are able to perceive the economic, social and political contexts of his words and actions. By immersing ourselves as far as we are able in his culture, we are better able to understand the ideological content of his teaching. By being attentive to the voices of today's poor, the demands of the gospel in our contexts become clearer.

Let us now apply the methodology by way of example. The texts selected for this purpose are those which are most frequently employed by the dominant ideology to argue against positions adopted by Christians working for fundamental social change.

Give back to Caesar what belongs to Caesar, and to God what belongs to God (Luke 20.25).

Jesus is teaching in Jerusalem where agents posing as religious enquirers are trying to entrap him into making a statement which would enable them to hand him over to the governor's jurisdiction. They ask a politically loaded question: should one pay or withhold Roman taxes?

The dominant ideology says that Jesus' response to the question shows that he believed that the pursuits of religion and politics should be kept entirely apart. The state has the responsibility of ordering civil affairs, and the church should not interfere with that task. The task for institutional and personal religion is to develop a sense of morality in people. Questions of the ordering of the economy are therefore not the concern of religious faith, and best left to the economists and politicians with the expertise to understand them.

Through our methodology we know that Jerusalem was the focus of the political party, the Zealots, who were committed to getting rid of the Roman administration and establishing a Jewish State. The residents of Jerusalem, for a variety of nationalistic, economic and ideological reasons, were generally sympathetic to this cause. Had Jesus answered the agents' question by saying that it was legitimate for people to pay the Roman taxes, he would have been taken as acknowledging Roman authority. This would have lost him the respect of the Jerusalem crowd. If, on the other hand, he had openly supported the popular movement to withhold taxes, he could have been arrested on a criminal charge.

Jesus is thus presented with what appears to be a 'no win' situation. He demonstrates his awareness of the trap, and his political astuteness, by appearing to affirm both positions! We can even detect an element of political irony in his response which suggests to people, 'If you acknowledge Caesar's authority by accepting and using his coinage as the basis of your economic life, by all means return that coinage to him by way of taxes!' This is certainly not advising people to eschew political and economic questions. To the contrary, those who heard his words would have picked up some carefully coded political advice, from the way that Jesus handled the situation, as much as through the words he uttered.

The dominant ideology generally goes on to link these words of Jesus with Saint Paul's teaching that 'the powers that be are ordained of God' (Rom. 13). The epistle suggests that those who resist governments, are resisting God and will be punished as a consequence. Christians should therefore offer unreserved obedience to the authority of the state.

We examine this contention in more detail when we look at the whole question of authority in the next chapter. But we should remember that St Paul was writing in expectation of Christ's imminent return to earth when all political authority would be rendered irrelevant. His views have to be balanced by those of Christians of a subsequent generation who, persecuted by the Roman state, came to consider the state as the embodiment of evil to be resisted by the Christian community.

To communities of the poor, themselves exploited by unjust systems of taxation which work in the interests of the rich and powerful, Jesus is speaking about the way in which imperialist regimes stamp their image not just on their coinage but on all aspects of human life and activity.[9] The coinage is so marked to indicate that it is the property of the regime, to be used by the regime as it sees fit. It does not belong to the people, who have no control over the economy. Justice will only be established when the emperor's image disappears and the economy works in the interests of the poor.

You will have the poor with you always (Mark 14.7).

A woman has anointed Jesus with an expensive perfume. It was suggested that the money used in its purchase would have been far better spent on meeting the needs of the poor. These are the words with which Jesus responded to that criticism.

The dominant ideology says that this response shows that Jesus was a realist about poverty. He is recognizing that it is part of the natural order and that no programme of economic assistance or social reform is ever going to fully alleviate it. Christians should follow his example, acknowledge that poverty is endemic to all social structures, and encourage those of means in the community to act charitably towards the poor.

This act of anointing is of immense cultural and political significance. Historically, the anointing ceremony had been used by the prophets of Israel when they were proclaiming kings. Jesus, immediately before his betrayal, is here being anointed as Messiah. Bystanders would immediately have made the connection with political precedents.

The patriarchal society of Palestine had very strict conventions about the manner in which men and women related to one another, and particularly how they touched one another. The fact that this anointing was performed by a woman was culturally outrageous. Equally offensive was Jesus' acceptance of her behaviour. Both he and the woman are ignoring cultural demands. Jesus was at dinner when this event occurred and then, as now in Palestinian society, meals were male occasions from which women were excluded. The men in the room express anger at the woman's intrusion, and their claim that 'this money would have been better spent on the poor', has a resentful ring to it. It diverts attention from the fact that a woman has anointed the Messiah.

In these circumstances, Jesus' words cannot be taken either as a proclamation that poverty is a permanent feature of society, or as a suggestion that the needs of the poor can be ignored. It is rather a recognition of the importance of people acknowledging his kingship as the opportunity presents itself, and an affirmation of the woman who broke the rules in order to do that.

Furthermore, there are mistranslations in our versions of scripture. The words 'you will have' and 'always' do not appear in the text. The more correct translations are 'you have' and 'continuously'. The text then suggests: *The poor you have with you continuously and you can do them good when you wish; on the other hand, you do not have me at all moments*. One can discern an ideological influence at work in the translation process itself.

The passage speaks directly to the situation of marginalized groups within our society, particularly to women. For here we have a woman, excluded from many aspects of social life, and most aspects of religious life, presented as the paradigm of Christian discipleship.[10]

To everyone who has will be given more (Luke 19.26).

This is a Wisdom saying which has been attached by way of commentary to the Parable of the Pounds (or Talents). The parable tells of a servant who was entrusted with some of his master's wealth but failed to realize a profit on it. He did not even deposit it in a bank where it would have gathered interest. The master takes away this servant's share and adds it to that of the person who has made the most profit.

The dominant ideology claims that Jesus is here reforming the Old Testament tradition which specifically condemns profit made from commerce and from loans at interest. He makes it legitimate for people to accrue wealth and to gain maximum profits. Furthermore, Jesus is affirming that those who do not use money wisely are the authors of their own misfortunes. Those who do, will be appropriately rewarded in the eyes of both society and religion. Margaret Thatcher used this parable in an attack upon Anglican bishops. 'Those who traded their talents and multiplied them were those who won approval,' she said, in vindication of the free enterprise system.

The parable in fact relates to a political event, fresh in the memories of those who heard it. Following the death of Herod the Great, his son Archelaus sailed to Rome to ask Augustus to confer the succession upon him. A delegation of fifty Jews followed to vigorously oppose this appointment. When he was successful and returned as king, Archelaus rewarded those who had managed his affairs in his absence, with political patronage. He gave them the government of ten cities, and so on. He also condemned the administrator who had not worked in his interests.

Jesus tells this story near Jerusalem where anti-Roman sentiment ran strongest. The political significance of the parable would have been obvious. The king is nowhere depicted as a model character. His appointment had been opposed by the people, and even his servant describes him as 'picking up what he has not put down', which is a proverbial description of those who exploit others. The servant is no better than his master. He has proved himself unworthy of trust, and breaks the code of loyalty by publicly exposing his master's economic exploitation.

Jesus is not commending the behaviour of either character. Both have behaved badly and he is not saying, 'If you wish to follow me, behave like these two rogues.' Rather Jesus is suggesting, 'If a corrupt king like Archelaus expects such a degree of loyalty from his followers, how much greater are the expectations of the Son of Man?'

Those reading the passage in the oppressive situation of the Nicaraguan countryside at the time of the Somoza dictatorship understood it differently. To them the words speak of the way that the unjust dominant ideology functions by, for example, taking away the little land that the peasants own when they cannot meet their bank demands, while lending huge sums to the large landholders so that they can accumulate even more. In contrast, if people substitute love for gain, the teaching's real meaning is revealed: those who have little love in them will lose everything; while those rich in love will inherit the earth.[11]

It is easier for a camel to pass through the eye of a needle than for a rich man to enter the Kingdom of God (Luke 18.25).

This saying occurs during a passage of teaching on the nature of riches and the need to renounce them, which begins with an aristocrat asking Jesus what he has to do to inherit eternal life, and concludes with Jesus telling Peter that it is those who have divested themselves of everything who will gain the Kingdom.

The dominant ideology regards this saying as far too hard, and has sought means of modifying it or explaining it away. One of the earliest attempts was to claim that the word *kamelon* (camel) was really the word *kamilon* (rope). If one is able then to reduce the rope to a thread, there is no obstacle to the rich entering the Kingdom. Another attempt, derived from a mediaeval sermon which had no basis in fact, was to claim that there was a Needle's Eye Gate into Jerusalem that a camel could only enter on its knees! Or again, as Lady Marchmain would have it in *Brideshead Revisited*: 'But of *course*, it's very unexpected for a camel to go through the eye of a needle, but the gospel is simply a catalogue of unexpected things.'[12]

In Palestinian culture the image is taken literally and indicates absolute impossibility. A rich person cannot enter the Kingdom through his own efforts, and cannot without assistance, dethrone his wealth.

The aristocrat and other bystanders belong to a tradition which regarded the use of wealth for building synagogues and orphanages and giving alms to the poor as a means to salvation. Jesus says that eternal life cannot be earned. It is inherited when people are converted to a loyalty deeper than that to their wealth. Wealth in this setting includes both the family property and that gained through the exploitation of others.

But Jesus goes further. He takes the traditional commandments which give prominence to family and property and reinterprets them. The commandment says that a person should not steal another's property: Jesus says one may have to leave one's own property behind. The commandment says that people should honour their parents which includes caring for them until they die. Jesus says one may have to abandon one's parents. The commandment says that one should leave one's neighbour's wife alone. Jesus says the disciple may be required to leave his own wife alone.

Two of the unassailable loyalties in Palestinian culture are to one's family and to the village home. Jesus is saying that in addition to renouncing wealth, unless one can also break with these, one cannot enter the Kingdom.

When the poor of Solentiname look at the wealthy in society, and analyse how that wealth was created, they see that it was in fact they, the peasants who created it. They sowed seed and harvested crops; they wove cloth and made shoes. When they migrated to the city, they built houses, skyscrapers, bridges and roads. Yet the wealth they created has been seized from them by a class of people who are creating nothing of value for that society. In many cases the wealth has been transferred through an exploitative economic system. In others it has been seized violently through the expropriation of land and life. Thus in an unjust society, wealth is a product of violence and exploitation, and it is because of this manner in which the rich have acquired their power that Jesus excludes them from the Kingdom.

CHAPTER THREE

Sightings of a New Earth
Biblical Parameters of a Just Society

Capitalism today has regrouped its forces and reaffirmed its claim to a moral base. The dominance of Reaganomics and Thatcherite policies in the North Atlantic stretching to the 'free enterprise' Labour governments of Australia and New Zealand provide the ideal climate within which capitalism flourishes. It is able to present itself as having a proven track record, and capable of rectifying any imbalances which may arise within the system. In contrast to capitalism's renewed vigour, there is an armchair quality about much of the criticism being directed at it. The capitalist propaganda machine has been very effective in labelling all dissent 'communist' and depicting socialist regimes as militating against human freedom and dignity. What appears to be the only serious political alternative in the field, Marxism, is thereby discredited and the 'proven' and workable capitalist model rolls on in the absence of any serious contender.

There is a vagueness about workable alternatives to capitalism amongst academics and activists alike. Their debates tend to centre around the classic options of socialism, with little serious attention given to other historic models or experiments, or to the forging of genuinely new options. Christians often have a highly developed critique of capitalism, but are less specific when it comes to spelling out what it is that they are working towards! They prefer to discuss principles or generalities rather than specific elements in the fashioning of a new society. So the Anglican bishops attending the 1988 Lambeth Conference speak of the need for the unjust structures of society to be changed into structures of grace. Until they are able to describe in detail what these structures of grace look like, and how they will function, this becomes yet another exercise in mystification.

Most Christians turn to the Bible in order to determine what their relationship to society at large should be. Not surprisingly, they turn up a range of answers. Fundamentalists insist that the present injustices and inequalities in society are inevitable results of the Fall, and cannot be remedied by programmes of economic or social reform. The visionary language of scripture does not refer to objectives which Christians should be practically pursuing, but to the characteristics of the Kingdom of God which will be established in the future without reference to human activity. At that time, all who are in a right relationship with God will be swept up into the Kingdom. Our efforts should therefore be directed towards ensuring that people are in this relationship. This is what Jesus' ministry was concerned about. There is obviously an element of present reality to the Kingdom, because Jesus was calling people into it in AD 28, but it exists in a spiritual dimension separate from contemporary politics and economics. On the basis of this analysis, one begins to understand why it is that biblical fundamentalism and capitalism walk hand in hand.

More liberal Christians discern in scripture only the imperative of love. Theirs is a romantic view of Jesus as a humble carpenter, wandering along the idyllic shores of an Eastern lake, living, teaching and offering love. If we wish to, we can rest with him in a shaded spot and experience the embrace of his love. It's a contemporary vision for an age which has become dehumanized, hollow, and alienating. As I heard one preacher put it, 'the gospel has a warm and fleshy touch.' The gospel is not so much concerned with issues of wealth and poverty and social justice as with the quality of our loving. It of course has a social dimension to it, in that love must undergird all human activities and structures. If we can become more genuinely loving people, the structures of our society will become more loving as a result. It is a popular view and there are many in positions of leadership in the church today who can be heard speaking about the Christ-event bearing love into our world, and who therein offer a romantic interpretation of Christianity.

Most contemporary Christian activists reject both these approaches in favour of an understanding that scripture actually demands that we take action against injustice. That being the case, there would seem to be two major schools of thought.

The first maintains that the Bible contains no economic, social or political blueprints for a new society. What we must do is decide which of the current secular options for a new society most faithfully represents biblical insights.[1] We need to evaluate the current analyses and strategies competing for our attention, and modify them, constantly subjecting them to a critique of the gospel. The assumption appears to be that because all political, social and economic systems are human creations, none can fully mirror the gospel. We need to make use of that which most approximates to the vision of the gospel, being constantly ready to make adjustments to it.

Others believe that scripture embraces not simply visionary language, but some very clear principles and organizational models about the structure and functioning of a just society. These are clearly revealed when one approaches scripture with the tools of structural analysis, cultural exegesis and contemporary testimony which we have developed. They enable us to discern the political and economic connotations of the words of Jesus, in a manner which other methodologies cannot emulate.

In this chapter and the next, we attempt this task, first by examining the details of the biblical vision of a new society expressed as 'a world renewed' or 'a new heaven and a new earth' or 'a world turned upside down' or 'the Kingdom of God', and then determining whether or not there exists a model which already embodies the totality of this vision.

The conceptual bases of the vision

Three biblical concepts stand out in terms of describing the relationship of the divine to the human, the relationships which exist between persons, and between persons and their communities. These words are *justice*, *peace* and *love*. In respect to justice, we need to note that in both Hebrew and Greek texts, the words justice and righteousness are the same word, and are used interchangeably.

While some Christians wish to see these three as separate principles for Christian living, or as three pillars of the Christian society, and emphasize their distinctiveness, they are much more inter-related than that. The terms overlap in meaning to such an extent that they might be better treated as three faces of the same reality. Righteousness/Justice, 'being right with God', is manifested to the extent that peace and love inform human existence. Peace, God's *shalom*, creates the conditions in which justice and love can flourish. Love is the 'greatest gift' which motivates and purifies all human activity.

It is characteristic of scripture, particularly the Old Testament, that in contrast to our Western tendency to banish principles to the realm of academic debate, it grounds principles by testing them in practical and quantifiable ways.

Righteousness/justice is one of the basic concepts in both Old Testament and New Testament writings. There has been a tendency in theological circles to equate righteousness with holiness; that is, to confuse it with spiritual and personal religiosity. But whereas holiness in the Old Testament is introduced as a religious term to which moral and practical considerations are added later, righteousness is an ethical concept which is related to practical behaviour. That it slowly comes to have a religious content as well is indicated by the way that some of the prophets at the time of the Exile and Return were using the word in the sense of 'salvation'.

The meaning of righteousness in the Old Testament is 'being in the right'. It is used of behaviour which can be determined by the judges as being right in particular cases. Throughout the development and usage of the term, this factor remains constant: the question of what is right or who is right needs to be independently arbitrated along the lines of judicial decisions. In origin, righteousness/justice has three facets to it. First, it means being in the right in a particular case. Secondly it implies legal status by getting a public judgment in one's favour. The righteousness so gained could be just as easily removed according to the claims of the later prophets. And thirdly, it refers to the quality expected of a judge in the exercising of his or her responsibilities. Particular stress is laid on the necessity for the judge to avoid bribes offered by the rich, and the tendency to respect the wishes of the powerful rather than redressing the wrongs suffered by the poor and the defenceless in the community. It is this notion of the protection and deliverance of the most vulnerable in the community which was extended into the much broader concept of salvation.

The idea of righteousness was originally grounded in the economic and social reality of a small nomadic community governed by specific laws informed by social convention. By the eighth century BC, however, the massive economic changes which had seen commerce located in towns and cities with the consequent development of a distinctively urban life-style, had eroded the customary and essentially rural morality. Large numbers of people had been dispossessed of their property through this process, and in consequence deprived of their civil and religious rights. The poor were being defrauded by urban traders, and ground down by wealthy employers in search of increased profits. The formulations of law, which had been relatively independent, now acted in the interests of the rich and powerful as an instrument of oppression.

In this altered situation it seemed to the prophets that the basis of righteousness/justice must reside in something other than custom, tradition and usage. Their contribution was to discern that righteousness and all its practical demands spring from the moral nature of God. They began to promote the idea of an abstract 'right': an objective reality so strong that although it could be resisted, it could never be defeated. Such a morality is more than an idea. It is a dynamic, practical personal energy which can be seen at work in the community.

In this period, righteousness was identified firstly in the public administration of justice. It was defined not in terms of a written and enforceable code so much as in the ability to recognize instinctively what is due to other people in order to enhance the rights of the human personality and the claims of humanity. This righteousness is understood both as an attribute of God and as an instinct in human nature, which God demands be manifested on earth through the establishment of social justice. The prophets also invested it with political content, in that it was a lack of justice in the nation which made it vulnerable to the attacks of others, and open to the possibility of utter annihilation. On the other hand, the possibility of justice being re-established by a messianic leader offered the hope of both survival and salvation.

It is to this tradition that Jesus refers in his New Testament teaching on righteousness/justice. He urges that the right action of his followers should exceed the right behaviour of the Scribes and Pharisees. He constantly refers back to the prophetic tradition, insisting that the motivation for righteousness is not a series of external laws, but an inbuilt concern for the welfare of others: a passion for justice which encourages the full flowering of the human spirit within the human community.

In the previous chapter we saw that Jesus' teaching on justice forced people to press beyond the demands of the law on matters of property and family, to a commitment of social and economic dimensions which was culturally shocking. Most scholars agree that Jesus set out the fundamentals of his teaching on justice in the Beatitudes. In St Luke's version, there are four blessings and four curses.

> Happy are you poor; yours is the Kingdom. Alas you rich; you are having your consolation now.
> Happy are you who are hungry now; you shall be satisfied. Alas for you who have your fill now; you shall go hungry.
> Happy you who weep now; you shall laugh. Alas for you who laugh now; you shall mourn and weep.
> Happy are you when people hate you, drive you out, abuse you, denounce you as a criminal; this is the way the world treats prophets. Alas when the world speaks good of you; this is how it treats false prophets.[2]

In St Matthew's Gospel, we find the impact of these words considerably softened by his addition of the words 'in spirit' following 'how happy the poor' (5.1–12). This undermines any perception of poverty and hunger in physical and material terms, and harmonizes Matthew's account with his Jewish ideology which saw no inconsistency between wealth and salvation. Some scholars suggest that the addition was not in fact Matthew's but that of early church editors. The words 'in spirit' were added by way of justification of the church's rapidly expanding middle-class base and its acquisition of both property and capital. Whatever the reasons, the tendency to 'spiritualize' the hard sayings of Jesus is of ancient origin. But to those hearing the words in their Palestinian context, the meaning is perfectly clear. Those who believe that their righteousness is confirmed by their wealth, their life-style, their personal happiness and their high standing in the community, are doomed. It is the poor, the hungry, the hopeless, the abused, the hated and the denounced whose righteousness spirits them into the Kingdom.

The links between Jesus' teaching and the eighth-century prophetic teaching are so obvious that there can be no doubting that Jesus used them as his basis in this instance. The relationship between justice and salvation becomes explicit. Salvation is a gift to the person who is actively seeking justice on earth, rather than to the person cultivating holiness in his or her heart.

The prophets carefully spelt out the different dimensions to justice. There is a concept of personal justice which we have already alluded to in the manner in which judges are expected to behave, protecting the interests of the weak and the dispossessed. The prophet Amos speaks of the poor person as one with nothing in his or her hands, whose rights are totally dependent upon the restoration to human dignity which justice imparts. And one of the most frequently quoted passages in Old Testament literature is from the prophet Micah, who alerts people to the fact that the demands of a just God are not fulfilled by providing altars with burnt sacrifices; yearling calves, thousands of rams, torrents of oil, and one's firstborn. On the contrary, the criteria by which people are judged are just actions, tender loving, and a humble disposition (Micah 6.6–8).

Justice is also understood in political terms. The spirit biased in favour of the poor, which is associated with the dispensation of individual justice, is expected to permeate the life of the nation as well. When the political establishment fails to take cognisance of justice, the prophet denounces it. This is the context of the prophet Jeremiah's confrontation with king Jehoiakim (22.13–19), who had begun to serve his own interests rather than the interests of justice. His obsession with the building of a gilded palace, and his exploitation of unpaid construction workers for this purpose, was at the expense of his responsibilities as the guardian of justice. The prophet reminds the king that his father used to judge the cases of the poor and needy in a manner which enabled the nation to flourish. But, the prophet charges, Jehoiakim possesses 'eyes and heart for nothing but your own interests, for shedding innocent blood and perpetrating violence and oppression'. Good government, on the other hand, is rooted in the proclamation and pursuit of justice.

There is a concern, too, for economic justice. In some ways this is the most basic justice of all, because civil and religious rights depended upon the way in which one participated in the economy understood as the manner in which the community organized its resources to meet its members' basic needs. The prophets were concerned about ways in which people were being *excluded* from the economy. The provisions of the sabbatical year, including the remission of all debts incurred in the previous six years, and the restoration of all property sold in that time to its original owner, were intended to ensure that people were able to participate in the economy. In addition to their support for these general principles, the prophets were outspoken in their condemnation of particular economic abuses, especially those within the cities. Micah denounces traders who use false measures and faked weights on their scales (6.9–14). He also condemns those whose only interest appears to be that of aggregating farms and houses, thus extending their control over the rural economy as well (2.1–2). His concern is echoed by Isaiah, who condemns those who try to establish monopolies, 'hoarding up house on house and linking field to field until they occupy the whole place' (5.8).

Then there is an emphasis on social justice: that justice which governs community or social relationships. For the prophets, this means that the rights of the poor in the community have to be safeguarded. Early in the Old Testament this was applied primarily in the cases of orphans and widows who had no means of support. The idea was later extended to include slaves, and strangers in the community. But as a greater differentiation in wealth occurred in parallel with the development of urban centres, so the meaning of 'poor' was further amplified to embrace all those people who were marginalized in the community. Justice for the poor, along with condemnation of the rich, is a recurring theme amongst the prophets. They are singleminded in their analysis that poverty is the direct result of exploitation by the rich, as witnesses this passage from Jeremiah:

> Like cages filled with birds, so are their houses full of what they have taken by fraud: this is how they have become great and rich. Fat and sleek they have grown; they went beyond words of evil: they did no justice, they trod upon the rights of orphans, they respected not the justice of the poor (5.27f.).

It is a feature of the prophetic analysis of wealth, that on almost all those occasions on which they comment on the injustice of wealth, the prophets associate it with violence. Jeremiah, confronting Jehoiakim, notes that his grandiose development projects perpetrate violence. Micah speaks of the cities 'whose rich men are crammed with violence' (6.12). Both the accumulation and preservation of such wealth involve violence. This is important to bear in mind, because it is the struggles of the poor for justice which the dominant ideology always portrays as 'violent'. The violence which created this injustice in the first place is never acknowledged.

The teaching of Jesus did not deviate from this analysis. He, too, was singleminded in his condemnation of the wealth which, through exploitation and violence, defrauds the poor. No amount of 'spiritualizing' or 'demythologizing' or 'historicizing' on the part of the servants of the powerful can ever modify his analysis and teaching on this issue.

The second biblical principle is that of peace. Peace is God's *shalom*. It is the value or blessing emphasized above all others in the biblical longing for the rule of the Messiah. The covenant the ancestors of Israel made with God was a covenant of peace. The messenger who will announce the arrival of salvation will come preaching peace. The Messiah is the Prince of Peace. On almost every occasion in the Old Testament when peace is mentioned, it is associated with justice/righteousness. Isaiah speaks of a restored Jerusalem in which the magistrates shall be peace, and the government righteousness (60.17). The psalms say that the messianic age will be a time 'when the righteous shall flourish, and abundance of peace, till the moon be no more' (72.7). Again, in describing the salvation that is to come, Isaiah says that 'the work of justice shall be peace, and the effect of justice security' (32.17). The links between justice and peace are very explicit.

The New Testament shares this messianic understanding of peace, and in both Acts and Ephesians, the ministry of Jesus is expressly referred to as the Gospel of Peace. Jesus is portrayed as the peacemaker who, by preaching peace to those near at hand and those far away, has reconciled them and has himself become the peace of all humanity (Eph. 2.13–18). St John's Gospel records that Jesus, before he was crucified, bequeathed his followers peace (14.27).

Peace is an active word. It is primarily employed in scripture not as we tend to use it to describe the absence of war and conflict. That is its secondary meaning. Its main meaning reflects its derivation from the Hebrew word for 'wholeness'. It is closely connected to concepts of health, well-being, prosperity and security. Its dynamic is to create within the community those conditions in which people may grow. The quest for peace is therefore the positive implementation of conditions and structures which are life-enhancing and conversely, the eradication of all those features which are destructive of life. In terms of the teaching of both the prophets and the New Testament, the establishment of peace is dependent upon the establishment of just social, economic and political structures.

This initial understanding of peace began to change early on in the Christian era. Some of the teachings of St Paul, for example, became the launching point for interpreting peace in a much more passive way, and these led to an association of peace with the personal tranquillity of the Christian soul assured of salvation. This in turn encouraged the view that the true Christians are those persons who have learnt to be 'at peace' with whatever social conditions, economic prospects or personal status God has bestowed upon them. This has been one of the more erroneous and destructive teachings of the church. It is an internalized and dependency-creating view which has but tenuous links with the biblical understanding of *shalom*.

The active dynamic of peace is attested to by the world's marginalized. The links between peace and justice were the subject of some of the most vigorous debates at the World Council of Churches' Assembly in Vancouver in 1982. Delegates from the West, threatened by the possibility of nuclear holocaust, tended to promote peace as the primary issue confronting humanity today. Delegates from the Third World pointed out that it was only now that people in the West were personally threatened with extinction that peace had even become an issue on their agenda. Thousands have died, and continue to die at the hands of ruthless Third World regimes, without a word of protest being raised. I remember a woman from Guatemala making this point very strongly in one of the working groups. She commented that we were permitted the luxury of sitting around in comfortable armchairs discussing peace issues, while in her country, a group discovered participating in the kind of discussion we were enjoying would be summarily shot! The 'peace at any price' call that some were articulating was met by the response, 'No. Not at any price.' Peace is more than the absence of war. Peace is the establishment of social, political and economic justice. There can be no peace, no reconciliation until justice has been established. That view is totally consistent with the biblical witness.

We can discern a similar relationship between love and justice. The New Testament emphasizes love above all else. Jesus taught that the entire Law was embodied in expressions of love: love of God, love of neighbour and the love of self without which the first two are impossible. The biblical understanding of love is that it springs from 'a renewed heart'. It calls for a personal rejection of those egoistic impulses which lead people to perceive all others as rivals, to seek always their own interests, to use others as a means of furthering personal ambitions, to treat them with neglect, and to 'neutralize' them if their interests conflict with ours. Love adopts a positive disposition towards the dignity and worth of every person, particularly those whom society deems unworthy, those who have injured us, and those who have no claim upon us whatsoever. In the Bible, love is not an emotion or a sentiment. It is an act of will, a determination to work positively and practically for the good and well-being, the *shalom*, of others.

In the Old Testament, while not completely identified with each other, justice and love stand in the closest of relationships. God's justice is manifested in his saving acts: salvation is offered on the basis of his love. Some commentators have regarded love as the end of God's purposes, and justice the means by which love is accomplished and fulfilled. It certainly has to do with ethical norms or standards. In the New Testament we find justice to be the test of a person's relationship to God. In response to the question, 'What is the ethical nature of God?', St John responds, 'Love'. Justice is that element within love without which it would be simply good-natured benevolence.

As with the other concepts we have looked at, Christian usage (or perhaps we should rather say misuse) has wrought considerable change. Our idea of love has been so individualized, romanticized and sentimentalized that it today bears very little resemblance to the way it is deployed in scripture. Many people shy away from its use altogether because of the totally negative meaning it has come to portray in Christian hands. It is another of the words which needs to be reclaimed for the sake of the gospel. One of my teachers, Joseph Fletcher, argued that in view of the misleading Christian views of love, our word 'justice', retaining meanings more faithful to scripture, should be substituted. We should therefore avoid the word 'love' when discussing Christian ethics. Love and justice are aspects of the one reality: justice is love distributed.[3]

What I have tried to do here is take one of the three basic concepts, righteousness/justice and show how *shalom* and love are related to it. One could have begun with any one of the concepts and followed the same process. The point is to illustrate how interwoven they are in meaning. But the important thing to note about them is that they are ethical concepts which provide an ethical foundation for the building of a new society. The biblical perspective is clear at this point: we do not take an economic structure and ask how it can be made to operate in a just manner. We begin with a concept of justice which is at once practical and dynamic and we construct an economic system upon it.

The priorities of the Kingdom of God

The Kingdom is the focal point of Jesus' teaching about justice, love and peace. The notion of the Kingdom and what precisely Jesus meant by it are the subjects of many scholarly works. It is generally agreed that Jesus spoke of the Kingdom as if it were a present experience, that he used it as a vivid contrast to the society of his time whether that of Israel as a nation or the Roman Empire, and that he indicated that its complete realization lay in the future. Without going too deeply into the debates, certain features of the idea of the Kingdom inform our vision of a Christian society.

The Kingdom is a present reality. Jesus announced its inauguration and said that some people were close to becoming members of it, while others were already in it. Still others were excluding themselves from it. In the way that Jesus employed the term, to be in the Kingdom is to choose to live under the rule of God, rather than the rule of others, whether that be the contemporary political order, or the religious establishment, both of which try to control conduct by law. The strength and the attraction of the Kingdom lie in the way that its members can live out its demands of justice, peace and love, without separating themselves from society at large. The reality of the Kingdom did not call for a retreat into an other-worldly spiritual realm. Rather, it offered people the possibility of going about their work in the world, living out new principles in the middle of a society whose values were discredited. It was not necessary physically to overthrow the corrupt order by guerilla activity as the Zealots advocated. The Kingdom constitutes a revolution in which people create a whole new life-style. We shall see later how early Christians modelled their communities on these principles.

The Kingdom is, however, only in its embryonic stage. It is a living, growing reality. Jesus uses a biological model in his parables to describe how the Kingdom functions. It is like a very small seed which will grow into an enormous tree. It is like yeast which slowly raises the entire loaf (Luke 13.18–21). Its principles push out to renew and transform all aspects of life: marriage, the family, the state, international relations, and so on. The basic dynamic of the Kingdom is not that it appears in a sudden blinding moment in the future: it is already here, gradually extending its claim over more areas of life. Thus, when the Pharisees ask Jesus when the Kingdom will come, obviously seeking structural manifestations of it, Jesus responds that the Kingdom cannot be physically observed, yet is something already at work in the world (Luke 17.20f.). At the same time, there remains a future dimension to the Kingdom, because it cannot be complete until all humanity and all its institutions and structures have been renewed in its power.

The nature of the Kingdom is inseparably bound up with the character of its members. St Matthew indicates that the primary characteristic of those seeking to enter the Kingdom is that they have their hearts set on justice (6.33). The realization of justice is therefore of the essence of the kingdom. That is why those not in search of justice, and those who perpetrate injustice, are excluding themselves from it. Many of Jesus' parables indicate that the Kingdom is not composed of those who think they are in it, the rich and the powerful, but of those poor, despised and rejected in whom it is established and through whom it is revealed to others.

Take the parable of the Good Samaritan (Luke 10.29–37). Christian social service agencies generally offer it as the ideal model of social work approved by Jesus. Margaret Thatcher has contributed to the debate by typically emphasizing the economic preconditions of social service: the Samaritan was only able to offer help because he had money in his pocket to cover the injured man's expenses at the inn! The parable certainly describes an appropriate way of responding immediately to the victims of physical or social injury. But at a deeper level, it indicates where the Kingdom of God is located: not amongst the violent who mugged the traveller; nor amongst the religious and legal establishments which pass human suffering by; but in the Samaritan who was to the Jews the most despised of people. The one thing we can say about the Kingdom with certainty is that its members are those who, by the world's standards of success, are failures; those who possess nothing; those whose experience of injustice has given them a passion for justice; and those whose lives are open to change, to the risk of living out principles which contradict the values of the world around them.

When we examine the values of the Kingdom, we discern that in most cases, they are diametrically opposed to the values of a society which favours the rich and powerful. The Kingdom is contemporary society turned on its head. Jesus describes it as a condition in which the first shall be last and the last first, where the greatest gives way to the least, where the servant is more important than the master, where the poor take precedence over the propertied, where the socially unacceptable become guests of honour. In this way he acknowledges and develops the Old Testament priority of justice for those excluded from the economic, and hence the social life of the community. The Kingdom is biased in favour of the disadvantaged. They are the measure of the just society. Our response to them is the test of the justice of our own motivation and behaviour.

Despite all the evidence to the contrary, there remain Christians who insist that the Kingdom is an entirely spiritual phenomenon, which bears no relationship to the structures of a transitory world. Their arguments are generally based on two disputed texts.

Where St Luke speaks of 'the Kingdom of God', St Matthew speaks of 'the Kingdom of heaven'. In speaking of a heavenly Kingdom, these Christians insist that a spiritual interpretation is clearly intended. Against their position, modern scholarship locates St Matthew's Gospel in its Jewish context. He is a Jew addressing Jews and therefore particularly conscious of the things which create offence in Jewish eyes. He doesn't want to alienate his readers before they have listened to his message. In the Jewish mind, to use the name of 'God' constituted a blasphemy. Hence Matthew avoids its use, choosing 'heaven' as a more acceptable alternative. He avoids offending his hearers, but in the process unintentionally confuses the meaning of Jesus' words.

Secondly, does Jesus not state unequivocally in St John's Gospel that 'My Kingdom is *not* of this world'? (18.36). This surely makes the Kingdom other-worldly? But what we have here appears to be a case of simple mistranslation. The Greek reads 'My Kingdom is not *from* this world.' In the words which follow, Jesus expands on this theme. 'If my Kingdom were from this world, my men would have fought to prevent my being surrendered to the Jews. But my Kingdom is not of this kind.' Jesus is indicating that his Kingdom is not a political movement aiming to replace the present order. As we have already seen, it is much more a process which reaches out to transform all aspects of human existence, including the political order. But it is not a political ideology for which people must be prepared to die! Jesus is emphasizing that his Kingdom does not have its *origins* in this world, which is quite different from saying that it has no *relationship* with this world.

Why did the church sanctify this mistranslation? The likelihood is that it was a deliberate act of falsification on the part of a church unwilling to countenance the possibility of the Kingdom offering a critique of the political orders of this world. That the concept of the Kingdom might have revolutionary overtones was unthinkable. To have made such an admission would have been to have allowed that the poor had a stake in the building and running of such kingdoms, and that state of affairs would have constituted a direct challenge to the political power, status and vested interests of the church. The mistranslation clouds the issue. It sent people then, and sends people still, in search of a mystical experience in a spiritual kingdom. This wild goose chase can only work to the advantage of the powerful.

The nature of authority

When discussing any kind of society, in terms of what already exists or in terms of our vision of what can be, the issue of authority is fundamental. We have to look at the way that the Bible in general, and Jesus in particular, handled this matter. We saw when we looked at the incident in which Jesus was confronted with the trick question about payment of taxes, something of his attitude. His ambiguous answer on that occasion did not comment directly on the legitimacy of Roman authority, or on any obligation of his followers to accept it. Indeed, given the context of the teaching, the dissatisfied citizens of Jerusalem may well have taken the response to mean that they need not recognize the civil authority.

A great deal of the Old Testament is given over to the history of the development of Israel, and the way in which authority was exercised. We can trace a movement from the individual charismatic authority of Moses, through the period of the judges deciding questions of justice, to the establishment of a monarchy, to the subjection of the nation to the authority of foreign powers, latterly that of the Roman empire. These changes in the manner in which authority was exercised evolved in historical process. But the Bible recounts that over one of the changes there was considerable debate.

The passage concerns the critical transition of Israel from a people to a nation; from the authority of the judges to the authority of a king. We find in the book of Samuel two quite separate accounts of this process, which represent two parties, the 'monarchists' and the 'covenanters'. These parties established the parameters of a debate which continued through Israel's history. We here look at the arguments advanced by the 'covenanters' because it was their themes which were taken up and developed into a critique by the later prophets (I Sam. 8.1–22).

The historical setting is at the end of the period of the judges, who were not primarily magistrates in our sense of the word, but popular tribal leaders. Judges were considered to have been anointed by God and therefore in a special relationship with him and able to interpret the meaning of the covenant. Each of the tribes might have several judges. The tribes were very much separate entities bound together by the Sinai covenant. There was no centralized administration or government. God had a direct relationship with his people and there were strong senses of independence and individualism, as well as local community. People participated beyond tribal boundaries, however, in the observance of common festivals and in the pursuit of social justice. In times of crisis they were able to surmount their differences to act powerfully as one people.

The passage recounts that the people of Israel, having observed the way in which the most powerful neighbouring nations organized authority around a central monarchy, asked Samuel to provide them with a king as well. Their vision at this point was limited to that which was already in existence, and which appeared to be working well in the interests of other nations. It represents a movement towards concentrating power in the hands of a single person rather than sharing power on a wider basis in the community. People are in fact asking to be released from the responsibility of making decisions: 'We want a king . . . to fight our battles.'

Jahweh God interprets these demands as a threat to the very basis of his relationship with his people. God's authority is about to be invested in somebody else. The covenant is in jeopardy as a result. Nevertheless God insists that the will of the people is paramount. He has given them freedom, and although their choice will lead to slavery and oppression from which they will cry out to him for deliverance, it must be respected.

Samuel tries desperately to dissuade people from this course, by spelling out the disadvantages of the proposed new system of authority. There is no doubt a 'reading back' from the subsequent experience of monarchy at this point in the passage. The disadvantages all have a remarkably contemporary ring to them. The population will be impressed into military service, and allotted the most dangerous frontline positions in order to defend the king. Men will be forced to work in agriculture and armament production to maintain the military establishment. Women will be directed to work as cooks, bakers and perfumers in order to provide for the administration's needs. The best land in the community will be expropriated and given into the possession of government officials. A system of taxation will have to be introduced to pay for the state apparatus. The basis of the system of production will be depleted as the best workers and best ploughing and transportation animals will be commandeered by the state. What it all adds up to, says Samuel, is that the people will exchange their present freedom for a form of slavery.

Despite this catalogue of disadvantages, the people still insist on a monarchy and Samuel anoints Saul as king. From this point on, the quest for political aggrandisement becomes an integral part of the new national consciousness. We see this particularly in the reigns of David and Solomon, two kings whose ambition was 'to make the nation great'. In the process, however, devotion to the monarchy tended to displace devotion to Jahweh God, and the nation drifted further away from the principles of the covenant which had been established with God's people.

It fell to the prophets to construct an analysis of what was happening to the nation. Hosea typically lays the entire blame for the corruption which has developed internally in the economic, political and religious structures and externally in foreign relations, at the door of the monarchy. With seven kings of the northern kingdom having been murdered by the year 737, he notes the instability of the system (7.7). Then he declares God's punishment for the crime at Gilgal, the place where the monarchy was instituted (9.15–17). Finally, he pronounces the end of the monarchy: 'In my anger I gave you a king and in my wrath I take him away' (13.9–11). Hosea's message was that the authority of the state cannot be given absolute obedience because it is Jahweh God who is lord of all. This entire authority structure must fall so that the land can be reborn!

The value of this passage is that it provides us with a critique of the way that authority is exercised by the state. It suggests that the construction of state administrative and military establishments necessarily leads people away from reliance on authority expressed on a religious or communitarian basis, into a state of personal slavery which is at variance with God's will for his people. We shall return to a more detailed discussion of the state later.

When we begin to examine the way that Jesus approached the question of authority, we are struck first by the way in which he opposed attempts to regulate human behaviour through legislation. We see this especially in his confrontations with the Scribes and Pharisees over the nature of the Law. Their understanding was that salvation could be won by observing the minute particulars of the Law. Jesus challenged that perception and took practical action to expose the weaknesses and injustices which flow from it. He walked further than the Law permitted on Sabbath, he defended his disciples when they ate corn in a field in contravention to the Law of Sabbath, and he healed people on Sabbath in breach of the Law. When taken to task for deliberately ignoring the Law's demands, Jesus responds with an explanation which sets all legal prescriptions within their human perspective. 'The Sabbath was made for man,' he says, 'not man for the Sabbath' (Mark 2.27). In other words, he points out that the Law of Sabbath had been originally instituted as a means of liberating people from an endless seven-day week of physical labour. Its purpose was to free people so that they could develop other than the subsistence and economic aspects of their lives. But as applied in first-century Palestine, the Law was no longer liberating at all. People were weighed down by its interminable prohibitions and injunctions.

Jesus is stating that the Law must serve human interests. So when he sees the Law obstructing human development, he does not hesitate to break the Law and to encourage others to do so as well. When Jesus breaks the Law by healing the sick man at the pool of Bethzatha (John 5.1–10), he tells the man to pick up his bed and walk, in the full knowledge that by so doing, the man would also be in breach of the Law. Indeed, St John's Gospel recalls that the man is immediately confronted by the legalists who tell him: 'It's Sabbath and you're not allowed to carry your sleeping mat!'

Jesus encouraged people to seek authority not in external laws but in interior human resources. In this respect, he stands in the tradition of the pre-monarchist covenanters where, under God, 'every person did what was right in his own eyes' (Judges 21.25). It was this understanding which prophets like Micah and Isaiah reaffirmed, indicating that divine authority is internally sited. It is when this authority prevails over earthly authority that the latter crumbles away and peace is established. Jesus would often demonstrate this principle through the technique of reflecting a question back to the questioners and having them answer it from their own resources. He tried to avoid being treated as a moral authority and dispenser of instant answers to all questions. There are examples of his resistance to this in St Luke's Gospel (12.13–15, 57–59). When a man in the crowd asks Jesus to pronounce on a question on inheritance, Jesus responds, 'My friend, who appointed me your judge, or the arbitrator of your claims?' And later in the same passage Jesus chides people for being able to read changes in the weather but not the signs of the times. 'Why not judge for yourselves what is right?', Jesus demands, and then goes on to illustrate the perils of people taking legal action to settle their differences. His implication is that people can develop the capacity to judge issues for themselves, and that there is no need to have recourse to the Law. Those who are living in the Kingdom have different values from the values embodied in the legal system!

Jesus always operated by making an appeal to people and never by coercing them. The Temptations in the Wilderness recorded at the beginning of his ministry were descriptions of strategies which could have commanded widespread acceptance and belief (Matt. 4.1–11). Turning stones into bread might solve the world's food crisis. (Some religious aid agencies still seek converts from amongst the hungry.) Throwing himself off the Temple would demonstrate his miraculous powers. (People still flock to the latest wonder-worker.) Or he could exercise political authority over all the kingdoms of the earth. (We all experience the tactics they use to ensure conformity!) Jesus rejected any suggestion of coercion in favour of making an appeal to the individual, who was free to accept or reject his claims. He adhered to this principle of voluntarism resolutely. In his conversation with the rich young man whom he loved and wanted as one of his followers, there is no manipulation, no coercion, no hint of moral blackmail. The young man decides the cost of following Jesus is too high, and he walks away (Mark 10.17–22).

We might like to note in passing that one of the dominant ideology's reactions to this story of the rich young man is to explain away the notion that wealth may exclude people from the Kingdom by inventing the suggestion that the rich young man was in fact the writer of the Gospel, Mark, and that he obviously must have retraced his steps to become a follower of Jesus. There is, of course, no biblical or historical evidence of this.

Jesus' teaching, that those who are in the Kingdom act on the basis of an internal authority rather than through reference to Law, was taken up and developed theologically by St Paul, particularly in his letter to the Romans. He asserted that people are saved by grace, not by Law. People act justly not because the Law tells them to, but by way of response to the love which God has showered upon them. But St Paul apparently misses the implications of Jesus' stance, for he chooses to apply this reliance on internal values and authority only to spiritual issues. This leads him into difficulties when confronted with the question whether the Christian saved by grace and a member of the Kingdom needs to obey the secular authority. We have seen that Jesus at best equivocated on this issue and was probably suggesting 'No'. St Paul, in contrast, has no hesitation in saying 'Yes'.

It is the Christian's duty, St Paul declares, to obey the secular authorities because civil government is part of the divine order. St Paul is attempting to apply the teaching of Jesus to his own immediate socio-political situation. He lived at a moment in history where the return of Jesus to judge the world was imminently expected, and where everything consequently had to be regarded as being provisional. The questions of who held power, and how power was exercised were not important questions because the present order was about to be swept away by the final realization of the Kingdom. So the words come easily to Paul: 'You must all obey the governing authority. Since all government comes from God, the civil authorities were appointed by God, and so anyone who resists authority is rebelling against God's decision, and such an act is bound to be punished' (Rom. 13.1–8).

St Paul was writing in this assured manner in AD 58. Twelve years later, as the Emperor Nero launched his persecutions against Christians, believers began to question whether *all* government did emanate from God! It tested common sense to the limit to accept that God had appointed Nero and that anyone who resisted him should be punished. When a subsequent Emperor, Domitian, tried to enforce emperor worship as the state religion, the contradiction became even more clear. How could Christians accept that their refusal to worship the emperor constituted rebellion against God? The Book of Revelation was composed around this time as a resource manual for persecuted Christians. Written in allegorical style so that the chief protagonists were easily recognizable, the book calls God's judgment down upon those who co-operate with the civil authority. Indeed the book goes much further, and speaks of the resistance necessary to bring the state to heel. This resistance will begin with the appearance of a Warrior for Justice, which is probably a reference to Christ. There is to be no co-operation with the evil and unjust regime, and those who follow the Warrior for Justice, must have the courage to resist to the death in order to establish justice for all. Should they die in the attempt, their martyrdom ensures that right will ultimately triumph.[4]

It is another of the tragedies of the church that St Paul's teachings, probably in the first instance based on a misapplication of Jesus' intention, and in vogue for less than two decades, should come to be regarded as the definitive teaching on the Christian attitude to authority. Despite the suffering caused by the Adolf Hitlers and Idi Amins of our world, some Christians refuse to deviate from the Pauline misinterpretation. For such people St Paul's teaching obviously takes precedence over the witness of Jesus, who nowhere suggested that we followed any authority other than that of his Kingdom in the quest for justice and peace.

Jesus' approach to authority was demonstrated in an incident which followed the occasion on which he had thrown the merchants out of the Temple in Jerusalem, and begun teaching in the Temple precincts. It is recorded in St Matthew's Gospel (21.23–32). The Chief Priests and the Elders confront him and demand, 'What authority have you for acting like this, and who gave you this authority?' As he often did in such circumstances, Jesus employs the technique of countering question with question. He poses in return a dilemma which they cannot answer without either exposing the falsity of their views on the one hand, or angering the Jerusalem crowd on the other! Jesus then tells a parable about a man who owned a vineyard and asked his two sons to give him a day's work. One son said he would go to the vineyard, but didn't. The other initially refused to work for his father, but after thinking about it, went. Jesus is reminding people that those who affirm legal authority and make all the appropriate gestures to it without intending to fulfil its demands, are excluding themselves from the Kingdom. And those who reject the Law, but are embodying in their behaviour the demands of the Kingdom, are already part of it.

The question, 'By what authority are you doing these things?' is a very ancient device for discrediting people. It immediately shifts the focus away from the truth of words and the integrity of action, and directs energy and discussion towards a labyrinth of questions aimed to establish acceptability, responsibility and verification. In the last analysis, it assumes control over what a person is saying or doing. It today is used as one of the ploys of the dominant ideology. Christians acting for justice will find this same question of authority posed not only by the state, but also by the church when it is acting as a servant of the state. Jesus' strategy was to refuse to deal with that question on the level at which it was presented. He could see that to do so was to play into the hands of the enemy. His response was to reveal to people the possibilities for human development present in a reliance for authority on an internalized experience of justice, rather than upon any legal code.

The characteristics of a developed humanity

Christians perceive in Jesus *the* model of what it means to be fully human. This model is not therefore a highly abstract one, but embodied in a human being, with all the contradictions that this involves. Some Christians wishing to see Jesus' perfection only as a confirmation of his divinity, portray the model he embodied as a distant goal, too difficult for sinful humanity to reach. That often causes people to overlook the specific revelation of Jesus as divinely human.

We see the human characteristics of Jesus on almost every page of the New Testament. He was a compassionate man. He was deeply moved by human suffering, by crippling disease, by victimization and injustice, by deliberate exclusion from the community. He was tireless in his efforts to identify with people, to be amongst them, and to make himself available to them. In order to be free to respond to them, he sacrificed the securities of a home, a family and an income. But we should not overlook that he was sometimes so tired that all he wished to do was to retreat to the desert to escape the pressures people placed on him and to renew his own vision and commitment. He wept both for reasons of personal grief, and over social injustice. He expressed a very deep anger bordering on bitterness over the hard-heartedness of some community groups and leaders. He appeared irritable and spoke rudely to people as he did with the Syro-Phoenician woman. And we should not forget that he stormed into the Temple and, with a certain degree of violence, set about those whom he considered had no right to be there.

Such characteristics enhance rather than diminish the humanity of Jesus. In him we see human attributes developed to their fullest extent and our vision of society must enable people to develop this potential as beings 'created in the image of God'. For Jesus, the development of humanity was depicted not primarily as an interior journey to be pursued in separation from the world, but as a wholeness forged through committed engagement in the concrete issues of the day.

The marks and characteristics of a divine humanity are best revealed in the healing miracles that Jesus performed. These accounts also provide us with examples of obstacles in the way of people becoming more fully human. Let's look at one of these miracles, the healing of a man who had been blind from his birth (John 9).

The incident begins with a discussion between Jesus and his followers on the nature of sin. The disciples express the view commonly accepted at that time and still held by some today, that there is a direct causal relationship between sinfulness and disease or deformity. So they ask whether the man's blindness is the result of his own sin, or the sin of others, perhaps his parents. Jesus says that neither is to blame. This man was born blind in order to reveal the power of God. For Jesus at least, the sins of the fathers are not visited upon their descendants in the shape of human deformity.

This is not to suggest that Jesus ignored sin. Throughout his ministry he acknowledged sin's reality and the way it prevented people from moving towards the discovery of their true humanity. He consequently regarded it as one of his roles to pronounce divine forgiveness for those whose sense of guilt had overwhelmed and immobilized them. By offering this forgiveness he restores them to fullness of life. He never underestimated the power of sin, pointing to the fact that all people are sinful in the sense of failing to live up to the standards of love, peace and justice demanded by the Kingdom. 'Let the person who has no sin cast the first stone', he said to a crowd impatient to stone an adulteress to death.

Our vision of society cannot ignore the reality of sin, nor the role that it plays in subverting genuinely human values and obstructing the progress of the Kingdom. In analysing the disordering and dehumanizing nature of our present society, the Christian has to give due weight to the nature and consequences of sin. Differentiation of wealth, cultural oppression, the manipulation of power on the basis of class, race or gender; and attempts to escape the pressures of life through materialism, sex, alcohol, drugs, and suicide, are not processes which occur in a vacuum. At their base are disordered, or as the Bible says, sinful personalities.

Scriptural reflection reveals a number of aspects to sin. In the Genesis story of the temptation of Adam and Eve in the Garden of Eden, their giving way to temptation and subsequent expulsion from Paradise to earn their keep through sweated labour, we have a myth which suggests that, from that moment onwards, all humans are born with a bias towards sinful behaviour. Historically this myth has been exploited to lay the blame of human sinfulness upon women, but feminist theologians are now redressing the imbalance this patriarchal propaganda has created. The concept of original sin remains a helpful one if we take it to indicate that each one of us is born damaged, less than the perfect embodiment of justice, peace and love. It then becomes vital to our struggle for humanity to recognize those points at which our lives have been damaged and to search for appropriate healing or restoration. Or if that is not possible, to learn to live creatively within the limitations that such damage has imposed.

The Bible abounds with stories about individuals who succumbed to personal sin; those who, given the choice, chose to do evil rather than good. Such sin does not, however, cut people off from the possibility of human development and salvation. We read that King David lusted after another man's wife and sent the poor man into the front line of battle where he was conveniently killed, so that David could offer his own variety of consolation to the grieving widow. There's a range of sins here related to sexuality, manipulation and exploitation. David survives to become a great folk hero, an ancestor whose lineage Jesus is proud to claim. One of the popular definitions of personal sin is 'missing the mark'. We, like David, aim to act justly, but in falling short of that mark, we sin.

Scripture also embraces a concept of corporate sin. The Old Testament in its patriarchal and sexist way often depicts the nation of Israel as a harlot. The entire community has fallen short of the demands of justice and peace. People have become 'stiff-necked', unable to turn and perceive the reality around them. Such behaviour is so offensive to Jahweh God that he punishes the entire nation, generally by sending an army of foreign occupation. In the New Testament, Jesus uses the term 'hardness of heart', which similarly suggests that the whole community has become closed to the truth and no longer open to the claims of justice.

Then, too, we can discern a notion of sinful social structures. In the way that we have seen Jesus dealing with the structure of Sabbath, or indeed with the religious establishment in general, we begin to understand that these are sinful in the sense they are not God-given but built by human endeavour. As a consequence they incorporate human shortsightedness, limitations and failings. Sometimes they reflect the corporate sin of a class or sectional interest, who employ the structure to further their ambitions at the expense of the interests of others. Thus, for example, a police force can be used to further the divisive policies of a government. Or a department of social welfare, established to alleviate suffering, can cause suffering through the way it deals with its clients. These processes happen irrespectively of the good Christian people who work within those institutions. The structures in that sense have a life of their own: their sinful characteristics are so woven into their fabric that a mere change of personnel is not going to ensure that they behave in a more human or liberating fashion.

A second element in this healing story is the understanding of human dignity which underlies Jesus' action. One of the striking things about Jesus' thought when we compare it to Old Testament thinking with its strongly communitarian bias is the way he emphasizes the unique value of the individual. He communicated this in his teaching by reminding people that their worth in God's sight is infinitely more than that of sparrows which are two a penny. So valuable is the human person that not one hair of one's head is without significance to God. He also communicated this insight through the way he approached people, treating everyone as a valued individual and challenging each person to make an individual decision about membership of his Kingdom.

It is not hard for us to imagine the conditions in which the man born blind had been forced to live until this point. Excluded from nearly all social, economic and religious functions and activities, he is a truly marginalized person. The only way that he could survive would be through the charity of others. This was generally handed out then, as it often is today, in a manner which erodes self-respect and personal dignity. But Jesus heals him and with the gift of sight appear the first possibilities of the man being able to take responsibility for his own life. It is only then that self-respect and dignity are established.

This is closely linked to another idea, that of participation. The Bible from its first pages portrays humankind as co-creators with God. Humans participate with God in the shaping of the world. In the opening chapter of Genesis, humans are made 'masters' of creation. In the second chapter, God bestows on humans the responsibility of naming the creatures of the earth. In Hebrew thought, the act of bestowing a name, or even knowing the name of another, was considered to give one the power over the other. The act of naming creation therefore carries with it an understanding of the exercising of power. Furthermore, we have already seen how important the notion of participation in the nation's economic life was to the Hebrews. All civil rights and religious benefits were dependent upon that participation. The prophetic vision is therefore one of a society in which all are able to participate fully.

In this act of healing we see Jesus removing all the barriers to the blind man's participation. When his sight is restored, the man is able to take part once more in economic and community life, and win back his rights. He is once more 'in the right': justice has been done to him.

We observe this process at work in every act of healing that Jesus performs. The miracles are not simply a demonstration of his power; a power, incidentally, which he shared with his followers. They are a demonstration of his belief that wherever humanity is being diminished through subjection to forces over which it feels it has no control, there must be an intervention to break the power of that domination. This is so whether that outside force is seen to be possession by evil spirits, physical deformity, or social ostracism. In all cases the external forces must be overthrown so that personal control over individual life can be re-established. This is dramatically illustrated in the healing of the ten lepers, who were so far outside the socio-economic structure that they constituted the most oppressed group of all. Healed by Jesus, they are able to enter the city once more and claim a clean bill of health from the Temple authorities. All their rights are restored at a stroke (Luke 17.11–19).

This participation, reflecting as it does human self-respect and dignity, is related to a further element, empowerment. Through his healing the blind man is given the power to cut loose from his utter dependence on others, to make his own decisions, and to take charge of his own life. Such empowerment is also a common feature of all the miracle stories. In the Bible, the empowering of one person does not necessarily involve another losing power in an absolute sense. A great deal of contemporary talk about the redistribution of power is based on male understandings of power as domination. Empowerment in that framework necessarily involves the powerless contesting and destroying the power-base of the powerful. One of the many contributions of feminine theology is to show that there are quite different understandings of empowerment, which need not be at the expense of other groups.[5] In this particular passage, and in others in the gospel, the redistribution of power involves the raising of a powerless person to sharing equal status and responsibility with those who are already powerful. In this way people cease to have power over one another.

Our blind man was not considered to possess the ability to so much as comment on the dominant ideology, let alone offer a constructive criticism of it. This was the domain of those who exercised ideological power, the Pharisees. After his healing, the formerly blind man is confronted by the Pharisees who wish to discredit Jesus. The man, in contrast to his former state, is now powerful enough to take them on at their own game. The Pharisees use every demeaning tactic from treating the man as an idiot to hurling personal abuse at him; but he calmly and confidently confronts them on the basis of their own ideological principles. In the end, they have to resort to physical force to drive him out of the area. As a 'sinner' he has had the effrontery to instruct the 'experts'. Such a state of affairs could not be allowed to persist, for if other people began to emulate this behaviour the whole ideological superstructure would be in danger of collapsing. Jesus, by empowering one person, has significantly altered the balance of power in the community.

Despite the efforts of some evangelical Christians to project a bleak and pessimistic view of human nature by harping on human weakness, unworthiness and failure, Christianity in fact has an optimistic view of human nature. It was Bonhoeffer, writing out of the horrors of the holocaust, who urged that instead of dwelling on the ugly shortcomings of humanity, we should be celebrating its beauty and strengths.

The gospel's optimism is reflected in the way it holds out to every individual and each society the possibility of change. Whereas some religious systems condemn people to a blind acceptance of their condition and offer no hope of rising above it, Christianity's concept of conversion of heart opens the possibility of striking out in a completely new direction. Nobody is beyond redemption. Anyone can change by having a heart and mind open to the Kingdom. Prostitutes, drunkards and turncoat tax-collectors were amongst those who gave testimony to this fact in Jesus' day. And there is no greater witness to the process than St Paul himself, the ardent persecutor of the early Christians who became the most fervent missionary of the gospel.

The possibility and the power of change are both centred in the Christian understanding of the resurrection. It is the doctrine of the resurrection, understood as a contemporary experience as well as an historic event, on which Christianity stands or falls. When

Christians recite in their Creed, 'I look for the resurrection of the dead', they are not expressing the vague hope that after they die they will be brought back to life again. They are celebrating life in its fullness *now*. They are looking around for signs of the resurrection: the cycle of renewed life in nature, the infectious liveliness of people whose lives had once been miserable, the liberation of our tired, outworn and oppressive institutions. For Christians all these are signs of resurrection power breaking through the deathliness of the world.

It was this same power, made available to the community at Pentecost, which changed the Christian community from a demoralized and grieving group of people, huddled together in an upper room in fear of public reaction, into a crusading community. Within a very few years they had established, first within Palestine and then in neighbouring areas, a network of communes. Within twenty years they had spread their influence through Asia Minor. They very quickly developed all the characteristics of a popular mass movement, and became so powerful that the Emperor Constantine eventually had to make this foreign religion from the far corner of the empire, the state religion. In the end, Christianity succeeded to the power of the Roman empire itself. And the whole of this historical development rested on an optimism about change and the creative energy of resurrection power.

The shape of community

The first Christians in Jerusalem established a pattern of community life based on what Jesus had told them and the way they had seen him behave. The life of the new Christian community contrasted starkly with that of the wider community in which it was set. It embraced people of the lower socio-economic classes who were in the process of freeing themselves from living by Law in order to live out the principles of the Kingdom within a country whose political and economic aspirations were leading it to disaster. These first Christians understood themselves to be embodying the resurrection and fashioning a new world within the old. It was not necessary to overthrow the old; they simply created new ways of structuring society which reflected the Gospel and which could be sustained while society around them was falling apart.

We can uncover very few of the details of these communities today, but their general principles are documented in scripture. They were small, self-governing units based on the communal ownership of property; what we would today refer to as communes. The Jerusalem commune is described in two passages.

The faithful all lived together and owned everything in common. They sold their goods and possessions and shared out the proceeds among themselves according to what each one needed. They went as a body to the Temple every day but met in their houses for the breaking of bread. They shared their food gladly and generously. They praised God and were looked up to by everyone (Acts 2.44–47).

The whole group of believers was united, heart and soul. No one claimed for his own use anything that he had, as everything that they owned was held in common. The apostles continued to testify to the resurrection of the Lord Jesus with great power, and they were all given great respect. None of their members was ever in want, as all those who owned land and houses would sell them, and bring the money from them to present it to the apostles. It was then distributed to any members who might be in need (Acts 4.32–35).

Even from these brief descriptions, the shape of the commune is clear. There was no concept of private ownership, all lands, possessions and goods being in common ownership. Previously privately-owned resources were sold and the proceeds put into a common fund. This fund was shared on the basis, not of equal shares, but according to need. There was an emphasis on unity, with public and private demonstrations of solidarity. The community offered testimony of the reality of its beliefs, particularly that in resurrection power. The life-style of the commune was of such calibre that its members were held in high public esteem.

A second feature of the communes was the way in which mutual solidarity was an external as well as internal feature. There is evidence of the way this worked in practice during the specific economic crisis eighteen years after Jesus' death. The effects of a disastrous famine in AD 47–8 were compounded by a sabbatical year in which the land had to lie fallow. The food supply was dependent upon what had been saved from previous harvests or could be imported. A Christian commune comprising in the main Greek converts had been established in the city of Antioch. They were alerted to the dimensions of the disaster by a delegation from the Jerusalem commune. The Antioch commune immediately came to the rescue, sending their surplus production in a relief operation led by Saul and Barnabas (Acts 11.27–30).

St Paul in his writings affirms this principle on at least four occasions. Commenting on the generosity of the communes in Macedonia, and on the way in which the Corinth commune had made a similar commitment, he says: 'This does not mean that to give relief to others you ought to make things difficult for yourselves. It is a question of balancing what happens to be your surplus now against their present need, and one day they may have something to spare that will supply your own need' (II Cor. 8.13f.). It is clear that by this time there was a fairly sophisticated mechanism in place through which communes separated by considerable distances could respond to external need in the same generous spirit that they handled their internal welfare programmes.

It was not long before these early experiments were overwhelmed by very powerful external forces which could not afford to let them succeed. But the experiments are also so contrary to the spirit and organization of contemporary capitalism that it too, must try and discredit them. The argument offered is that this early form of Christian organization proved so unworkable, and such a dismal failure, that its members were eventually forced to face up to reality and build more appropriate structures. The Christian commune model from the first century may be of historical interest as a failed experiment, but it is certainly no model for contemporary Christians to espouse with any degree of seriousness. But as the Latin American theologian José Miranda has pointed out, the fact that the Sermon on the Mount failed does not deprive it of its normative character. Scripture attests to the fact that communism is obligatory for Christians, and the fact that the early attempts at communal living failed does not modify the requirement.[6]

Miranda suggests that Christians today must try to discover why this first attempt failed, and learning from the errors of the past, make sure that our future attempts to build communities of justice and peace do not founder on the same mistakes. This is one area in which, in comparison to other sciences, theologians have proved amateur. We document the successes of Christianity; only rarely its failures. Yet in the scientific laboratory, it is often the patient documentation of failed experiments which eventually reveals a way forward. Much work has to be done to determine why it was that the first Christian communes failed to survive the pressures against them. Marx has suggested it was due to their neglect of a political strategy, so that in the end, they were forced to compromise with stronger ideological and political forces.

On a more positive note, we might remind ourselves that the conviction that the ownership of property is inconsistent with Christian values has remained an important perception in the church, albeit held by only a minority of Christians. The writings of Church Fathers like Clement of Alexandria, Basil the Great, Ambrose, John Chrysostom and Augustine, all provide us with critiques of the damaging effects of private ownership.[7] And throughout Christian history groups of Christians have emerged to treat the early teaching seriously and to pattern their communities upon those of the first Christian communes. That such initiatives continue to this day is another sign of hope for the church.

We can also learn from the compromises the early church made with the dominant ideology of the day. One of the major compromises can be detected in St Paul's insistence on the necessity of hierarchical structures. The establishment of such hierarchies within the Christian communes with St Paul's support can be seen as a return to those patriarchal values and modes of organization which Jesus had rejected in his model of the Kingdom. Perhaps with Paul considering himself to be a person of some pre-eminence in the Christian movement, and constantly having to defend himself as a result against accusations of naked ambition, this compromise became inevitable. His assertion that all government comes from God provided powerful ideological underpinning for the contention that within the commune there needs to be a definite hierarchy of roles. Apostles (and he declares himself to be one) are given first place, prophets second, teachers third, miracle-workers fourth, healers fifth, and so on down through helpers, leaders and linguists. Given that Jesus had declared that in the Kingdom the hierarchies of this world would be stood on their heads, this innovation within the communes could only be justified on the basis that the apostles were number one because they were the least important people in the community. Their increasing willingness to make authoritarian declarations, coupled with their authoritarian behaviour, showed that they in no way believed themselves to be so.

The same fiction is maintained in ecclesiastical hierarchies to this day. The Pope is 'the servant of the servants of God', but rarely acts as if this were his actual status! Whatever St Paul's motivation for imposing this order, and whatever the ideological processes at work which encouraged people to accept its imposition, the new situation runs counter to the teaching of Jesus and eroded the 'democratic' character of the original communes. What it facilitated in the long run was an easy integration of the religious apparatus into the hierarchical structures of the Roman empire. From that moment, and for centuries to come, Christian attempts to return to a communitarian base necessarily involved a direct challenge to the existing order.

On the other hand, although he stoutly resisted applying the model to his own life, we do have St Paul to thank for a specific vision of the way the new society ought to function. He uses the analogy of the human body (I Cor. 12). This particular passage follows a format common in Paul's time for political commentaries. Were it not for the fact that Christ is mentioned in the text, it could have stood as a political statement in its own right. As it is, it is a statement of how the Christian commune should be modelled on a co-operative basis. As in the body every organ has a vital role to play in creating an harmonious unity, so each member of the commune has a particular function to fulfil.

St Paul makes a number of assertions about these functions. First, although made up of many diverse parts, the body acts as a single entity. Secondly, the body is not identified with any one of its many parts. If the body were composed of equal and similar units it could not function at all. It requires great diversity, and it is the harnessing of this diversity which gives the body its character. It is not possible for one organ to say to another, 'I have no need of you,' and for the body to survive. There has to be a mutual recognition of need, and co-operation. Thirdly, Paul notes that it is the apparently weakest parts of the body which are the indispensable ones, and it is the least honourable parts which are adorned with the greatest care. There is a parallel here with the teaching of Jesus about the priority given in the Kingdom to the apparently weak and dishonourable members of the community. And fourthly, Paul suggests that a characteristic of the body is a communal dimension to the recognition of pain and the celebration of joy. 'If one part is hurt,' he says, 'all parts are hurt with it. If one part is given special honour, all parts enjoy it.'

This beautifully poetic description of the co-operative community is in distinct contrast to models which are based upon intense competition and the survival of the fittest. While in other places Paul may be tempted to use competitive images like running a race, or putting on armour for battle, his model of community does not permit of a winners versus losers mentality. In the Christian community, individualism gives way to the principles of co-operation, to acceptance of mutual dependency, to recognition of weakness, to the making public of private pain, and the common celebration of achievements. It was a far call from the structure he was actually responsible for creating, but then Paul, like the rest of us, had to struggle with the contradictions he embodied. His vision nevertheless remains an important guide to the way a co-operative Christian society can function.

On the basis of this overview we are able to identify the broad parameters of the society the Christian should be seeking to establish. The basic foundations of society are ethical principles of which justice, reflected in personal, social, economic, political and international relationships, is the most important. This justice calls for a sharing of resources in a manner which empowers people, enhances human dignity and creates the optimum conditions within which full humanity, the kind we see in Jesus, can develop. Christians should therefore be committed to co-operative, highly participatory and voluntarily accepted forms of organization in which there is no place for hierarchical, authoritarian or coercive structures. While local expressions of community may differ, they would share a basis of common ownership and mutual inter-dependence embodying these principles and encouraging the widest possible diversity. Such a society cannot be established through revolutionary violence. Jesus insisted that it is already a present reality which only requires its claims to be extended to ever more areas of human activity.

CHAPTER FOUR

Old Wine in New Bottles
Christian Critiques of Capitalism and Socialism

Some voices insist that the Christian vision for society is already embodied within one of our current political alternatives. Today's world is popularly held to be divided into two major camps, 'the free world' and 'the communist world' competing for our attention. These can be further broken down into predominant ideological tendencies or differing expressions of capitalist-based societies and socialist-based societies. One economist has designated the main ideological streams as *laissez-faire* or free market capitalism, Marxism, social market or mixed economy capitalism, democratic socialism and economic conservationism. This latter designation refers to the 'small is beautiful' approach to economics.[1] Although we have gone some way towards developing a critique of both capitalist and socialist models, we should at this point pause to ask whether it is possible, perhaps with modification, for these major perspectives to carry us in the direction of our vision? One way of pursuing this task is by examining the way that churches have responded to the two competing options.

Capitalism as a Christian option

In the first chapter we looked at the way in which the gospel is conveyed in capitalist categories in Western societies, and identified some of the arguments raised in defence of that process, and some of the critiques which have been developed against it. It will by now be very clear to the reader that it is the argument of this book that the capitalist mode of organization embodies very little of the biblical vision of the ideal society. On the other hand, the Christian churches have appeared amongst that system's strongest

supporters. This is true of Christian bodies which are as diametrically opposed to one another as the Roman Catholic Church and
the newer fundamentalist churches. Historically speaking, the
theology of the Roman Catholic Church has provided some of the
bases for capitalist development, and the Fundamentalists, it
might be argued, are themselves a product of the capitalist
system.[2] In view of the fact that the vast majority of Christians in
the West continue to support this option, it has to be treated
seriously.

It has been convincingly argued that many of the features of
capitalism run counter to the vision of a truly developed humanity.
The model, far from creating just social, political and economic
structures, through its twin obsessions with the primacy of
economic growth and the maximizing of profitability, creates a
series of powerful economic centres. The capitalist structure
channels resources to these centres at the expense of surrounding
areas. It is consequently a feature of capitalist development that
towns and cities flourish on the resources drawn in from rural areas
which, as a consequence, tend to be comparatively under-
developed. As the economic centres expand and require ever
increasing resources, so the infrastructures of the rural community
– transport, education, employment, commerce and so on – come
under pressure. In many instances the country store and the
country school disappear as life becomes centred on the metro-
polis. This model of development necessarily leads to underdevelopment and to all the social and economic crises which
accompany it.[3]

This initially secular critique of capitalism has been shared by
both Third World and First World theologians. The Cuban
theologian Sergio Arce Martinez accuses the church in the West of
having committed itself to an ideologized faith which, in contradiction to the gospel, has become part of 'the bourgeois, imperialist, capitalist disorder'.[4] That contention is amplified in his Presbyterian Church's statement of faith which says that

the capitalist system of social organization, in order to endure,
has to maintain a manipulated and enslaving education that
produces egoists who distort the meaning of human life and see
as the supreme ideals of human life, unending consumption,
insatiable satisfaction of getting rich, materialistic fetishism and

the drive for luxury and ostentation. As a result this brings about a dehumanized society where the most ferocious competition is of utmost importance and in which its victims are inculcated social evasion by means of drugs, sexual license, gambling and alienating religiosity.[5]

A similar critique has been offered by one of the best-known development theologians in the West, Charles Elliott. He writes that the churches 'give to Western capitalism and its attendant social structures a legitimacy and moral authority' which have acted as 'the legitimizer of a series of relationships which lie at the heart of the structures of injustice'.[6] We saw in an earlier chapter how this operates at an ideological level.

This process is illustrated by reference to the development of the church's teaching about private property. We have noted elsewhere the rapidity with which the practice of the early church and the teaching of the Church Fathers about the communal ownership of property was abandoned in favour of the church itself becoming a major political power and property owner. Once in this position, the right to own private property needed to be vigorously defended.

This right has been consistently maintained in the social teaching of the Roman Catholic Church. It appears, for instance in the Vatican II document, *Gaudium et Spes*.

> Since property and other forms of private ownership of external wealth contribute to the expression of personality and afford opportunities for social and economic service, it is a good thing that some access to them should be encouraged whether for individuals or for communities.
>
> Private property or some control over external goods gives a certain elbow-room for personal and family independence and can be regarded as an extension of human liberty. Since it also provides incentives to responsible work, it is in some sense a condition of civil liberties.[7]

In linking the flowering of the human personality, the concept of liberty and civil liberties themselves to the institution of private property, the church is putting its weight behind some of the fundamental tenets of capitalism. There is no biblical justification offered for this stance. Under challenge, the church can offer only the legitimization which tradition, in this case property-owning tradition, provides.

On the other hand, the church has been forced to recognize that the institution of private property has legitimized relationships which are unjust. The entire class structure of society, from feudalism through the development of capitalism to the present day, is based upon this right of ownership of property and the resources that go with it. It is but a short step from the right to own property to the right to defend one's property against the attacks of those who would remove it. Hence the development of a body of law and institutions such as the police force and the army to protect it at a local and a national level needs also to be justified.

In an attempt to ameliorate some of the more destructive effects of private ownership, the church has emphasized another principle: that a person should not regard private property as only his or hers, but as something whose benefit should accrue to others. Private possessions are intended to benefit the common good. So without in any way challenging the right to own property, the church is able at the same time to affirm that in the world's under-developed regions where vast estates are poorly cultivated or left uncultivated for purposes of gain, a 'redistribution' of the land amongst those able to make them productive is permissible. Such confiscation must, of course, be accompanied by appropriate compensation to the owners![8]

Once the church proved willing to defend the institution of private property, it was duty bound to defend the class structure which was based upon it. Here again there was a convergence of theology and the liberal or capitalist ideology, with both affirming that the class system sprang from the Natural Order and was therefore a natural element of society. Being itself both a landowner and a political power, the church protected its own interests by always siding with the ruling or owning class against the interests of other classes. Thus the concept promoted by the socialists that two classes, the owners of capital and the sellers of labour, were naturally hostile to each other, was anathema to the church. This was spelt out in the document *Rerum Novarum*.[9] Socialism was depicted as engendering an unnatural class conflict by deliberately exciting the envy of the poor towards the rich. The socialist objective of creating a society of equals had to be rejected because the church believed that it is a condition of human existence that 'in civil society the lowest cannot be made equal with the highest'. Christian teaching had certainly undergone a total transformation on this issue from the days in which Jesus had declared that in his Kingdom the lowest would be made the highest, and the hightest relegated to the lowest status.

Leaving the question of an unjust class structure aside, does not capitalism at two points in particular reflect our vision of the new society? Its emphasis on individualism surely reflects the weight and value that Jesus gave to the individual, and its commitment to the preservation of freedom surely provides the milieu, by way of contrast to totalitarian regimes, in which human development can be promoted?

Capitalism's emphasis on the individual differs markedly from the biblical focus. In describing the free market economy as a condition in which there are a few winners and many losers, a spokesman for one of New Zealand's major transnational corporations was highlighting the competitive nature of the enterprise within which one may have opportunities for development at the expense of others. That point was amplified by All Black rugby hero and economic entrepreneur Andy Haden in a 1985 television debate, when he declared that the value of the game of rugby is that it is an intensely competitive and physically bruising activity which forms men capable of relating to the Real World where economic success is dependent upon beating the other fellow or the opposing team.

We have seen that while Jesus placed enormous emphasis on the development of each individual to their potential as created in God's image, this development was neither at the expense of other people, nor through the perpetration of injustice or personal injury. We have also seen that the early Christians took his teaching to mean that communities should function co-operatively rather than competitively. Capitalism is right to stress the value of the individual, but in its basic understanding of development as first and foremost an economic process based on competition between individuals, it parts company with the biblical understanding of the process.

Capitalism likes to present itself as the only political system which can guarantee real freedom. Rival systems can be maintained, capitalists insist, only by denying people's basic human freedoms and imposing rigorous and oppressive mechanisms of control. We earlier noted the way that capitalists maintain that personal freedoms are intrinsically linked to the free enterprise economic system. They believe that if we abandon that system, we also throw away our freedom.

The economist Milton Friedman has been one of the most influential advocates of capitalism in our day. His monetarist policies have been adopted by Conservative and Labour led governments alike. For him, freedom in a political sense means the absence of the power of one person or one group to coerce another into behaving in a certain way. We have already seen that the absence of coercion is one of the fundamental characteristics of the way that Jesus dealt with people. So in trying to ensure this condition, capitalists are at least being true to the gospel! The preservation of freedom therefore requires that strong centres of power be as far as possible eliminated. That which cannot be altogether eliminated must be dispersed through a system of checks and balances. If we can remove the economic system from the control of political authority, the free market can become a check on unbridled political power, rather than a reinforcement of it. A free market, because it provides people with what they want, rather than with what other people think they want, becomes itself a guarantor of freedom. Underlying most critiques of the free market, says Friedman, is a lack of belief in freedom itself.[10]

While in no way wishing to diminish the value of freedom, opponents have pointed out that at the early stages of industrial development, the concept of freedom manifested as the freedoms of thought, speech and conscience which undergirded free enterprise, were essentially critical ideas which replaced the values of a decaying society. But once these became the dominant values and were institutionalized, they lost both their critical function and their ability to tolerate criticism. So we have reached a stage today where free institutions and democratic principles are used to limit individual freedom, to repress individuality, to disguise the reality of political and economic manipulation, and to create narrower boundaries of human experience.[11]

In this situation, what some would regard as the most basic freedom of all, the freedom from *want*, is not being met by capitalism. Instead the vested interests of the economic system create false needs, promoting an endless succession of new and rapidly obsolescent products through high pressure advertising and sales techniques. At the same time, the most basic human needs, food, shelter, work, education, go begging. Under capitalism, the idea of freedom includes the freedom to starve, the freedom to be homeless, and the freedom to be unemployed, the implication being that people suffering in these ways are not so much victims of exploitative systems, but of their own freedom to choose not to take advantage of the benefits of capitalism. Criticism of the system has to be channelled through capitalism's democratic institutions: The freedom to protest is therefore permitted only within strictly defined limits. 'If you don't like the system,' we are told, 'you are perfectly free to change it through the ballot box.'

That capitalist institutions provide only an illusion of freedom can be tested both by personal experience and historical analysis. In 1981, the South African Springboks sent a rugby team to New Zealand, an event which was to prove one of the most divisive and violent in the latter nation's history. The South African regime presents itself as the last bastion of freedom and democracy in Africa, and elicits support from the Free World on the basis that it alone can protect the vital sea routes around the Cape of Good Hope. If the South African free enterprise government falls, the sea lanes fall into the hands of the Russians! Rugby is one of the most powerful ideological symbols of the white racist regime. In South Africa, as in other countries, its administration is almost entirely in the hands of those who ally themselves with the free market economy. The freedom to promote sporting tours irrespective of their moral or political implications is integral to that ideology. And it was on the basis of that argument that the Conservative New Zealand government in power at that time welcomed the tour.

Thousands of New Zealand citizens took to the streets to express their opposition to the hosting of ambassadors from such an unjust and oppressive regime. The street marches, which began as relaxed and good humoured events, had by the end of the tour taken on all the characteristics of pitched battles and community riots. As consensus broke down, so the state had to rely more and more on its coercive apparatus in order to protect its understanding of freedom. The police force, and later the army, were employed to impose limits upon freedom of both assembly and speech. The constraints were enforced at almost every point. On one protest I found myself in the front line, face to face with the police. Their tactic was to verbally abuse the protestors in the most degrading possible way. Protestors had to maintain strict silence in the face of this assault on their dignity, for any who responded were immediately arrested on the charge of using offensive language! Freedom of speech had been reduced to the freedom of state agents to say anything they pleased, and the freedom of the public to remain silent.

Capitalism therefore tends to endorse only those freedoms which enhance its control over people's thinking and behaviour. Critical ideas have to be suppressed; workable alternatives to free enterprise have to be portrayed as unworkable. At the international level we see this demonstrated time after time by the United States of America, which regards itself as the greatest defender of human liberty. Yet in practice, the freedom to proclaim ideas has to be constantly checked by the fear of subversion. Internally, we saw this at its worst during the MacCarthy era when writers, actors, artists, politicians, teachers, priests and even the military and intelligence services themselves were accused of 'un-American activities'.

The processes which capitalism uses to protect its understanding of freedom become even clearer at the international level. They can be observed in the way that the United States 'respects and protects' the freedom of Latin American countries which it regards as an important part of its sphere of influence. In many of these countries there is a long history of United States intervention which has generally resulted in support for the very kind of dictatorial regime whose concentration of power runs counter to the ideal of freedom. This is matched by vigorous opposition to popular liberation movements, notwithstanding how democratic they are.[12] Thus when Salvadore Allende's Marxist regime came to power through the ballot box in Chile, the United States immediately began to deploy overt economic power and covert political action to render the new government unworkable. This lethal combination of a capital strike which paralysed the economy, and CIA backed action to foment social unrest, was carried out in the knowledge that the Latin American solution to such 'problems' is generally a military coup. History records exactly how successful these tactics were to prove against a democratically elected regime!

We see similar tactics being employed against the Nicaraguan regime. It must also be shown to be unworkable, lest other countries are tempted to experiment with socialist options. Millions of dollars of private and state funds are invested in the training and arming of 'democratic' elements; the Honduras based terrorists fighting a guerilla war against a government confirmed in office by popular vote. Provocative United States naval exercises are held off the Nicaraguan coast, the CIA makes attempts to blockade Nicaraguan ports, the US Administration tries to isolate the country diplomatically, and intense efforts are being made to subvert the Nicaraguan economy. When popular elections are held, it becomes imperative that the United States discredit them as 'rigged' despite evidence to the contrary from parliamentary observers from 'free world' countries. When Nicaragua lodges an appeal through one of the few avenues for justice open to it, the World Court at The Hague, the United States President announces, when the Court finds in Nicaragua's favour, that his country will no longer participate in World Court proceedings.

The case of Nicaragua is of particular interest to Christian activists, because in contrast to the Cuban revolution where the institutional church was one of the bastions of capitalism which had to be overthrown, in Nicaragua, liberation theology and the popular church helped pave the way for change. Christians hold key roles within the Sandinista government as a result. Capitalism is particularly conscious of the threat posed to its dominance by liberation theology and the popular church. In 1980, Republican strategists meeting in Santa Fe produced a paper on American foreign policy objectives for the 1980s. Known subsequently as the Sante Fe Document, it specifically states that Latin America, like Western Europe and Japan, is part of America's power base. It sees liberation theology and the Roman Catholic Church, to the degree that it has been infiltrated by this theology, as a major force against American ideological domination in Latin America. It therefore regards the active countering of liberation theology as a key thrust necessary if the United States is to maintain its influence.

The role of the Church in Latin America is vital to the concept of political freedom . . . Unfortunately Marxist–Leninist forces have utilized the Church as a political weapon against private property and productive capitalism by infiltrating the religious community with ideas that are less Christian than communist.[13]

The Document maintains that the church therefore needs to be encouraged to return to its 'proper' role of promoting political freedom understood as private capitalism, free trade, and economic security for United States' interests. It further makes it clear that if propaganda fails to achieve this objective, wars of national liberation will have to be launched in order to restore correct order.

One of the methods which the Reagan administration employed for combating this anti-capitalist stance by the church was to encourage the rapid growth of fundamentalist and pentecostal missions to Latin America. It is from 1980 onwards that press reports begin to comment on the literally planeloads of missionaries being transported from the United States to this region. These missionaries act, whether consciously or unconsciously, as ideological agents of the United States of America. In promoting a literalist and unquestioning faith, the separation of faith and politics, overt support for right-wing regimes, and in refusing to become embroiled in questions of human rights abuses, these Christians stand in stark contrast to the witness of the Roman Catholic Church, and pave the way for acceptance of United States economic and political objectives in the region. Little wonder, then, that the press reported that General Augusto Pinochet of Chile, infuriated by the persistent criticism of his regime by the Roman Catholic Church, planned to leave that church and join a pentecostal evangelical sect.[14]

History shows, then, that capitalism is not willing to defend freedom of choice in an absolute sense. Indeed, if the freedoms which it advocates produce a counter-ideology which is threatening to its interests, almost any tactic from subversion to outright violence is regarded as perfectly legitimate and morally justifiable in the defence of those interests. It goes without saying, of course, that these same tactics employed against capitalism are declared to be both illegitimate and immoral! In contrast to the freedom that Jesus offers people in his Kingdom, the capitalist practice of freedom is no freedom at all.

Thus while two of its bases, the emphasis on individualism and the proclamation of human liberty, appear to parallel those concepts in our biblical vision of the new society, neither in fact does so. Furthermore, its other characteristics run counter to our vision of a developed humanity. Its acceptance of a class structure produces distorting and exploitative relationships, which create the very social and economic injustices that Christians are called to redress. Its glorification of competition is the antithesis to the biblical concept of co-operation. The way it exploits the earth's natural resources for the benefit of a few and to the disadvantage of the world's poor countermands the Christian concern for respect for all of creation. Its stimulation of artificial needs in the pursuit of profit, its vision of unlimited economic growth, and its willingness to defend and promote itself by force and coercion if necessary, cannot legitimately claim Christian allegiance. The communities it has created bear little resemblance to those envisaged by the prophets, or created by the first Christians.

Socialism and the Christian vision

Many Christian activists have come to feel that it is in socialism that the Christian vision for society is most faithfully reproduced. In addressing socialism we are not dealing with an homogeneous system. While socialists may share the broad outlines of a socialist vision, they differ markedly when it comes to strategies for achieving and maintaining power.

We have already noted the way that the bulk of Christian teaching, and especially that of the Roman Catholic Church, has effectively supported the capitalist ideology. As the injustices of international capitalism became more apparent and the Third World church's critique of that system became more strident, and as many members of the church not only espoused socialist principles but became directly involved in political struggles to establish socialist regimes, so the Roman Catholic Church has had to modify its position substantially. Indeed, in some instances an accommodation with socialism has been essential to its very survival.

Its reasons for opposing socialism in the first place were as much political as theological. In the mid-nineteenth century, the church was still a political power to be reckoned with. Popular advocacy of the new socialist principles like the abolition of private property constituted an enormous threat to both the church's income and its power base. Similarly, the accumulation of power in the hands of a

secular state envisaged by popular socialism was anathema to the
church, and led to the identification of socialism as an enemy
which had to be quickly crushed if the church were to maintain its
political power.

The Roman Catholic Church's position *vis-à-vis* socialism is
outlined in a succession of papal documents beginning with *Rerum
Novarum*. This statement 'On the Condition of the Working
Classes' appeared in 1891. In it, socialism is condemned for
artificially creating inter-class hostility, for doing away with
private property and goods, for replacing the God-given structure
of the family with the state as the basis of social organization, and
for agitating for equality in society where the Roman Catholic
Church holds it to be a fundamental condition of human existence
that such equality can never be established.[15]

The 1931 encyclical *Quadragesimo Anno*, 'On Social Reconstruction', was issued at a time in which many Roman Catholics
had come to feel that with some of the modifications which had
been made to socialist ideas, they could now be accepted without loss of Christian principles. Pius XI denies this vehemently,
insisting that socialism and the gospel can never be harmonized
because socialism conceives of human society in a way 'utterly
alien to Christian truth'. The terms 'religious socialism' or
'Christian socialism' imply, he said, a contradiction in terms.
'No one can be at the same time a sincere Catholic and a true
socialist.'[16] This pronouncement remains part of the magisterium to this day.

It was when Pope John XXIII opened a window to allow some
fresh air to blow down the corridors of the Vatican, and unleashed
one of the most profound institutional revolutions the world has
seen, that the official position against socialism was modified in a
major way. In a succession of documents, but more particularly in
the 1961 encyclical *Mater et Magistra*, 'On Recent Developments
of the Social Question in the Light of Christian Teaching', the
Pope undertakes this exploration. Firstly, he acknowledges the
need for the state to intervene to promote the common good in
situations where life is dominated by economic power. Then he
affirms the process of 'socialization', the natural tendency for
people to join together to achieve objects which are beyond the
reach of the individual. Finally, he draws a distinction between
philosophical teachings which may be in the church's view false,

and historical movements working for profound changes of the kind the church applauds.[17]

There are the beginnings of an accommodation here. Socialization is not socialism, but there is an affirmation of the principle of human solidarity in the achievement of social justice in contrast to capitalism's individual competition. The state is granted permission to intervene to limit the effects of centres of economic power in a way that runs directly counter to capitalism's understanding of economic power being a check against political power and the source of all human freedoms. And finally the way is opened up for the church to work in some kind of partnership with an ideology it may continue to regard as false by Christian values, but which is seeking to establish forms of social justice which do reflect those values. Whereas up to this point Roman Catholic statements had attempted to give the impression of 'balance' by criticizing *laissez-faire* capitalism as well as socialism, there was no doubting that its real interests lay with the capitalist system. This was confirmed as much by its economic behaviour and its support of particular political regimes, as by its social teaching. But now the emphasis is beginning to alter significantly.

With Pope Paul VI, the critique of capitalism in general and the support for socialist movements becomes much more specific. Capitalism is a system which

> considers profit as the key motive for economic progress, competition as the supreme law of economics, and private ownership of the means of production as an absolute right that has no limits and carries no corresponding social obligation.[18]

This Pope questions capitalist assumptions about the relationship between increasing wealth and social progress, and that technological advance will make the world a more human place to live in. Having offered a critique of the most exploitative features of capitalism, he endorses the socialist principle of the enforced redistribution of resources and wealth according to the demands of social justice. Building on the principle established in the Vatican II document *Gaudium et Spes*, and no doubt with some of the vast landed estates of Latin America in mind, he says:

> If certain landed estates impede the general prosperity because they are extensive, unused or poorly used, or because they bring

hardship to peoples or are detrimental to the interests of the country, the common good sometimes demands their expropriation.[19]

Once again we find capitalism's insistence on the absolute right to private property, for so long defended by the church, being modified by a new understanding of the gospel's call for social justice.

But these affirmations do not constitute a wholesale endorsement of socialism *per se*. In a subsequent document, *Octogesima Adveniens*, issued in 1971, the Pope notes that while Marxism appeals to many because of its will for justice, equality and human solidarity, it remains incompatible with the Christian faith. The Pope warns:

> It would be illusory and dangerous . . . to accept the elements of Marxist analysis without recognizing their relationships with ideology and to enter into the practice of class struggle and its Marxist interpretations, while failing to note the kind of totalitarian and violent society to which this process leads.[20]

The clear implication is that within Marxist ideology, analysis and practice are so closely linked, that for Christians to lay claim to using Marxist analysis without accepting the Marxist strategy for implementing the new society is not really possible. Yet, as José Miranda[21] has argued convincingly, the church itself appears to have achieved precisely this by in its own documents employing a Marxist analysis without committing itself to a Marxist solution! From *Quadragesima Anno*, the document which declares that Catholics cannot be socialists, onwards, the church's analysis of economic society and industrialization has been essentially Marxist. Roman Catholic social thinking begins to declare that society is divided into classes in which some own the means of production while others, able only to contribute their labour, submit to the decision-making power of the owners. It also acknowledges the inevitability of conflict between the two classes ('struggle' in Marxism, 'confrontation' in the church's documents), and the necessity of building a new society (for Marx, 'a classless society'; in pontifical doctrine 'a society free of classes'). The Marxist analysis is also used in the recognition that structures need to be transformed, as well as persons and attitudes, and that social problems should be approached with 'an historical mentality'.

What is good enough for the official church has been enthusiastically adopted by Roman Catholic theologians and social reformers in the Third World. Despite admonitions to the contrary, a Marxist analysis, and in some cases a Marxist prognosis, has appeared to offer the only solution to deepy embedded social injustices. Almost without exception, the works of the liberation theologians have been based in that analysis. The Latin American church in particular has produced a series of statements and reflections, many of them Marxist in character, which have had a profound effect upon the whole theological tradition of the church. Thus as early as 1968, Roman Catholic priests who were delegates to the Cultural Congress in Havana were able to declare:

> We Catholic priests . . . being convinced
>
> that imperialism today, especially in the Third World, is a dehumanizing factor which destroys the foundations of the individual's dignity, threatens the free expression of culture, militates against the genuine forms of human development, and creates a situation of underdevelopment which is becoming daily more acute and more oppressive:
>
> that though Marxism and Christianity differ over the interpretation of man and the world, it is Marxism which provides the most precise scientific analysis of imperialism, as well as the most effective stimuli for mass revolutionary action;
>
> that the Christian faith means love, which must be expressed in effective service of each and every human being;
>
> that the priest Camilo Torres, by dying for the cause of revolution, has given the most noble example of a Christian intellectual's commitment to the people;
>
> We commit ourselves to the anti-imperialist revolutionary struggle to achieve the liberation of each and every human being, accepting all the consequences it may bring.[22]

While not all were willing to state their views so unequivocally, the Third World insisted that whatever structural changes were made, must benefit those who are the poor and the dispossessed in the community. In countries where the gap between wealth and poverty was growing daily, the need for the church to be visibly the church of the poor was paramount. This provoked a massive deinstitutionalization of the church, principally through the establishment of basic Christian communities. It was inevitable that one day, someone at the centre of institutional power should also be convinced that the church should not only preach poverty, but live poverty.

When Albino Luciani was elected Pope in 1978, and took the name John Paul I, it appeared that such a man had arrived. Convinced that the church must be the church of the poor, having as a first act dispensed with the pompous ceremonial through which Popes were crowned, he initiated an inquiry into the wealth of the Vatican. Within a month he was dead. His death remains controversial. It has been suggested that he was killed by those who stood to lose most from the financial reforms he proposed to carry through,[23] even though the most recent investigation claims that the Pope died from neglect at the heart of one of the world's largest Christian communities.[24]

In any event, his Polish successor, John Paul II, has promoted none of the reforms which would have modified the church's compromise with the institutions of capitalism. The Vatican's window on the world has been very firmly shut, and the blind drawn as the conservatives regroup and are restored to power. The Pope whose life has been spent opposing Marxism has given contradictory signals to the faithful. On the one hand, in his address to a packed Yankee Stadium, he could proclaim that 'it is not right that the standard of living to rich countries should seek to maintain itself by drawing off a great part of the reserves and energy and raw materials that are meant to serve the whole of humanity', and so re-affirm the stance of his recent predecessors. On the other hand, he could give the church's blessing to the rabidly right-wing group, *Opus Dei*, and issue admonitions against both liberation theology and the active involvement of clergy in liberation struggles.

Pope John Paul II's major contribution to the debate has been in the document *Laborem Exorcens*, 'On Human Work'. Some commentators have seen this as an attempt by the Roman Catholic Church, not for the first time, to discover a 'third way' which surmounts the difficulties posed by both capitalism and socialism. One writer is daring enough to suggest that in the expectation that capitalism will pass and that socialism will no longer be regarded as its natural heir, 'the Pope has before him the dazzling prospect of a new order, under the spiritual hegemony of Roman Catholicism'.[25] It might be wise for the pontiff to recall that on the last occasion when the church thought it was promoting a 'third way' it ended up supporting fascism!

The Anglican and Protestant churches have experienced less difficulty accommodating to socialism. Within the Lutheran and Calvinist traditions, the doctrine of 'the two kingdoms' allowed a clear distinction to be drawn between spirituality and temporality. Socialism in consequence posed less of a threat than it did to the Roman Catholic Church.

In England, Christian movements which claimed to work only from the teachings of the Bible had played a formative role in establishing the democratic tradition. The followers of John Wycliffe – the Lollards – propagating their teaching through the Poor Preachers, had through the fourteenth and fifteenth centuries criticized the institutional church for abandoning scripture and becoming overly concerned with master and servant relationships, property and money. The branding of twenty-one Lollards at Burford Church, for having read the Bible in English, indicates the threat the church perceived in the Bible falling into lay hands and becoming the source of radical ideas, and the extent to which it was willing to go to prevent that happening!

The influence of Wycliffe's teaching can be detected in the Peasants' Revolt of 1381. The priest John Ball went far beyond Wycliffe in the application of the teachings, inciting the population to kill the nobles as a prerequisite to the establishment of social equality. Ball developed a form of popular education based on easily-remembered rhymes like 'When Adam dalf and Eve span, Who then was a gentilman?' A contemporary account chronicles the way that the revolt, led by Ball, Wat Tyler and Jack Straw, entered London, wrecking the establishments of the nobility, killing the Flemings and Lombards who controlled sectors of the economy, and executing the Archbishop of Canterbury.

The Puritan Revolution of 1642 felt that the English Reformation, which had gone some distance towards dismantling oppressive authority and freeing up the intellectual climate, had not shared power on a wide enough basis. It gained for the middle class a political influence commensurate with their economic role in the community. It initially established parliamentary control over major policy decisions, limited the powers of the monarchy and the aristocracy, and dismantled the church hierarchies. Later, more radical objectives would be pursued with the abolition of the House of Lords, the execution of the King, the confiscation and sale of crown and church lands, and the establishment of a Commonwealth under the leadership of a Protector. The Revolution, which held power for twenty years, embodied biblical understandings of the inherent equality of all within the community.

One group which initially supported the Revolution, but later came to part company with it because of its failure to establish sufficient freedom and equality, was known as the Diggers or the Levellers. This small group of artisans, farm labourers and small tradespeople had a far more radical vision which called for a revolutionary reorganization of society. They sought not only religious equality but universal suffrage including the participation of women, the abolition of private property and its redistribution amongst the poor, and communal dwelling and cultivation. The name Diggers originated in the revolutionary act on 1 April 1649, when Gerrard Winstanley and his followers began to dig and plant uncultivated common land at St George's Hill. The justification for this is set out in Winstanley's *The True Levellers' Standard Advanced*, which is an apocalyptic vision of the free and just society, and embodies ideas which would be later embraced by the French and American Revolutions.

So there had developed in England a tradition which was at least sympathetic to the new socialism. Tony Benn regards this Christian tradition as the forerunner of the Labour Movement in Britain.[26] Christians like Charles Kingsley and F. D. Maurice, believing that the socialist movement should be 'christianized', established the English version of Christian socialism. This holds that while socialism is the most democratic political option, it needs to be supported by moral, intellectual and spiritual education. Christian socialism began to engage in practical relief programmes amongst the poor. It established co-operative workshops and opened a Working Men's College. It tended to be treated with indifference by the church at large, rather than with hostility. It never grew to dominate the church's social thinking, but it made an influential contribution to it. In demonstrating the compatibility of socialism, gospel and church, it opened the way for the church to influence working-class education, co-operative legislation and the Trade Union movement.

It therefore comes as no surprise to find Anglican bishops treating Marxism as less than the threat that Roman Catholic bishops have determined it to be. The summary of the 1978 Lambeth Conference's discussion on this point recognizes that Marxism at its best is concerned with human issues which Christians cannot ignore. These issues include:

1. The gross inequality in the enjoyment of the resources and products of the world both between individuals and groups in a society and between societies.

2. The importance of structures in forming the minds and shaping the destinies of those subjected to them.

3. The widespread sense of helplessness engendered by the failure of politics and institutions (including ecclesiastical institutions) to provide a compelling objective for mankind or a realistic programme for striving after it.

Marxism is attractive to many, because it has a passion for people's welfare, a sense of the sins of society and of the powerful, and an absolute conviction that history has a purpose which can be related to human fulfilment. In these ways it can be said to have the support of scripture.[27]

The summary goes on to urge Christians to resist the labelling of radical critiques of society, and especially criticisms to do with matters of ownership and control, and the manipulation of truth, as 'communist'. The danger here is that by implication the capitalist alternative is seen to be both 'right' and 'Christian'. Capitalism and Marxism have each made promises which have been unfulfilled, and Christians should develop a critique of both based on the reality of God, the importance of people in all economic and social planning, the significance of other than economic elements in the construction and working of society, the priority of freedom in human affairs, and that dimension of human experience which suggests that life cannot be satisfied through material possessions.

Such a critique must also be applied to Marxism in order to reveal its 'mistakes':

its godlessness, its rejection of revelation, its ultimately degrading view of man as no more than a creature of economic circumstances, its motivation of hatred towards those of a different 'class', its fear of the dissident and non-conformist.[28]

The Protestant churches, with their Calvinist concepts of a church free of powerful hierarchies, are in theory at least, even more open to acceptance of the socialist model. Engels somewhat surprisingly regarded the Salvation Army as an important ally in the struggle for socialism. He commented on the way that the Army had returned to an early form of Christianity, appealing to the poor as the elect. He saw it as taking battle with capitalism in a religious way and so fostering a form of class antagonism which might one day alienate the well-to-do who support it! In contrast today the Salvation Army is one of the most conservative bodies in relation to liberation and justice issues.

By far the most cogent arguments in support of socialism have emanated from the World Council of Churches. While the Council's social teaching is not binding upon its member churches in the manner of the Roman Catholic magisterium, it has nevertheless been extremely influential. Christians in the member churches, in the absence of a word from their own tradition, have often had to look to the Council's statements on social, economic and political issues for guidance. The body to which I belong – the Church of the Province of New Zealand – has not within my memory made a significant statement in any of these areas. But the Council certainly has, and it is to the Council that I have had to turn in order to explore within a theological context, some of the most pressing issues of our time.

Critics of the World Council of Churches often attempt to portray it is a crypto-Marxist organization, part of the Kremlin's plot for world domination. The strong stands it has made against racism, economic exploitation, and militarism, together with its support for popular liberation movements and human rights, has made it a natural target for the political right. That the Council has an ideological bias, it freely admits. But it insists that its obedience to God as Lord means that no ideology can be ultimate and that it has to submit both itself and its ideologies to God's judgment. It has explained its stance in the following way:

Since its formation in 1948 the WCC has sought to express its major concerns in statements that are ideological in nature and intention. The WCC knows itself to be committed under God to the peace and unity of all humankind ('that we may all be one'); to a new social order ('a just, participatory and sustainable society'); to liberation for the victims of oppression and from everything that threatens the humanity of God's children (the Programme to Combat Racism, the Community of Women and Men in the Church, etc); the eradication of poverty, ignorance and disease, and so on.[29]

The Council has maintained admirable consistency in its analysis of contemporary society and in spelling out its vision of a just, participatory and sustainable society, in a programme which has more recently been designated 'Towards the justice, peace and integrity of creation'. It has always acknowledged that full humanity cannot develop in isolation from the world, but only within the context of concrete social, cultural, political and economic realities. It has paid careful attention to those factors which work against the interests of human fulfilment.

One of its most significant studies identifies four elements in the process of dehumanization.[30] Firstly, there is cultural oppression with consequent cultural deprivation which prevents freedom of human expression. Secondly, there is linguistic monopoly and deprivation. Language, a tool for shaping the world and liberating people, can become an instrument for preventing diversity and institutionalizing oppression. Then there are those structures of society, politics and economics through which some people exercise uncontrolled and irresponsible power over the rest of the community on the basis of class, ownership, inherited wealth, or positions of power and influence shaped by previous relationships of dominance and dependence. Being human involves the participation of all in the development of one's community and the use of its resources. Finally, the failure to face the true necessities, implications and possibilities of conflict, by insisting on compromise or consensus which ignores the reality of structural violence, for example, can be a means of further oppression.

This radical analysis of cultural and linguistic oppression, of domination on the basis of class, wealth and imperialism, which suggests the inevitability of conflict, obviously draws on Marxist analyses. Indeed, it is hard to see how anyone wanting to understand the relationship between structures of oppression could proceed without using the social science tools which Marx devised. This embryonic analysis has been further developed within such World Council units as the Programme to Combat Racism, and the Commission on the Churches' Participation in Development. The latter, through a series of consultations and studies,[31] has become ever more specific in its critique of the capitalist model of development. It portrays capitalism as the pursuit of an unjust model which delivers few benefits to the masses, and makes them passive recipients of the development process. It acknowledges that only radical political and economic structural changes will ever be able to eradicate poverty. And it points to the most successful model of development as one in which the poor become agents of their own development, identifying their own needs, mobilizing the necessary resources and shaping their own history against the interests of the powerful and the advantaged.

Particularly influential in the development of the Council's thinking at this point has been the work of Brazilian educator Paulo Freire, who worked for some years in the WCC's sub-unit on education. Freire's theory and practice of awareness creation, referred to as conscientization, originally based on literacy training amongst oppressed peasant communities, has been developed as a remarkable model of social change. His action-reflection-action methodology enables oppressed groups to unmask the reality of their oppression. The interweaving of action and analysis, with commitment to a concrete struggle being the necessary first step, leads to the establishment of popular movements for change. Such change is generated and controlled by those traditionally the powerless in the community, rather than as has been historically the case, by powerful elites.

The emergence of forms of political participation and the establishment of new political frameworks spring from a new consciousness which the oppressed develop about their rights and their capacities. This approach places people at the centre of the revolutionary process, rather than structures and structural change. Indeed, Freire tends to talk in terms of transformation rather than revolution. The just society, which in terms of his vision mirrors many elements of a socialist society, will not be achieved simply through structural change. A new internal consciousness has to be developed within people so that they are not only motivated to act for change, but are also empowered to resist the oppression which new structures may engender. One of the lessons of history for Freire is that very often, when the powerless have achieved power, they have had experience of no model other than that of the former oppressor, which is thereby maintained in place.

Paulo Freire's understanding of the process of change therefore takes issue with those who insist that the economic system is the determinant one, and that if that is changed, all the other structures of society must change as a result. Freire places greater emphasis upon culture. Culture relates to a person's inner consciousness. As we have already seen in the case of New Zealand, the domination of one nation by another, particularly through the processes of colonization, has involved attempts to destroy the indigenous culture, and to demand conformity to the alien culture. Freire says that in these situations, the indigenous culture is suppressed and becomes 'the culture of silence'. On the other hand, putting people in touch with their culture once again stimulates the emergence of a new consciousness, a new person, and ultimately a new society. To follow through the New Zealand example, the current Maori renaissance, based upon a rediscovery of culture and language, has unmasked the reality of a century and a half of European oppression, and has inspired a movement for political change, which would see sovereignty over the entire country and its resources restored to the Maori people.

Despite its critique of capitalism as the source of oppression, its advocacy of the 'socialization of the means of production', and its support for Marxist-based liberation struggles in countries like Mozambique and Zimbabwe, the World Council is careful never to suggest that in socialism or Marxism, we can discover the ideal form of human organization. While affirming principles which can be seen as socialist, even Marxist in origin, the World Council is just as aware as the Roman Catholic Church that many of the proclaimed socialist successes have been at the expense of opportunities for human development. While socialist models of development offer advantages over capitalism in terms of social justice, they also must be subjected to a critique of the gospel.

These Christian critiques of socialism echo some of the secular critiques. In practice, the inauguration of a socialist regime has not necessarily spelt an end to oppression. Some socialist theories hold that it is impossible to move directly from a capitalist society to one which is genuinely socialist or communist. There must be a series of intermediate stages, one of which is that the state must secure on behalf of the population all resources, assets and institutions, along with the power of controlling the economy and the political process. It is not possible for the people to seize these and manage them rationally in the first instance. But this state control is only an interim measure. The state's function is to so redistribute wealth and devolve decision-making amongst the people, that in the end the state itself would, in Marx's words, 'wither away' and cease to exist.

What happens in most cases, however, is that having acquired power, the state is very reluctant to let go of it! To the extent that the state replaces the former capitalists as the owners and controllers of the means of production, distribution and exchange, state socialism becomes in effect state capitalism. The USSR is a particular example of this. There the state, with its absolute control over industry, finance, health, the arts, the military and the secret police, is able to exercise a manipulation as great as, if not greater than capitalism's.

Not all socialist regimes get stuck at this point, though. The Cuban revolution, which we noted earlier was retrospectively Marxist–Leninist, in addition to meeting the basic needs of its people in terms of housing, employment, health and education, has encouraged an exceptionally high degree of voluntary effort and popular participation. It promoted this initially through its street and village level organization of Committees for the Defence of the Revolution. More recently, the concept of *Poder Popular*, People's Power, has been established. Aware of the tendency for central bureaucracies to take over the functions of voluntary associations, this attempt to institutionalize the revolution devolves a great deal of administrative power to popularly elected assemblies serving local communities and regional structures. Compared with our local authorities, these have considerable autonomy and enable the community to both control its own destiny and contribute towards national development. I visited one locality where the residents, concerned by the noise and pollution created by a bus assembly plant, voted to close the plant and relocate it outside the city, with transport provided for the workers. Such solutions do not present themselves as real options in the capitalist West. The Cuban model still has its limitations in that state power and authority are still very much a reality, and certain decisions, like those concerned with defence, are not devolved to the community. However, the movement is in the right direction.

Another strand of socialist thinking transfers power into the hands of associations or collectives of workers. Bakunin's question, 'If the proletariat is to be the ruling class, over whom is it to rule?'[32] alerts us to the fact that one group of people still exercises power over another. His critique of the Marxist theory of the state, in addition to attacking the idea of the state *per se*, points to the way in which a privileged elite of scientists and doctrinaire revolutionaries impose their preconceived idea of social organization upon the people, and conceals its virtually dictatorial powers through the fiction of pseudo-representative government which claims to express the will of the people. This perception, offered prior to the foundation of any Marxist state, some would feel to have proved itself too accurate for comfort.

In neither of these understandings, state or worker control, do we have a distribution of power through the community with everybody able to participate meaningfully in the decision-making process. Both therefore involve a diminishing of our biblical vision of a co-operatively functioning society. Nor does the Leninist concept of an elite revolutionary vanguard seizing power on behalf of the oppressed appear consistent with our vision. For us it is important that people be liberated to shape their own history, not that others, no matter how well intentioned, shape it for them. Related to this issue is the socialist understanding of the nature of participation. As we discussed earlier, socialism's vision is usually constructed by an elite, and people participate in the implementation of their vision. In our understanding, by way of contrast, people must be able to participate at the level of articulating the initial vision, not merely during the process of its implementation.

The major objections to socialism must hinge on its attitude to authority. In so far as it structures itself on the basis of an authority invested in institutions and laws which are backed up by instruments of coercion, it has to run counter to the way we understand Jesus to have interpreted authority as an internal question, and a response to the Kingdom's demands of justice, peace and love. For the Christian, the appeal is to internal authority, often referred to as conscience, rather than to any external authority.

Christians also raise questions about means and ends, particularly questioning whether a peaceful and just society can be established through violent and unjust tactics. There is no indication in the teaching of Jesus that he supported violence against persons. Indeed, when his followers wished to defend him by force of arms, he declared that his tactics were not those of violence, for those who live by the sword will die by the sword (Matt. 26.51–55). Our biblical vision leaves no room for separating our strategies and tactics from our objectives. The methods we employ to achieve the vision have themselves to be embodiments of the vision. Thus we cannot establish a peaceful and just society through tactics which regard human life as expendable.

There appears to run through all authoritarian socialist literature the assumption that change will need, if not to be imposed from above, at least to be directed from above. Liberating the structures will create a new, liberated personality. This is the opposite of the naive Christian approach – that good people will produce good structures – which we have already rejected. Nor is the opposite true, that good structures must produce good people. Structures can certainly facilitate or hinder human development. But side by side with structural change, there needs to be the establishment of a new set of human values, and the kind of interior consciousness which Freire refers to, which for want of a better term, we might refer to as human spirituality.

Our vision really begins at the opposite end from authoritarian socialism. The Kingdom of God demands a radical change in personal commitment and life-style and consciousness, and adherence to a set of values, which in Jesus' time at least, were the opposite of those of authoritarian systems. The development of the Kingdom depends not upon the sudden overthrowal of one set of social, political and economic structures and their replacement by another, but on the members of the Kingdom gradually extending its claims over all systems and structures, transforming them in that process.

Both the World Council then, and the Roman Catholic Church, remain cautious about socialism because they are unwilling in the first instance to accept any ideology uncritically. Thus in World

Council studies on the poor and oppressed as agents of change, it is argued that Council support for alternatives to capitalist domination 'does not mean commitment to any absolutist ideology or closed theories of history'.[33] Similarly, Pope Paul VI argued that the weakness of all ideologies becomes visible in the concrete systems through which they express themselves. Thus bureaucratic socialism, technocratic capitalism and authoritarian democracy are unable to escape the materialism, the egoism and the constraint which accompany them.[34] The clear implication is that all ideological formulations place limits upon human development. Our search for a Christian society must therefore draw us towards a non-ideological expression of community, should such an entity exist.

Speaking of utopian visions, Paul VI suggests that while some people may use them in order to retreat from concrete tasks in order to take refuge in an imaginary world, utopias ought not to be ignored.

> This kind of criticism of existing society often provokes the forward-looking imagination both to perceive in the present the disregarded possibility hidden within it, and to direct itself towards a fresh future; it thus sustains social dynamism by the confidence that it gives to the inventive powers of the human mind and heart; and, if it refuses no overture, it can also meet the Christian appeal. The Spirit of the Lord, who animates man renewed in Christ, continually breaks down the horizons within which his understanding likes to find security and the limits to which his activity would willingly restrict itself; there dwells within him a power which urges him to go beyond every system and every ideology.[35]

In suggesting to us that, pressing beyond system and ideology, we pursue the utopia which our biblical vision lays out before us, the church is pointing us in a most unexpected direction.

CHAPTER FIVE

Like a River in Flood

A Liberationist Vision for Society

The one vision of society which has always declared itself to be anti-ideological and open-ended, and which has insisted upon giving priority to people, life and action rather than to theory and to system, is a vision which has been very much misunderstood. Its adherents are distinguished by their refusal to subjugate themselves to an authority, particularly in the matter of theoretical positions. On this basis they have particularly resisted the idea of authority embodied in a political party which guards and interprets theory in a protective and ultimately oppressive way. The tradition believes that a society shaped by a party protected and state institutionalized ideology must by its very nature be oppressive. This tradition goes by many names. It has often been called libertarianism. In terms of contemporary community action it is sometimes called community transformation. Because it provides the basis of a great deal of action for human liberation, it might well be called liberationism. Its most common title, however, is anarchism.

This latter term is a generative word, producing an almost totally negative reaction in people. There are very good reasons for this. Because anarchism offers a real alternative to both capitalism and authoritarian socialism, it has been systematically denigrated and subverted by the political and ideological apparatuses which have most to lose from the realization of the liberation it holds out to people. So in common usage, the descriptions 'anarchy' and 'anarchist' have become almost totally devalued. When a New Zealand Anglican bishop claimed that church groups addressing racism were leading the nation towards anarchy, I suggested he was using that word in a scaremongering and manipulative way.

He responded that because both the Oxford Dictionary and all reasonable people understood the term in the way he employed it, he would continue using it as an image of negativity and of the destruction of the values that right-thinking people hold dear. Which I suppose at least reveals the ideological captivity of 'reasonable people' and the Oxford Dictionary! In the discussion which follows I use the terms anarchism, libertarianism, and liberationism and their respective adjectives to describe this tradition.

We had better begin by clarifying what we are *not* talking about. We are not using the term 'anarchy' in the way politicians of the Left and the Right use it to describe industrial, economic or social chaos. What they most often mean by it is that people have gone on strike or taken to the streets to demonstrate against the injustice of their oppressive policies! It is consequently part of their propaganda battle to denigrate anarchism and make it appear unworkable. Nor are we talking about nihilism, that form of blind negativism which developed into a movement in Russia towards the end of last century. Nor are we referring to that manifestation of anarchist thought known as Propaganda of the Deed which eliminated powerful individuals through terrorist action. Anarchism embraces many streams, all of which are deliberately misrepresented by their critics, and is such a comprehensive idea that it cannot be identified with, or judged by, any one particular example of its vision.

In our scientific milieu, insisting as it does that everything must be quantifiable and able to be grasped in its totality, the fact that anarchism has no corpus of doctrine and refuses to make dogmatic pronouncements, runs so counter to contemporary education that people are generally not equipped to give it serious consideration. Indeed, to appreciate it properly, an entirely different mindset from that of its capitalist and socialist rivals is required. That is what renders debate with them difficult and sometimes futile. Anarchism's refusal to discuss issues at the level of abstract theory, and its emphasis on spontaneity of action, set it apart. Because there are no dogmas to which anarchists must adhere, it encourages enormous diversity. In a sense, there are as many understandings (one cannot speak of 'theories' in this instance) of anarchism as there are anarchists, and obviously, no anarchist writings can be regarded as definitive or authoritative in the manner that Marx can be treated in relation to the socialist tradition. Nor does it offer the scientific mind a pre-packaged description of the way the new society will operate. It insists that people must build and implement their own vision and that appropriate economic and political structures will emerge in that process. It encourages diversity on such a scale that it is even able to envisage different economic systems operating in different communities! All this is anathema to those who seek uniformity rather than diversity, structure rather than flexibility, a good theory rather than effective action, institutionalized authority rather than freedom.

'Show us a working model of anarchism!', its critics demand. We earlier saw that this demand is a constituent element in the dominant ideology's resistance to change. We have all been encouraged by that ideology to believe that, before any change at all is possible, we need a detailed blueprint of the new society, together with a full checklist of its advantages and disadvantages over what we already have. If we were to take a historical view, however, the new capitalist system did not replace feudalism through the blueprint and checklist process. It was the product of evolving social, economic and political structures. But now that it is in a dominant position, it tries to create the impression that it has always been with us, and that for want of a better alternative, it always will.

Perhaps liberationism's most basic problem is that it offers people, conditioned to rely on the authority and expertise of others, the possibility of too much freedom! There is plenty of evidence around to show that anarchism can and does work. During the Spanish Revolution of the mid-1930s, the anarcho-syndicalists established collectives in a number of the country's regions. These were not isolated one-off experiments but widespread and effective initiatives. They embraced over 1600 agricultural collectives in Aragon, the Levante and Castile alone, as well as the collectivization of all industry and public services in Catalonia and seventy per cent of that in the Levante.[1]

The Barcelona tramways system is a typical example. A private company comprised of some sixty routes and employing 7,000 workers as drivers, conductors and mechanics, over 6,000 of whom were members of the CNT, the National Confederation of Labour, an anarchist-led organization built around the principles of libertarian communism, it formed itself into a collective after street battles and barricades had paralysed the city. Establishing a federalist form of organization which linked all workers to a vision for the industry, it had 700 trams instead of the usual 600 back on the tracks within five days of the fighting having ceased. Gradually old cars were repaired, new ones built, track relaid, overhead cables rehung, dynamos repaired, and a new safety and signalling system installed. The wages of workers were raised and fares were lowered. Yet between 1935 and 1936 there was an average increase of nearly fifteen per cent in monthly receipts. The system carried 50 million more passengers in 1936 over an extra 1.6 million kilometres. In other words, the anarchists operated a more extensive, less expensive and more profitable public service than that offered by its former capitalist owners.

Similar successes were reported in those parts of the textile, forestry, water, gas and electricity industries which were collectivized. Of particular interest in an age which now wishes to privatize medicine are those collectives which socialized medicine. The Syndicate for Sanitary Services in Barcelona included over 1,000 doctors, 3,000 male nurses, 330 midwives, 600 dentists, 80 specialists, 700 pharmacists, 220 veterinary surgeons, and so on; in total over 7,000 people organized on a libertarian co-operative model. One needs to compare this model of health delivery to that of Thatcher's Britain which in terms of management now relies on an elite of successful managers from fields other than health and excludes the medical profession almost totally.

The problem was not that these anarchist collectives did not work, but that they worked too well! The real possibility of these local successes being elaborated on a national basis, replacing state power with community co-operation, became unthinkable to those groups which could not contemplate, let alone survive the demise of the authoritarian state. Betrayed by the Marxists, and ultimately defeated by the fascists, the Spanish anarchists nevertheless demonstrated that the libertarian model of social and industrial organization provides a workable alternative.

Then too, the libertarian ideal has been espoused by many Christian communities which have managed to survive for remarkably long periods within hostile environments, living out their vision in the midst of a society whose values they reject. Walter Map, writing in 1179 about the Waldenses who persist to this day, perceived them as a major threat to established order. 'They have no fixed habitations,' he said. 'They go about two by two, barefoot, clad in woollen garments, owning nothing, holding all things common like the apostles, naked, following a naked Christ.' And he went on to warn that people should not be taken in by their humility because if once admitted as Christians they will eventually drive out the majority.[2]

The Waldenses were typical of the many Christian groups and movements which sprang up as a response to the comparative wealth generated in Europe from the twelfth century onwards. Renouncing property, power and privilege, embracing voluntary poverty, and identifying with the poverty-stricken masses, they attracted enormous followings.[3] One group, known as the Brethren of the Free Spirit, which despite its title was of particular appeal to women who challenged the power of the institutional church, adopted mystical anarchist beliefs, resisting all doctrines and authorities. Their views persisted right through to the Reformation, and were echoed by later movements such as the Ranters. Very much in the nature of a persistent underground tradition, and always regarded as heretical by the church, the movement was to profoundly influence one of the fathers of the modern anarchist movement, William Blake.

Christian libertarian and anarchist communities still flourish today. Amongst the better known ones are the Catholic Worker, a series of communities in North America; the Sojourners Community in Washington DC; the Tennessee Farm which boasts some five thousand members; and the Community of the Ark in France. In addition there has been a proliferation of small anarchist communities like that calling itself 'Where Two or Three', in Australia or 'Pinch of Salt' in England. By far the most striking feature of these communities is their commitment to non-violence. This goes some way towards exposing the falsity of the assertion that anarchism is essentially a violent and destructive movement.

The permanence of the anarchist ideal, and the persistence of libertarian communities, suggests that here may be an option for human development whose day has yet to come. The odds against appear enormous. I was able to study political science at university without anarchism ever once being mentioned by my teachers, not even as a historical oddity, let alone a contemporary option. That indicates the degree to which the dominant ideology maintains its control over the educational establishment! But as popular dissatisfaction with both capitalist and socialist working models increases, and as the churches develop their critiques of the dehumanizing elements of both, so anarchism is being rediscovered as a development option which lies close to the heart of the gospel. For this reason, we need to examine it in some detail.

While the work of classical anarchist thinkers like Bakunin, Proudhon and Kropotkin remains essential reading, Christians have been strongly drawn to two strands of liberationist thought. One has its origins in Russia and embraces the emphasis Tolstoy placed on non-violence and that which Berdyaev placed on freedom. The second has its origins in the tradition of English dissent and includes the two founders of modern anarchism, William Godwin and William Blake. Godwin, a nonconformist clergyman, wrote *An Inquiry Concerning Political Justice* in 1793. He popularized his ideas in a novel, *Caleb Williams*, which was serialized for British television several years ago. Godwin's work, standing in the tradition of radicalism, explored the themes promoted by Winstanley's Diggers; religious equality, universal suffrage, the redistribution of land among the poor, communal ownership and the abolition of private property. His book is generally regarded as the first full exposition of anarchist ideas.

Godwin married the libertarian Mary Wollstonecraft whose 1792 book, *A Vindication of the Rights of Women*, challenges the domination of stereotypical sex roles, patriarchy and hierarchical systems, establishing a basis on which many groups campaign today. The Godwins' daughter Mary married the poet Percy Bysshe Shelley. Mary's novel *Frankenstein or the Modern Prometheus* explores libertarian themes, while Shelley in poems like *Queen Mab*, *The Mask of Anarchy*, *Song to the Men of England* and *Ode to Liberty* gave lyric form to critiques of civil and religious oppression.

The artist, mystic and poet William Blake completes the circle in that he was a close friend of Mary Wollstonecraft and illustrated one of her books. Blake, also standing in the dissenting religious tradition and the libertarian political tradition, similarly rejected all forms of imposed authority and 'celebrated freedom both in its negative sense of being free from restraint, and in its positive sense of being free to realize one's potential'.[4]

Creating the environment for human development

The word anarchism literally means 'without a ruler', or 'without government'. But this does not imply, as its critics try to maintain, that it is entirely without orderly ways of managing its affairs. What anarchism is basically rejecting is the assertion that it is necessary for some people to rule over others, whether as individuals or as groups. Pierre-Joseph Proudhon, another of the founders of modern anarchism, expressed its basic position succinctly when he said, 'Whoever puts his hand on me to govern me is a usurper and a tyrant. I declare him my enemy.'

In adopting this stance, anarchism parallels the teaching of Jesus that authority is to be discovered in a person's interior resources, not in an appeal to external law. We have noted the way in which Jesus urged those who accepted the principles of the Kingdom to reject the legalistic and authoritarian approach of the Scribes and Pharisees. Anarchist writers have been equally clear in their analysis of the destructive effects of law upon the human personality. Peter Kropotkin, observing that law was employed for three kinds of protection, the protection of property, the protection of persons and the protection of government, showed that not only did law fail to achieve its objectives, it was hurtful to human life. The laws of property protect certain vested interests, the laws of government protect particular elites in power, and the laws of persons, ostensibly in place to protect them, are used to deprive people of their liberty, to maim or to kill them. Leo Tolstoy, perhaps the best known of the Christian anarchists, observed the violence inherent in the practice of the law. This violence is not so much that of human passion, but is an organized and much more subtle reality. 'Laws', he wrote, 'are rules made by people who govern by means of organized violence, for non-compliance with which the non-complier is subjected to blows, to loss of liberty, or even to being murdered.'

Anarchists often draw a distinction, then, between law that is imposed upon life, and law that is inherent in life. Herbert Read[5] argued that every modern scientific advance has demonstrated that 'nature' is penetrated by 'law', and that the anarchist task is to discover the true laws of nature and live in harmony with them. He understood the most comprehensive law in nature as that of equity, the principle of balance and symmetry which guides the growth of forms along the lines of greatest structural efficiency, and constantly illustrates the principle by the harmony and shape it gives to the development of plants, the human body, and the universe itself. Christians can immediately link this insight to their understanding of creation, where the Creator-God nurtures, sustains and shapes creation through laws of natural development. This should not be confused, however, with the scholastic notion of Natural Law which became the basis of the Roman Catholic church's teaching, which in its original formulation was an attempt to discern inherent law through the application of rational faculties, but which, like the Old Testament Law, hardened into external formulations used to control and modify human behaviour.

Another contemporary anarchist, Giovanni Baldelli,[6] sees authority as practised in anarchist communities as the recognition of competence within a certain field, and the right to take and carry out decisions with the consent of every person whom that decision affects. In such an understanding authority is not in conflict with freedom, but the means through which positive freedom can be implemented without risking slavery or resorting to violence. He sees people in various regions with common interests and problems banding together to deal with them. There may then develop cultural authorities, free associations like churches, sporting groups, artists' guilds and so on, which are concerned with the creation, development and preservation of values. Economic authorities could be established to co-ordinate demand and production and to maintain just and efficient distribution.

Anarchists are clearly committed to a society which makes it possible for all members to become involved in the decision-making processes. They also try to build in safeguards to ensure that nobody's interests can be compromised. This perception closely reflects the style of participation we identified in biblical witness, and in the actions of Jesus to remove the barriers which prevent people from participating in the community. In fact only the liberationist or anarchist approach offers the degree of participation we are seeking, in contrast to capitalism's under-standing of participation in the economy on the basis of class distinctions, and socialism's concept of participation in order to implement a vision which has been predetermined by an elite.

The World Council of Churches' programme 'People's Participation in Development' has maintained that development which is imposed upon people is itself a form of violence. True progress can only occur when people themselves become the agents of their own development. These beliefs, along with the programme's determination to see the power of decision-making devolved to the widest possible spectrum of the community, has led the Council to question both socialist and capitalist development. That the Council's view is indistinguishable from that of anarchism at this point is not accidental. It has for forty years reflected on the implications of scriptural witness and Christian tradition for discipleship in today's world. And it has observed and evaluated the failures of the two major ideologies competing for commitment. That it should have arrived at what is virtually an anarchist understanding of development might in terms of historical analysis be regarded as inevitable.

The devolution of effective power to the local community is a cornerstone of anarchist thought. In rejecting the right of any authority to make decisions on behalf of people without their direct consent, anarchism has specifically rejected the role played by the modern state. In this respect it presses socialism towards the achievement of its goal – communism – in which the state, as Marx declared, would wither away. Critics of anarchism seem unable to conceive of forms of social, political and economic organization which are not statist in basis. It is as if they believe that the development of nation states at a particular moment in history was an embodiment of Natural Law to be treated as a permanent and unchangeable reality, rather than as the embodiment of particular understandings of authority and control. Nation states were then, and remain today, an effective way of centralizing political and economic power. Luigi Fabbri, offering an alternative to this, spoke in terms of posing strenuous opposition to the centralist spirit which is characteristic of all party and statist political thought. Instead, social life should be organized on the basis of solidarity and free agreement expressed as a form of federalism which moves out from the individual to incorporate the municipality, the commune, the region, the nation and the international.[7] There is no need for the state as we experience it.

Both the concentration of power in the state, and the power to coerce people which the state possesses, are seen as forms of violence, in the manner that the Book of Revelation regards the power and authority of the Roman state. Both Blake and Godwin understood that the basic question is not the form of state, but the very existence of the state itself. The state's objective is to mould people into 'good subjects'. Godwin believed that if a person's natural development were not interfered with by the state, the person, instead of being conditioned, would mould the environment in accordance with her or his innermost aspirations of peace and liberty. The state offers what is in effect a caricature of society, and produces people who are a caricature of humanity. This state moulded and controlled aberration of humanity seems to mirror the condition of those in Jesus' time who were held to be possessed by demons. Such people have no control over their lives, and behave in ways they do not themselves choose to behave in. We saw that Jesus' response was to intervene to break the power of that domination, so that people could take full control of their lives once more. Or as Paulo Freire puts it, people act to become the subjects rather than the objects of history.

The state is as a consequence seen as one of the chief obstacles to human development, and anarchism's objective is to create instead an environment in which full human development becomes a possibility for the first time. Not only does this imply the need for space in which humanity can mature, but a milieu of freedom which encourages that maturity. Michael Bakunin wrote:

> I am a fanatic lover of liberty, considering it as the unique condition under which intelligence, dignity and human happiness can develop and grow . . . I mean the only kind of liberty that is worthy of the name, liberty that consists in the full development of all the material, intellectual and moral powers that are latent in each person. . .[8]

He went on to elaborate an anarchist understanding of freedom in his *Revolutionary Catechism*,[9] which identifies human reason as the criterion for truth, human conscience as the basis of justice, and individual and collective freedom as the only source of order in society. Bakunin insists that freedom is the absolute right of every adult man and woman to seek no other sanction for their acts than their own conscience and their own reason, being responsible first to themselves and then to the society which they have *voluntarily* accepted. He contests the popular view that the freedom of one person is necessarily limited by the freedom of others, arguing that the exercising of individual freedom in fact confirms and expands the freedom of all. 'Man is truly free only among equally free men; the slavery of even one human being violates humanity and negates the freedom of all.' He believed that the freedom of each individual is only in reality realizable in so far as all people experience equality, and that this achievement of freedom through equality is what we understand by justice.

Such a view of freedom takes us far beyond anything that the ideologies – even that of free enterprise – are willing to allow humanity. Ultimately the ideologies cannot permit us the freedom to reject them! What we have in Bakunin's writings is an emphasis on human development and its relationship to freedom which parallels Christian thought. The kind of freedom he argues for is akin to the freedom proclaimed by the resurrection. Resurrection means that humanity can no longer be contained, no longer held down. As demonstrated in the person of Jesus, it offers a model of humanity no longer even constrained by the physical environment.

In one of the more controversial and influential theological works of the early 1960s, Paul van Buren depicted Jesus as the truly free man who brings freedom to others. In exploring the meaning of the resurrection, he wrote of Jesus in terms of a free man who died as a result of the threat that the truly free personality poses to people who are themselves insecure and bound. What Christ's resurrection did was to make freedom 'contagious'. The disciples in communicating the story of Jesus were not simply recounting the life of an extraordinarily free man who had died. 'In telling the story of Jesus of Nazareth,' he says, 'they told it as the story of the free man who had set them free.'[10]

The Russian philosopher and theologian Nicolas Berdyaev devoted his life to what he called 'hammering out a philosophy of freedom'. The traditional Christian notion of free will – the ability to choose between good and evil – is not freedom at all for Berdyaev, because it presupposes a norm outside the person by which the distinction between good and evil is determined. Nor, in his view, is freedom to be equated with individualism which can be merely a form of slavery to egocentrism. He rejects both capitalist and socialist understandings of freedom: capitalism because its stress on economic freedom and unlimited right to possess private property destroys the human personality, and freedom along with it. In capitalism, freedom becomes a privilege of the ruling classes. On the other hand, he rejected socialist views of freedom, especially those which developed in Russia following the Revolution. Such regimes cannot help but be authoritarian and cannot allow real freedom to develop. His personal experience at the hands of the regime lead him to conclude that the socialist idea of revolution inevitably leads to terror and 'terror is the loss of freedom, the loss of everybody's freedom, the loss of freedom for all'.

Writing towards the end of his life, Berdyaev declared himself 'of religio-anarchist tendency'. Some commentators describe him as a mystical anarchist. His understanding of freedom undoubtedly springs from anarchist roots and when he became a believing Christian, he attended the Moscow meetings of one of the groups associated with mystical anarchism, 'The Seekers After God'. Although he would subsequently return to the Orthodox church into which he was born, his anarchist leanings persisted and he rediscovered in the church's understanding of authority, a basis for his own views on freedom. The Constitution of the Orthodox church, built on principles of self-government, led it to become the first church to resist and then to reject the claims of an external authority, the papacy. Authority in the arena of Christian truth is vested in the hearts and minds of those within whom the Spirit of Christ dwells, who constitute the Orthodox church. This rejection of external authority in the Christian life remains faithful to the teachings of Jesus. It is salutary for Christians in the West to be reminded that the authoritarian mode which their churches have adopted is not the universal Christian view!

This libertarian objective of creating an environment free of constraints within which the human personality can develop to its full potential cannot be in conflict with our Christian notion of human development. Furthermore, as anarchists begin to spell out the principles on which the new society should be based, they very closely resemble the co-operative model of functioning which St Paul offers the Christian community.

Peter Kropotkin promoted sociological concepts of anarchism based on the insights of natural science. One of his best known works, *Mutual Aid: A Factor of Evolution*,[11] opposes the then popular Darwinist concept that the struggle of the strong against the weak with only the fittest surviving, is the sole basic natural law. Such a theory inevitably leads to the conclusions that the right to life does not extend to all creatures, and that the needy, the damaged and the disabled have to resign themselves to their situation.

Kropotkin argued that alongside the struggle for existence in nature there is another principle, demonstrated in the way that weaker species come together in social groups, to ensure their preservation through instincts of sociability and mutual aid. He identifies this principle in the plant and animal kingdoms, providing numerous examples, including one documented from New Zealand in which an enormous flock of sparrows force a preying hawk to flee for shelter! He goes on to trace the principle of mutual aid through the forms of social organization amongst primitive humanity, to the shape of the mediaeval city, to the co-operative elements displayed in the village life and labour organizations of his day. Had it not been for this spirit of co-operation and mutual aid, he insists, humanity could never have survived.

Side by side with mutual aid runs another principle: the self assertion of the individual. This also is a progressive force in humanity, something on which both capitalism and liberationist anarchism would seem to be in agreement. But where capitalism wants to harness this individualism to its economic system, thereby placing strict limits upon it, Kropotkin views it as exercising the critical function of breaking through the bonds of all that constrains humanity. True personal development only be-comes possible when this individualism is given recognition, and when through free choice it co-operates with other free beings. It is therefore in the field of ethics that the richness of mutual aid lies fully revealed. As Kropotkin sees it, a person is guided in behaviour not merely by love 'which is always personal, or at the best tribal', but by the perception of 'oneness with each human being'. Rampant and self-centred individualism consequently has no place in anarchism. It is a person's sense of unity with all creation which motivates one to act co-operatively for the good of all. It is this understanding of the unity of all life which has encouraged the development of close links between anarchism and 'green' ecological and environmental movements over recent years.

Such a view is totally consistent with the Christian understanding of the Spirit of God indwelling and manifested through the whole of creation. Furthermore, the church has taught that the whole purpose of creation is to facilitate the development of the individual. Thus, for example, Paul VI declares:

> The Bible from the first page on teaches us that the whole creation is for man, that it is his responsibility to develop it by intelligent effort and by means of his labour to perfect it, so to speak, for his use. If the world is made to furnish each individual with the means of livelihood and the instruments for his growth and progress, each man has therefore the right to find in the world what is necessary for himself. . . All other rights whatsoever, including those of property and of free commerce, are to be subordinated to this principle.[12]

In the same way that St Paul emphasized organic and cellular principles of growth and organization, contemporary anarchists have often promoted a cellular and organic view of development. Hence we find Colin Ward outlining a form of organization which begins with what is local and immediate, and which links with other initiatives in a network which has no centre and no directing agency. As the original cells grow, so new ones are created.[13] Indeed many, Ward included, push this imagery further, arguing that anarchist society is not something which has to be created. Rather it 'is always in existence, like a seed beneath the snow, buried under the weight of the state'. Anarchism is seen not as utopian speculation but as an ever present reality manifested in countless apparently unrelated events and movements in which people claim freedom for themselves. This is one of the responses which can be made to the claim that anarchism does not work. It can be observed at work wherever repressive and authoritarian institutions are being replaced by people-centred structures promoting human liberty. As another modern anarchist, Paul Goodman, put it: 'A free society cannot be the substitution of a "new order" for the old order; it is the extension of spheres of free action until they make up most of social life.'

If this begins to ring a few bells for Christians, it is probably because our perception of the Kingdom of God is exactly the same! We might recall from chapter three the way that Jesus insisted that his Kingdom could not be observed replacing the present order: it is like a tiny seed which, although giving the impression of insignificance, germinates to reach out and transform all aspects of life. At this point at least, Christian and anarchist perceptions are indistinguishable.

In Western society, where the damaging effects of capitalism are becoming ever more apparent, this move towards cellular and co-operative ventures has accelerated. In New Zealand during the late 1970s and early 1980s, for example, capitalism's burgeoning unemployment crisis provided impetus for the creation of alternative means of survival: work co-operatives, housing co-operatives, food co-operatives and credit co-operatives. While these share much in common with similar movements elsewhere, in the New Zealand case they offered the additional advantage of enabling Maori people, the chief victims of social and economic crises, to penetrate beyond the dominant culture to recapture some of the communitarian values by which they lived prior to the introduction of capitalism. Within these co-operatives, the anarchist principles of devolution of power, non-authoritarian structures, participative decision-making and mutual aid can be seen at work. So attractive have the principles become that even some of the largest capitalist enterprises appear to be adopting them, speaking of worker-participation, co-operative ventures, and so on. In their case, the exploitation of the terminology generally springs from no other motivation than that of the possibility of increasing production and profitability. It is generally an illusion of power-sharing and mutual aid which attempts to conceal where real power and control lie.

We see other anarchist principles at work in the efforts of consumer groups to liberate some of our more oppressive institutions. The efforts of community-based groups to establish community control over the system of health delivery, which in the hands of professionals and transnational pharmaceutical companies thrives on illness, can be seen as extending the principle of freedom in a way that breaks down institutional power. So too are those women who are claiming their freedom in the area of reproductive rights, against the power of male professional hierarchies, and drug companies which have used them as human guinea pigs in testing contraceptive drugs. So are the attempts to deschool society through the establishment of alternative schools; and styles of community or social work which aim to enable citizens to claim freedom and the power of decision-making over more and more areas of their lives. In an age of media controlled mass conformity, the establishment of counter-information services and neighbourhood newspapers which provide a voice for the voiceless, can be seen as extending that freedom. So can the countless movements which aim to establish dignity and liberation for various groups oppressed within capitalist societies: women's liberation, black liberation, children's liberation, homosexual liberation, and animal liberation! All provide confirmation that anarchist principles are alive and well.

Towards communities of common ownership

'A perfect society', wrote St Basil, 'is that which excludes all private property. Such was the primitive wellbeing which was overturned by the sin of our first fathers.'

Anarchism shares this analysis that the institution of private property is the most exploiting and dehumanizing of relationships. It regards common ownership as the one alternative which will establish justice in this respect. Alexander Berkman promoted an anarchist vision like that of the early Christian communes in which the private ownership of the means of production, distribution and exchange have been abolished. Speaking within an industrial context, he limited personal possession to the things a person actually used. Thus while a watch would be personally owned, the watch factory would belong to the people. Land, machinery and public utilities would be collective property which could not be bought and sold. The actual use of resources is to be considered the only title, and such title is in respect to possession, not to ownership.[14] He sees coalminers being in charge of the coal mines, not as owners of them, but as the competent operating agency. Similarly, railroaders would run the railways, sailors the shipping. He explores the anarchist concept of people taking responsibility for that in which they are competent. As Bakunin once put it, in the matter of boots, he regarded the bootmaker as a competent authority, but he reserved the right to make a free choice about which pair of boots to buy! In Berkman's vision, with the socialization of natural resources, land, factories, transport and products, there can only be a form of free exchange on the basis of what people need, and what can be supplied. There is no necessity for profit; no need for money as the medium of exchange.

The anarchist ideal is often criticized in relation to its economic base. This is because economists, whether of capitalist or socialist predisposition, tend to think in terms only of monolithic systems. Anarchism, on the other hand, upholds the principle of diversity in all aspects of life and community living. It therefore offers no single economic blueprint, but encourages communities to establish economic bases which embody the principles of equity, justice and freedom. Anarchism entertains the possibility of a community experimenting with different economic systems at the same time.

It is sometimes said that libertarian proposals necessarily involve a return to earlier forms of social and economic organization, which could not possibly work in this day and age. This again is part of the propaganda waged against them. What liberationist anarchism is concerned about is the human scale of production, and the elimination of strong centres of economic power. E. F. Schumacher's 'small is beautiful' theory of economic conservationism (not conservatism!) has attracted widespread interest. The head of one of New Zealand's largest transnational corporations recommended it as basic reading for all his employees! And one of the more unexpected developments in international economics has been a return to principles of barter which do away with the requirement of monetary exchange. Thus New Zealand implements a 'lamb for oil' deal with Iran. The United States barters military hardware in exchange for Saudi oil. One quarter of India's overseas trading in 1985 was on the basis of barter. That such a system is not only working successfully within the constraints of capitalism, but looks like being promoted on a much wider scale, indicates that this form of exchange is a viable way of organizing an economy, even on the international level.

In developing their models, anarchists look both to those forms of economic organization which have proved workable, and to a careful analysis of the deviation from principle which has caused others to fail. When questioned how production would be organized, libertarians respond, 'On the basis of free contracts and free exchanges'. When it is asserted that libertarian communes must by definition be so small that they would be incapable of organizing large enterprises anarchists respond that there can be no preconceived solutions, but that contemporary technology is constantly creating new possibilities. In terms of the economy, no practical solution which is in accordance with the free choice of the new society, and which enables diversity, can be excluded. It envisages the testing of differing models as the basis of larger-scale production. And when it is pointed out that certain activities cannot be organized other than on the basis of centralized planning – a national transport system, or an international postal service, for example – anarchists readily agree. Their concern is that there should be no centralization of power through which vested interests can dominate and exploit people. The international postal service actually provides a working model of what anarchists are talking about. National postal systems have their own form of organization, their own technologies varying from simple to complex, and vastly different standards of 'efficiency'. Yet without any external authority insisting that they do so, they choose to co-operate with each other on a voluntary basis. That co-operation ensures that a letter posted in one country, irrespective of its ideology or economy, will arrive at its destination in another.

There is a determination in anarchist action to establish and maintain community accountability. This is one of those principles to which the dominant ideology pays lipservice, but which it studiously avoids putting into practice. When, several years ago, the New Zealand police force was coming under heavy criticism for its public behaviour, the Commissioner of Police went on record as saying that the police force represents the community and is accountable to the community. But this is demonstrably *not* the case. There is no machinery through which the police force can exercise accountability, and none through which the community can ensure that its priorities are heeded by the police. Thus, in those cases where a member of the community has been assaulted by the police, or worse, has died in police custody, the improprieties are investigated not by the community, but through the process of an internal police enquiry. In the event of the public outrage which seems to be occurring ever more frequently, the government establishes a commission of enquiry, which may consist of a lone lawyer! In our first chapter we traced the way in which within the system of state government, instruments of coercion like the police force are in reality made accountable to the political establishment, not the community.

Because in an anarchist society these instruments of coercion would normally have no place, the question of community control of police would not arise. It is for the community to decide what form of policing, if any, is appropriate. But the principle of accountability of those structures which are regarded as necessary is essential and liberationist anarchism's concept of power-sharing and participation ensures that this accountability is protected.

An ethical basis for society

There have been three major streams of thought within anarchism on the relationship between ethics and the community. The first, pioneered by Proudhon, takes ethical premises as its point of departure. In this stream the value of *justice* has generally been regarded as the ethical base. The second stream, of which Bakunin is a representative, is libertarian and sees the concept of *freedom* as that from which all else is derived. The third stream, represented by William Godwin in the eighteenth century, and Paul Goodman in our own, makes *happiness* the central concern, and derives ethics from this principle. Some anarchists think that in the work of Errico Malatesta, these three bases are brought together in a value-pluralist synthesis. No matter which of these approaches the anarchist may adopt, however, ethics remains fundamental.

Giovanni Baldelli writes in the tradition of Proudhon. He insists that only an anarchist society can be a truly ethical society, and only an anarchist personality an ethical personality. He explores the nature of a society built on ethical principles which include the primacy of the human person, the sacredness of human life, the rejection of coercion, means not being justified by the end, and the unacceptability of double standards. It is difficult to envisage Christians arguing against any of these principles which, Baldelli insists, cannot be imposed but which must flow from an act of free choice and operate as an act of faith. Such principles have to be worked out in the theatre of human action and forge a unity of style and judgment in a person's life. He goes on to demonstrate how these principles apply to society's concerns of freedom and authority, work and wealth, value and exploitation, and wrongs and reparations.[15]

We have already alluded to the way that Bakunin felt that unfettered freedom provided the only milieu within which true human development could be achieved, and how in his *Revolutionary Catechism* he states his understanding of freedom. 'If there is one fundamental principle of human morality,' he writes, 'it is freedom. To respect the freedom of your fellowman is duty; to love, help, and serve him is virtue.' He makes this ethical understanding of freedom the basis of the new society. Henceforth, he insists, 'the political and economic structure of society must now be reorganized on the basis of freedom . . . order in society must result from the greatest possible realization of individual liberty.' And he goes on to spell out how this ethical principle informs political organization, social organization, and revolutionary policy.[16]

William Godwin's writing on the nature of justice[17] makes difficult reading these days because he uses concepts and categories which have been abandoned by modern thought. Nevertheless two of his convictions remain as cogent now as they were then: that humankind is inherently good, and that humanity can choose ethical norms as the basis of society. Godwin viewed the moral evils which exist in the world as the direct consequence of the political institutions which have created them. If humanity is to advance, people have to be enabled to develop a capacity for independent judgment. Such independence is not possible when human understanding is corrupted by ideas like 'patriotism' or forced to submit to external authority. He also maintained that the source of crime, vice and injustice in society springs from a person's lack of knowledge. In so far as it is government which imposes authority, fosters patriotism and prevents the development of independent judgment, government is the real source of crime, vice and injustice. Godwin insists that all the moral and legal evils which defenders of strong political institutions maintain are prevented or at least ameliorated by those institutions, are in fact caused by them!

To be virtuous, Godwin says, is to feel the right emotions. Right emotions are those which people experience when they see the facts of a situation clearly. Knowing the facts involves possessing particular knowledge and rejecting the false generalizations which have been created by the political institutions. How remarkably contemporary he sounds! If we undertake an analysis of these right emotions, he continues, we find that they are in harmony with two principles, those of the greatest happiness and of impartiality.

The origin of society is to be found in humanity's need for mutual assistance. The moral principle on which society is based is that of justice, which means that we seek to employ all our skills for the development of others. In other words, we are seeking some kind of 'general good'. Yet this general good is not a principle which is above or beyond humanity, to which it must aspire: what is experienced as good and just between individuals is good and just for society.

Running through all Godwin's moral thinking is a tremendous optimism about humanity. Neither good nor bad is born into us, he asserts, and human perfectibility is a real possibility. 'Perfectibility is one of the most unequivocal characteristics of the human species, so that the political as well as the intellectual state of man may be presumed to be in a course of progressive improvement,' he writes. This progress depends upon two things: the removal of those external factors which create 'evil' characteristics in humanity, and the awakening of the human mind to the possibilities of rational and free choices. We shall see when we look at anarchist strategies, the important role that education plays in this process.

Malatesta, it has been argued, synthesized all three approaches.[18] He described anarchy as 'this society of free people, this society of friends' and referred to the law of solidarity governing the future of humankind. In the natural world, species survive and make life more pleasant either through individual struggle or through what he calls 'association for the struggle' against all those factors antagonistic to existence and wellbeing. It is through common struggle that there developed in humanity a social feeling which enabled it to transform the conditions of its existence. This social feeling constitutes the very basis of humankind's moral nature. So he concludes that 'Solidarity, that is the harmony of interests and of feelings, the coming together of individuals for the wellbeing of all, and of all for the wellbeing of each, is the only environment in which Man can express his personality and achieve his optimum development and enjoy the greatest possible wellbeing.'

The marks of an anarchist society are, in Malatesta's view, a society without government, a society which maintains itself on the basis of free and voluntary co-operation, a society which relies on the spontaneous action of interests, and a society which is entirely based on solidarity and love. He speaks of anarchy having equality of conditions as its basis, solidarity as its beacon, and freedom as its method. 'It is not perfection,' he wrote, 'it is not the absolute ideal which like the horizon recedes as fast as we approach it: but it is the way open to all progress and all improvements for the benefit of everyone.'

All these streams of anarchist thought are agreed about one thing: human society demands an ethical base which will shape its social, political and economic structures. That is a conclusion with which Christianity could not possibly disagree.

Anarchism's transformative and revolutionary strategies

The rejection of the proposition that the end justifies the means is almost universally shared by anarchists. The dominant anarchist tradition has always insisted that the strategies employed in working towards the new society must be totally consistent with the vision of that society. As Emma Goldman put it: 'No revolution can ever succeed as a factor of liberation unless the *means* used to further it be identical in spirit and tendency with the *purposes* to be achieved.' She made this comment in the course of her assessment of reasons for the failure of the Russian Revolution. Clearly for anarchists there has to be a unity between idea and action, in much the same way that Christians insist on a unity between belief and action. Nor does the parallel stop there, for both anarchist and Christian insist that the truth of their convictions is to be demonstrated in the way they live them out within the present society.

We have noted already that anarchists lay great store by education as a fundamental strategy. Sometimes it is said that this optimism about people being open to reason, to being grasped by the power of ideas, and by an act of free choice changing their behaviour, is naive. It therefore behoves Christians to recall that Jesus shared this optimism and this strategy. He, too, believed that building a new world called first for interior changes within the individual. He saw that the rigidity of the form of education espoused by the Scribes and Pharisees shackled people's hearts and minds. At the time of his temptation he rejected approaches which could have motivated people into personal change through material acquisitions, superstition or compulsion. Instead he challenged them with the power of a liberating idea and with the witness of a liberated life-style, so that by an act of free choice they could enter the Kingdom.

Godwin, who had unsuccessfully attempted to establish a school after he had left his church post, was aware of the domesticating role that education played in his day. He was the first person to examine the way that state-controlled education threatens human liberty, and he was an original thinker in terms of his counter proposals for a liberating form of education. He regarded state-controlled education as essentially conservative; concentrating on what is already known rather than what is yet to be discovered; keeping pupils in a state of subservience to the teacher rather than encouraging them to make discoveries for themselves; and being manipulated by the government in power to 'strengthen its hands and perpetuate its institutions'. There are quite remarkable parallels here to the return to the form of domesticating 'basic education' which conservatives are currently fostering on the one hand, and on the other to the critique of contemporary education developed by Ivan Illich, and the model of education for liberation pioneered by Paulo Freire.

True education, Godwin insisted, has to be based on a desire to learn, and people perceiving value in what they are learning. This is by way of contrast to education based on the fear of authority and other constraints. Traditionally, the master of a subject makes the knowledge he has accumulated available to the pupil. Godwin perceived things differently:

> No such characters are left upon the scene as either preceptor or pupil. The boy, like the man, studies because he desires it. He proceeds upon a plan of his own invention, or which, by adopting, he has made his own. Everything bespeaks independence and equality. The man, as well as the boy, would be glad in cases of difficulty to consult a person more informed than himself.[19]

Paulo Freire in our own generation has similarly analysed the way in which education is employed either to maintain the existing values, culture and structures of a society's dominant class, or to liberate people from these. He designates the one form of education as the 'banking' model in which the teacher is seen as possessing all the information, and pupils regarded as 'empty vessels' waiting to be filled. The teacher has an active role, the learners receive passively. Moreover, the teacher decides which selections of knowledge should be divulged. In contrast there is the 'problem-posing' model of education in which all function as both teachers and learners and a framework created for creative thinking and action in relation to commonly experienced problems.

No other political movement has assigned a more significant role to educational principles within both its theory and practice than has anarchism. From the early writings of Godwin, through those of Tolstoy and Josiah Warren, to the contemporary thought of art critics Herbert Read and sociologist Paul Goodman, education has been regarded as a liberating tool. Goodman has described from nursery to university the degree of flexibility which must be demonstrated if education is to be genuinely liberating within an unfree society.[20] Herbert Read has argued that the virtues of the liberated life are better developed through art than through the teaching of information.[21] For anarchists, liberating education is a powerful strategy for social change: it is both a demonstration of the principles and the benefits of anarchism, and itself an act of social transformation.

Popular propaganda always depicts anarchism's strategies for change as universally violent. We need to examine this assertion, for we have already seen that if the ethical basis of society is seriously pursued, the means employed to establish the just and peaceful society must themselves be peaceful and just. Violence is therefore ruled out. It was on the issue of violence that some of the early anarchists parted company with the Marxists. The latter proclaimed that the corrupt state had to be overthrown by violent means. It was Bakunin who pointed out in response that the state ruled by Bismarck and that proposed by Marx were identical in one respect: there is the same deployment of military power, and the same deployment of armed force against the masses.

On this issue we must allow anarchists to speak for themselves. Peter Kropotkin, in responding to the charge that anarchism is *the* party of violence, showed that violence becomes characteristic of all parties when they lose confidence in other strategies and fall victim to despair. He documented a particular twenty-year period to indicate that by far the greatest number of violent acts, and the worst degree of violence, had been perpetrated by monarchist, republican, social democrat and socialist regimes. Against this background, anarchist violence paled into insignificance. Emma Goldman, in one of her essays, shows how anarchist violence has either been a product of the capitalist press, or instigated by state authorities, including the police, as a way of discrediting the movement. She goes on to express the anarchist position:

> Anarchism, more than any other social theory, values human life above things. All Anarchists agree with Tolstoy in this fundamental truth: if the production of any commodity necessitates the sacrifice of human life, society should do without that commodity, but it can not do without that life. That, however, nowise indicates that Anarchism teaches submission. How can it, when it knows that all suffering, all misery, all ills, result from the evil of submission?[22]

Liberationist anarchism believes that the violence of the present age has to be resisted. Submission to it merely reinforces its claim upon us. In commenting on this situation, Emma Goldman quotes from a report of the killing of Sir Curzon Wyllie by a Hindu assassin: 'We may deprecate terrorism as outlandish and foreign to our culture, but it is inevitable as long as this tyranny continues, for it is not the terrorists that are to be blamed, but the tyrants who are responsible for it. It is the only resource for a helpless and unarmed people when brought to the verge of despair. It is never criminal on their part. The crime lies with the tyrant.' In such instances, the response is understood as an act of liberation from an overwhelmingly violent situation.

We find Kropotkin constantly returning to the anarchist principle of respect of human life, and insisting that all coercion, torture, punishment and other expressions of violence, are contrary to humanity's interests and have no place in the new society. Baldelli echoes this stance when he says that 'the renunciation of violence and deception . . . is the first and fundamental condition to the achievement of freedom and peaceful social existence as well as to their preservation once achieved.'

Baldelli calls this renunciation of violence 'The Way of the Meek'. Meekness is not understood in a passive, submissive sense, but is a positive commitment to harmlessness, and a conscious choice not to participate in violent competition and self-seeking. The meek, who are in most cases themselves victims of violence and deception, are by these choices establishing a new moral value.

Thus it is that the victims of the present dehumanizing society begin to shape the liberating society yet to come. Baldelli argues that the tactic in this process is that of permeation: 'ethical' people can begin to reclaim the present seats of authority, by working within them from an anarchist perspective to replace 'power' with 'freedom'. Jesus' witness within the power structures of his time, particularly that of the religious authority, might be described in precisely this way: reclaiming the authority of religion for humanity by replacing power with freedom! And we might also note the connection to the biological model of change. Australian anarchists Richard and Val Routley have described just such a model through which the existing useful state institutions are reclaimed for anarchism, while those which are unnecessary or unsatisfactory are allowed to die.[23]

The tactics of permeation cannot work, though, in situations of entrenched and oppressive power. It is on this point that all strategies for change, and particularly those opposed to violence, experience great difficulty. In Baldelli's view, naked power applied too heavily and upon too sensitive material engenders what he calls 'anti-power'. 'Anti-power' he says, 'is the motive force of genuine revolutions. Being a fruit of desperation, it dissipates as soon as hope returns and, being unethical, it becomes power as soon as it is triumphant.' Anti-power manifests itself either as deathlike resistance, or as a striking back to recall society to justice and peace. It proves itself 'deadly and inhuman solely against that which has been proven deadly and inhuman.'[24]

Bakunin related this 'striking back' to a destructive urge which he recognized within his own personality, and subsequently elevated to a political value. This urge is not seen as a negative force, however; rather as an essential prelude to creation. As he put it in his typically apocalyptic style:

> There will be a qualitative transformation, a new living, life-giving revelation, a new heaven and a new earth, a young and mighty world in which all our present dissonances will be resolved into a harmonious whole. . . And therefore we call to our blinded brothers: Repent! Repent! The Kingdom of God is coming nigh. Let us put our trust in the eternal spirit which destroys and annihilates only because it is the unsearchable and eternally creative source of all life. The passion for destruction is also a creative passion.[25]

It was but a short step for some anarchists on this basis to begin to advocate first the destruction of property, and then the elimination of persons, as a legitimate revolutionary tactic. We find in the *Principles of Revolution*, a work which has been incorrectly attributed to Bakunin, the revolutionary depicted as an agent of righteous extermination, making a 'list of those condemned to death' and expediting their sentence 'according to the order of their relative iniquities'. Anarchists who came to be known as 'Propaganda of the Deed', in the belief that no act of rebellion is without value, and that each act of rebellion proclaims the revolution, set about destroying the symbols of entrenched power. For them, there were no 'innocent bystanders': people who by free choice were associating themselves with the centres of power must suffer the consequences of the choice they have made.

Thus King Umberto I, who had been responsible for atrocities against the Italian revolutionary movement, was assassinated by a weaver who

> rose alone above the general indolence, and alone faced the symbols of so much infamy. With a stroke he put back history, wayward and arrested, back on the path of its future, towards its destiny. That gesture spoke to the confused masses . . . the king who is glory, myth, power is like any other man, only a miserable bag of fragile flesh and bones. A single revolver shot can reduce him to litter the way he did with you. . . A king dies and another takes his place. But the king who picks up the crown with his father's blood on it learns prudence, moderation, wisdom.[26]

It is unfortunate that the reputation of anarchism is today judged almost exclusively in terms of this particular tactical approach, which has certainly never been the dominant one in anarchist thought. It was a tactic espoused by independent Italian anarchists against the advice and convictions of leaders of the movement like Malatesta, whose last written words were a rejection of this kind of violence. 'He who throws a bomb and kills a pedestrian, declares that as a victim of society he has rebelled against society. But could not the poor victim object: "Am I society?"'.[27] Even so, we have to recognize that Propaganda of the Deed anarchists are not arguing for the perpetration of mindless acts of violence and destruction in order to bring about chaos and confusion. They argue that only specific acts of counter violence can put an end to the massive violence which unjust regimes inflict upon their subjects. Individual acts of rebellion, Galleani insists, have to be evaluated conscientiously in the light of the historical moment, the causes of unrest, the social context, and the immediate and remote repercussions of the event. Only then can a proper assessment of Propaganda of the Deed be made.

Christian anarchism

In contrast to the violence of Propaganda of the Deed, the distinctive contribution of Christian anarchist thought has been its unswerving commitment to non-violence. This calls upon Christians to make acts of personal resistance whenever the state attempts to coerce or co-opt them into its destructive agencies. For Tolstoy this meant resistance to military service. 'Governments', he said, 'assert that armies are chiefly needed for external defence, but that is not true. They are needed first of all against their own subjects, and every man who performs military service involuntarily becomes an accomplice in all the acts of violence the government inflicts upon its subjects.'[28] He here echoes Blake who, noting the way in which war had developed into contests between large civilian rather than small professional armies, perceived that war had become basic to the health of the state. Not only were civilians being annihilated in the process, but states were employing armies to perpetrate violence against their own citizens rather than for national defence. That this has now come to be regarded as fairly standard practice is confirmed by analysis of the recent history of many governments. The only deployment of the New Zealand armed forces in the last ten years, other than for United Nations' peace-keeping duties, has not been to repel external aggression but to control its own citizens. The army has provided support for police action both in the eviction of Maori people from their traditional lands and in the protection of the Government/Rugby Union alliance during public protests against the Springbok Tour of 1981.

Tolstoy asserted that what made Christianity unique was its commitment to non-violence.[29] In an essay written in the last year of his life,[30] he describes how all previous arrangements of life were founded on the power of rulers and maintained by violence. Violence, including killing in self-defence, or in defence of one's country, or the execution of criminals, became an inevitable condition of social life. Christianity substituted love as the highest law of life, acknowledging all people as equals, and advocating forgiveness and the returning of good for evil. 'Thus,' he writes, 'Christianity in its true meaning, acknowledging love as the fundamental law of life, directly and definitely repudiated that very violence which lay at the base of every previous arrangement of life.'

Tolstoy felt that the early church had quickly abandoned Christianity's most fundamental teaching. Leaders had been so conditioned by centuries of violence that not understanding what Christianity was demanding, or understanding only too well, they concealed the truth from people and 'took from Christianity only that which was not repugnant to their established mode of life'. The church tried to unite Christ's renunciation of violence with Hebrew teaching which allowed it. It succeeded so well that the violence which was incompatible with Christ's teaching 'came to be considered both by those suffering coercion and those imposing it, not only not repugnant to the Christian teaching of love, but completely lawful and in accordance with Christian teaching'.

What is required, Tolstoy argues, is a return to Christ's principles of non-violence. This involves three simple, natural steps. First, we must ourselves stop doing direct violence, and also prepare ourselves for this. Secondly, we should not take part in any violence done by other people, or in preparation for violence. And thirdly, we should offer no approval of any violence whatever.

We have already seen that there have throughout Christian history been small communities which have resisted violence and challenged the right of the (violent by definition) state to regulate human behaviour through law. Typical of these was the Hopedale Community in Massachusetts, whose minister, Adin Ballou, insisted that while human and divine government are realities, Christians are called to live under God's rule. Compared to divine government, civil government has no intrinsic authority, no moral supremacy and no rightful claim to human allegiance. Ballou therefore urged Christians to withdraw from participation in state affairs and from the management of the state's activities. He said that it was the Christian task neither to reform nor purify nor subvert the state; rather it is to supersede the state with the

Kingdom of God. Nor did he regard Christian refusal to participate in government or to support state institutions like the police and the army as an act of antagonism. Christians are not to go out of their way to offend civil power, or to provoke arguments with good people. Instead, they are called upon to be moral agents of the Kingdom of God and to demonstrate its 'more excellent way' in their quality of life and social organization.

Tolstoy, Blake, Ballou and Berdyaev all reached the same conclusion: that master and slave, ruler and subject, oppressor and oppressed, are victims of the same spiritual affliction. Berdyaev went on to explore this understanding within a theological context. The essential contradiction of human existence is that humanity has an immense drive towards freedom, yet a deep love of slavery. 'Master', 'slave' and 'free person' are three structures of consciousness. Neither of the first two can exist without the other. The free person exists in himself or herself. Much of Berdyaev's thought is concerned with the nature of human personality: it is indestructible, exceptional, original, authentic, potentially universal, subject to no law. As with Christ, who was the ultimately free personality, 'only the free man is a personality and he is that even if the whole world would wish to enslave him'. He regarded the basic and guiding principle of the Kingdom of God as creative autonomy. At this point he differs from Tolstoy and Ballou for whom that principle is non-resisting love.

Berdyaev, who freely acknowledged that it was Tolstoy who had alerted him to the condition of human slavery in the modern world, made two further points about it. While the crude forms of violence perpetrated against people to deprive them of their freedom are readily identified, the even larger role played by psychological violence tends to be overlooked. The system of upbringing may deprive a person of freedom. Hardened public opinion may act as a form of violence against people. Whenever a person becomes a slave to public opinion, morals, custom, or to judgments or opinions imposed by society, there is a degree of violence present. Berdyaev noted this particularly to be the case in the media of his time, insisting that the daily newspaper exercises a psychological compulsion upon people in a manner that enslaves them and deprives them of their own freedom of conscience and independent judgment.[31]

Secondly, he notes that people commonly have an illusion of freedom. 'Psychologically,' he says, 'the easiest thing of all to accept as freedom is the absence of movement, the habitual condition.' Any movement for change exercises a certain degree of force upon both the material environment and persons. The *status quo* in society is generally represented as a restful or peaceful state, free from force. Social change on the other hand is generally depicted as a violation of freedom and the application of force. Berdyaev notes as a consequence that an institution like slavery which has become habitual and hardened through time may not appear to be violent, whereas a movement with the aim of abolishing slavery may appear extremely violent.

In similar vein, William Blake concluded that the most pernicious form of slavery was the power of the ruling class to determine the consciousness of the people. He referred to the dominant ideology as 'mind forg'd manacles', showing how political and spiritual authority and the superstructures constructed upon them create chains of illusion. Like Godwin, he perceived that the law imposed by the ruling class is never a remedy for social and moral disorder. Quite the reverse, it causes those disorders. The alliance of state and church imposes a moral code on humanity which can only lead to deception, hypocrisy and violence.

These considerations of the reality of structural violence paved the way for subsequent explorations, like those of Paulo Freire, into the processes through which oppressed people become conditioned to accept the oppressor's view of reality, and therefore themselves help to maintain the structures of oppression in place. Freire also points out that often when oppressed people who have suffered great violence come to establish their own liberating society, having no experience of any other model than that of the oppressor, they end up reproducing elements of the old violent structures. This has been demonstrated in our day with the establishment in the Middle East of a Zionist state, by people who were victims of the world's most terrible and inhumane treatment. The institutions of this state now perpetrate upon people of another race similar forms of harassment, punishment and oppression to those which Zionists themselves once endured.

This serves to remind us yet again of the complex problems which face Christians determined to maintain a non-violent stance in the face of intrinsically violent structures and processes. We shall explore this question further when we examine the strategies that Jesus employed. But we are here affirming resistance and non-violence as genuinely anarchist strategies. There have been a number of significant Christian attempts to establish witnessing communities based on these principles. One of the best known is the network of communities known collectively as the Catholic Worker. Amongst its founders were Dorothy Day, Peter Maurin and Ammon Hennacy, all both Roman Catholics and Libertarians.[32] The community's newspaper, also called *The Catholic Worker*, may well be the most widely circulated of today's libertarian journals. It has consistently promoted radical Christian pacifism, has refused to pay taxes, and has fostered forms of non-violent direct action. There are currently more than twenty rural and urban Catholic Worker communities in North America which offer hospitality to the outsider, and serve as bases of resistance to the dominant ideology.

In Protestant circles the best known of the communities is the Sojourners Community. Its origins are to be found in the struggles against American involvement in the Viet Nam war in the late 1960s, when many Christians sought ways of confronting American imperialism. The community is now located in Washington where it lives the gospel out amidst the poor, consistently witnesses to peace, and publishes its own magazine promoting non-violence, *Sojourners*.

The anarchist tradition, then, has much in common with Christianity, and offers Christian activists a model of change far more in harmony with the scriptures than either capitalist or socialist alternatives. Indeed, Berdyaev contends that *only* Christianity is able to create a truly just society. But he notes two characteristics of the radical change required. The first is that social transformation is dependent upon personal transformation, and the second is that change cannot be imposed upon society. It has to be voluntarily accepted by individuals.

He goes on to place special emphasis upon creativity as *the* human vocation: the making of something new which has not been created before. Creative activity, borne on the wings of imagination, is liberating because it demands self-forgetfulness and sacrifice. Rejecting the ethics of law, which he regarded as pre-Christian, Berdyaev develops what he called the ethics of creativeness which seeks to transform the world of science, art, politics and the economy through creative acts which enhance the meaning of life.

In his spiritual autobiography, he records words which will speak to many contemporary Christians:

> I find myself in complete rupture with my epoch. I sing freedom, which my epoch hates; I do not love government and am of religio-anarchist tendency, while the epoch deifies government; I am an extreme personalist, while the epoch is collectivist and rejects the dignity and worth of personality; I do not love war and the military, while the epoch lives in the pathos of war; I love the philosophic mind while the epoch is indifferent to it; I value aristocratic culture while the epoch degrades it; and finally I profess eschatological Christianity, while the epoch recognizes only traditional-contemporal Christianity.[33]

In the course of training Christian social and community workers, I have discovered increasing numbers of students, disillusioned with the bureaucracy and the inhumanity of present structures, turning to the diversity which liberationist anarchism offers, as well as the opportunities it provides for living out the gospel in the contemporary world. The following declaration I came across indicates the direction which many Christians are taking:

A Positive Programme of Christian Anarchy

Devolution of authority
Decentralization of power
Distribution of wealth
Demythologizing of work
Deschooling of society
Degree of technology
Development of land

Christian anarchism as counter-culture

Christian anarchism, as its numerous expressions of community have demonstrated, offers a counter-cultural perspective from which the oppression of both capitalist and socialist ideology can be analysed and addressed. It is counter-cultural in a number of senses. In the first place, its starting point is not a social, economic or political theory. It springs instead from what we might call the religious impulse to understand the nature of humanity, and to create the optimum conditions within which humanity can develop.

Secondly, it sets out to create an ethical society, free from the present constraints of authority, hierarchy, patriarchy, bureaucracy and coercion. It understands that the human personality develops as an ethical entity through making free choices and acts of faith, without recourse to external law.

Thirdly, it insists that the strategies and tactics employed to move towards the new society must themselves embody the vision of that society.

Fourthly, it talks of dispersing rather than seizing power. This means that change is not dependent upon some historic moment when all the forces for change are aligned. Anarchist principles can be lived out in community now as the old order decays.

Something of its spirit is captured in the basic ecclesial communities which have become a feature of some Latin American Roman Catholic communities and which offer a deinstitutionalized experience of the church. It is certainly visible within the multiplicity of attempts that Christians are making to create and experiment with new life-styles. A World Council of Churches' Consultation on new life-styles in 1980, commenting on the role of people's movements and groups committed to establishing a just society, said:

> What is emerging from their variety is a new value system which, though still embryonic, is tending to replace the established system of values which is felt to be dehumanizing and oppressive.
>
> Thus, while individualistic attitudes prevail in societies which are based on authoritarian, hierarchical and bureaucratic values, the groups committed to change tend to gather in communities and collectives, making people's participation, horizontal communication and shared leadership the basis of their action.[34]

The report goes on to comment about the un-hierarchical and non-authoritarian values of these communities, and the way that the value system already present within the movements, but not yet realized by the world at large, acts as a sign of hope. All of this is consistent with anarchist objectives and strategies, as is the motivation and goal of freedom.

There is even some evidence of major Christian denominations moving in this direction. Some Roman Catholics are interpreting the principle of subsidiarity, attributed to Pope Pius XI, as consistent with libertarian views:

> It is a fundamental principle of social philosophy, fixed and unchangeable, that one should not withdraw from individuals and commit to the community what they can accomplish by their own enterprise and industry. So, too, it is an injustice and at the same time a grave evil and a disturbance of right order, to transfer to the larger and higher collectivity functions which can be performed and provided for by lesser and subordinate bodies. Inasmuch as every social activity should, by its very nature, prove a help to members of the body social, it should never destroy or absorb them.[35]

The idea that a higher organization should not usurp functions that a lower organization more representative of the community can perform was amplified by Pope John XXIII in the documents *Mater et Magistra* and *Pacem in Terris*. In the former he argues for observance of the principle in the area of the ownership of goods and the equitable development of economic life within the community. Addressing the question of aid to less developed areas of the world, he enunciated a principle which is presumably of far wider application: that in terms of development, citizens themselves should be encouraged to accomplish as much as is feasible. In the latter document, the Pope applies the principle of subsidiarity to international relations, arguing that while it is the responsibility of the world community to tackle the major social, economic, political and cultural problems, such institutions must not limit the sphere of action of local authority, or take its place.

Subsidiarity implies the placing of limits upon the power of the state. That theme was taken up and developed by the Roman Catholic bishops in the United States in their controversial 1986 statement *Economic Justice For All*. In an apparent rejection of totalitarian and statist approaches, the bishops applied the principle of subsidiarity when they argued that 'in order to protect basic justice, government should undertake only those initiatives that exceed the capacity of individuals and private groups acting independently. Government should not replace or destroy smaller communities and individual initiative.'[36]

It was significant also that the 1988 Lambeth Conference of Bishops of the Anglican Communion suggested that where local and national government cannot deliver adequate services, the poor can achieve significant progress when they take matters into their own hands. In deliberating on Christianity and the Social Order, they address the issue of coercion as exemplified in structural violence, the imposition by powerful states of their policies and military bases upon smaller states, and the way that states institutionalize violence against their own people. They acknowledge that states acting in this way lose their moral authority. While not admitting to the critique that states by their very nature behave in this violent and coercive way, they nevertheless point out that the breakdown of centres of power, far from being a bad thing, can release remarkable energies. They quote the example of a Latin American city which between 1960 and 1984 constructed $173 million of public housing while the informal sector created $8,319 million of unauthorized housing. They comment:

> Rather than fight official bureaucracies, people are taking action for themselves. The hopes, the skills and the ingenuities of the poor are being harnessed to the development of their own communities, and governments are having to accept it. These communities have disregarded ideologies and political platforms as they have sought to construct their homes and to open markets, bypassing the legal process on the way.[37]

In pointing out the value of community-run and community-accountable initiatives in business, housing and transportation, in suggesting that they are in a sense beyond ideology, in allowing that these must occur outside the law, and in recommending them as a model for community development, the bishops are adopting a liberationist stance.

In a commentary on the United States' Roman Catholic bishops' pastoral letters on peace and the economy,[38] Phillip Berryman suggests that the time may be ripe to 'explore and develop the affinities between Catholic social teaching and anarchist thought'. Noting that the principle of subsidiarity is somewhat anarchist, he finds that the church's teaching has much in common with the communitarianism of some anarchist thinkers. Where anarchism calls for human scale communities rooted in local history, ecology, language and tradition, regards the local body of citizens as the basic political unit and rejects the notion of one's primary loyalty being to the Nation-State, it has points of contact with Roman Catholic social thought. He also points to the way that writers like E. F. Schumacher and Ivan Illich, activists like the Berrigan brothers, and movements like the Catholic Worker, have managed to marry anarchist and Roman Catholic positions.

As the institutional church, faced with the dehumanization which the political options it has espoused have engendered, begins at last to suggest that liberationist initiatives may provide a way forward, we can justifiably ask whether the idea of the Christian counter-culture, critical and liberating, is not about to come into its own!

CHAPTER SIX

Direct Action Against the Treasury
The Strategies of Jesus

There is a deep resistance amongst Christians towards analysing the strategies that Jesus himself employed in any terms other than those of a pastoral ministry to individuals in personal crisis. On frequent occasions in the course of the training programmes we have sponsored, Christians have maintained the view that whenever Jesus happened across people in distress, he invariably dealt with them on a one-to-one basis offering them love, forgiveness, healing and salvation.

This emphasis on individualism has characterized Christian mission and ministry for centuries. It is reflected in all the church's activities from its preaching of the necessity for individual conversion, to forms of social service structured to solve personal crises or to enhance the individual's sense of self-worth. For example, the largest denominational social service agency in my city spends a disproportionate share of its budget of several million dollars on 'personal services', to the detriment of community-based programmes.

This obsession with dealing with individuals has all but blinded the church to the need for structural change. Even when it does attempt to address that question, it tends to do so from an individualistic perception.

The most frequently employed analogy of Christian social service is that of dedicated people performing ambulance work at the foot of a cliff, binding up the wounds of those unfortunate victims who happen to have toppled over. Some Christians take the further step of asking how we might prevent people falling over in the first place by constructing some kind of protective fencing at the cliff's edge. A few progress to the uncomfortable conclusion that people are not falling over at all, but are being pushed over (whether intentionally or by accident) and that there is a certain degree of cynicism involved in Christians being party to a destructive institution on the one hand, and then holding up their hands in horror when they discover the mutilated victims at the foot of the cliff on the other. But rarely do Christians question the very existence of the cliff itself, or advocate the use of gunpowder and earth-moving equipment to reshape it into a gently graded hillside.

This focussing of attention upon the individual is an example of the way in which the dominant ideology insinuates itself into our thinking and begins a process of domestication. In riveting our attention on the personal and the individual to the exclusion of all else, it successfully diverts us from the possibilities of structural and political action. As a result, Christians are socialized into a naive, and from the perspective of the powerful, a non-threatening view of social change: that destructive and dehumanizing structures will be reformed through the actions of loving and dedicated Christians working within them. They hold to this strategy in spite of the fact that there is practically no historical evidence to support it. And as a consequence of that, the field of effective social change is left wide open to other ideologies.

This is not to deny the importance of ministering to individuals in need or to diminish the emphasis which Christianity places upon the personal. Both are to be clearly identified and substantiated in the Gospels. It is rather to argue that because Jesus began with the personal and dealt with private hurts, it is easy to lose sight of those dimensions to his ministry which highlighted private woes as public pain. Christians therefore need to look in some detail at the methodologies which Jesus espoused.

The Gospels tell us that at around the age of thirty, Jesus spent time examining appropriate strategies for his work. We might recall in passing that the age of thirty was considered relatively advanced in a society where life expectancy was much shorter than it is in ours, and that Jesus was an ageing rather than a bright young reformer! Jesus undertook this reflection in the course of a forty day fast, the spiritual and personal dimensions to which need to be acknowledged. But what the Gospels describe as the Temptations in the Wilderness are, divested of their mystical elements, the account of a person analysing methodologies for mission and action (Matt.4.1–11).

We are told that Jesus rejected three particular strategies. The first was that of providing enough bread to satisfy the world's hunger, which we might see as the equivalent of international aid and development programmes globally, and locally, as state-sponsored income-maintenance programmes. The second was the temptation to prove by leaping unhurt from the Temple roof that he was a person worthy of the full trust of the community. Our modern equivalents may well be those technocrats who urge us to have faith in their schemes of modernization and resource development. The third possible strategy was that of exercising political power on a universal scale. We don't have to search far today for talk of world government or world domination and for examples of their advocates struggling to 'liberate' each other's spheres of influence.

Jesus rejected all these strategies and the roles which accompanied them: resource provider, miracle worker *per se*, and world leader. What the Gospel passage on the Temptations does not identify, however, are the strategies which Jesus did elect to implement. We have to dig a bit deeper to identify these in the course of his three-year public ministry.

We can examine Jesus' strategies from three perspectives. There are first the strategies he employed to challenge the dominant ideas of his day and to proclaim an alternative world view. Today we would refer to this as the counter-cultural or *ideological* arena. Secondly, there are the strategies he used to create and maintain an *organizational* base for his work. And thirdly there are the *direct action* strategies which he sometimes used in their own right as examples of the new society he was advocating, but were also means of highlighting the contradictions within the dominant ideology; or techniques for ensuring the solidarity of his organization.

Strategies in the ideological arena

Many Christians use the word 'ideology' in a pejorative sense to describe systems of thought which appear opposed to the Christian faith. This is a typical manifestation of the confused history of the word which first appeared in the English language in 1796 and which has often since then been applied to abstract, impractical or fanatical theories. The term is much in need of rehabilitation and it is here being used in the more open sense of a World Council of Church's working definition which bears repeating:

> Ideology is a system of thought or blueprint used to interpret society and man's place in society, the function of which is either to legitimate the existing structures of society or to change them.[1]

Whether one accepts the World Council's suggestion that there are of necessity ideological elements within Christianity, or the more positive assertions of those who maintain that theology is the critique of the ideology of Christianity,[2] the World Council's definition enables us to understand the sense in which Jesus was ideological. In his teaching he was offering people an alternative interpretation of the nature of the world and of humanity's place within it, to that which was being promoted by the establishment of that time.

In our second chapter we noted very briefly some of the constituent elements of that ideology of first-century Palestine and the power base that maintained it. We now need to clarify these a little more.

In Palestine the set of ideas employed to explain the world and to establish a value base for personal morality was derived from biblical texts. Given that the bulk of the population was illiterate, those deemed to have authority in the process of the interpretation and application of texts were in a position of enormous power. They acted, in fact, as ideological agents.

There were two basic texts, the Torah which comprised the first six books of the Old Testament, and the Prophets. There were also two schools of interpretation. The first was the preserve of the priests who regarded the texts as a closed selection and who promoted an increasingly conservative reading of them. This very conservatism created the space for the emergence of the scribes as the dominant force in ideological formation and maintenance. The role of the scribes was to publicly read and comment on scripture in the sabbath by sabbath services in local synagogues. As a consequence they developed a very close relationship with the people.

In explaining and interpreting the texts, the scribes drew on sources which were not admitted by the priests. There was first, that ever-increasing body of literature which the scribes themselves were producing within their tradition, the Targumic texts. But they also drew heavily from two other traditions, Wisdom and Apocalyptic literature.

These traditions brought about subtle shifts of ideological emphasis. For example, the Wisdom literature of a book like Job, in its concern for the marginalized in society, and its searching for an explanation of why those who had been most faithful were by comparison to the faithless suffering most, changed the focus from the health of the community to the plight of the individual. That shift encouraged people to think in terms of individual rather than community salvation, and of the development of codes of personal morality, an area in which the scribes delighted to offer advice.

The apocalyptic texts introduced to Israel ideological elements from abroad, particularly from Persia. These texts were produced against the background of profound political disillusionment amongst the Jewish people. They had been subject to wave after wave of foreign oppression and each time it appeared that liberation was within their grasp, their hopes were dashed. Apocalyptic literature tries to restore national confidence, steeling people for specific religious and political struggles. It is resistance literature at its best, acknowledging both the outrages of the past and the suffering of the present situation, but promising a new dawn, a final glorious victory. The writings mark a break with the older prophetic tradition which had suggested that God would intervene to directly alter the course of history in response to people's faith. The new literature proclaimed that a predetermined but secret plan is being worked out and that all will be well. The people should take heart.

At the time of Jesus the influence of the apocalyptic movement was at its height, and it had become the most important element in the way in which the scribes interpreted the texts. It was reflected in the stress laid on messianic deliverance: the notion of the saviour whose advent would be signalled by disasters and wars, but who would defeat the hosts of evil and inaugurate the messianic kingdom.

The ideological function of the priests was centred at Jerusalem to which they journeyed on a roster system to fulfil their duties in the Temple. Their task was to officiate at the rituals which, based on animal sacrifice, were held to eliminate pollution and re-establish national and personal purity. In any culture the language and symbols of ritual are vehicles of ideology, so the priests' influence was considerable. Furthermore, it extended into the local judicial system where they were required to determine questions of pollution and purity, and to the economic and political affairs of the state, by virtue of their other role as civil servants.

The basic structure of Israel's ideological blueprint was simple. There was a three-tiered universe. Above lay the heavens, the dwelling place of God and his angels. In the centre was the earth, the domain of humanity. And underneath lay the sea or the abyss, inhabited by demons. This structure was symbolized in the Temple itself where the Court represented the sea, the Holy Place the earth, and the Holy of Holies the heavens. The Temple was a pillar supporting the heavens in their proper place. It thus acted as the axis of the universe, the place where heaven and earth meet. Holiness radiated in concentric circles from the Holy of Holies to the Temple Mount, to the city to the countryside. Jerusalem was as a consequence the most powerful of ideological symbols.

Given this dominant ideology and the power of the agents who transmitted it, how did Jesus address the ideological situation? The most elementary reading of scripture indicates that Jesus perceived the ideology in the hands of the Pharisaic party to be an instrument of oppression. Scripture also describes how he set about both confronting and subverting that ideology.

We should at the outset note the way in which Jesus took steps to avoid both the official condemnation and the public alienation which would occur if he were seen to be espousing radical ideas which threatened the whole basis of the tradition. A dominant ideology normally possesses very effective mechanisms for neutralizing anyone who challenges its supremacy, and the Jewish ideology was no exception. The charges of blaspheming and of being a political stirrer would later be laid against Jesus. While these charges may be evaluated as effective in terms of eliminating Jesus from the scene, they arrived too late to counteract the power of the counter-ideology which had been implanted amongst his followers.

Jesus' strategy in this respect was publicly to declare that he was not concerned to change anything but was, on the contrary, a staunch defender of orthodoxy. At the beginning of his public ministry Jesus made that declaration: 'Do not imagine that I have come to abolish the Law or the Prophets. I have come not to abolish but to complete them. I tell you, until heaven and earth disappear, not one dot, not one little stroke, shall disappear from the Law until its purpose is achieved. Therefore the person who infringes even one of the least of these commandments and teaches others to do the same, will be considered least in the Kingdom of Heaven . . .' (Matt. 5.17–19).

Jesus addresses himself directly to the ideological sourcebooks, the Torah and the Prophets. He affirms their traditional place in the scheme of salvation, and categorically asserts that the person who even infringes the regulations, let alone sets out to alter them, has little chance of salvation.

However, in the verses which immediately follow these, Jesus takes some of the particular requirements of orthodoxy, 'You shall not kill', 'You shall not commit adultery', 'You shall not break solemn oaths' and so on, and begins to radically reinterpret them. He insists that the anger which leads to violence and the lust which leads to adultery are as 'sinful' in the eyes of the Law as the acts themselves.

Jesus presses deep into the nature of the Law in order to highlight its contradictions. In concentrating all its attention on prohibitions, it neglects the questions of human motivation and human spirituality. The Law allows anger to the point of physical violence; it condones lust to the moment of adultery. Jesus' concern, on the other hand, was to promote a fully developed humanity free from the desire to coerce, manipulate or exploit others. Although he has made a fundamental alteration to the Law, his action is cloaked in the claim that his interpretation is not a deviation from orthodoxy but rather, the true orthodoxy. He promotes change while ruling out the possibility of change.

Part of Jesus' ideological strategy was to establish himself as a notable authority in the field of scriptural interpretation which was the preserve of the priests and the scribes. One way of doing that would have been to have infiltrated the ranks of the ideology-makers and to have begun to influence the process of interpretation from within. While infiltrating the priesthood would have been difficult because of its hereditary nature, he could easily have become a scribe, who were either self-supporting on the basis of a trade or a small business, or else assisted with public funding. But if he ever did consider this approach, Jesus rejected it.

That does not mean that he chose to work entirely outside the institution. He maintained an ambiguous relationship with the establishment, identifying with it at points through his affirmation of the tradition, his attendance at synagogue and his observance of the feasts, yet deliberately distancing himself from its power structure and adopting the role of critic.

Challenging the authority of the scribes in the confrontations he had with them became part of the strategy for establishing his own competence and authority. He issued these challenges in a number of ways. One was to continually suggest that the so-called experts were leading people into error: that neither they themselves understood the issues, nor did they possess the ability to open other people to the truth. Quite the opposite. The end effect of their misunderstanding and misinterpretation of the tradition was to place obstacles in the way of the quest to become divinely human.

On other occasions Jesus chose to out-scribe the scribes! There are numerous incidents in scripture where he engages the scribes in their own particular form of argument and comes out the winner. This suggests that he had studied the scribes' methodology so closely and became so skilled in its application that he was always confident of being able to beat them at their own game.

St Matthew's Gospel provides us with a classic example of these skills in an incident where the scribes lay a clever trap for Jesus, but end up outmanoeuvred and entrapped themselves. Towards the end of his ministry Jesus is found teaching in the Temple precincts (Matt. 21.23). Those who regarded themselves as being in authority challenged him directly. 'What authority do *you* have for acting like this? And who gave you this authority?' Jesus responds that he will certainly answer that question if his adversaries first answer a question he has for them. And he poses an unanswerable theological question about the baptism of John. Was that baptism a divine or a human event, he enquires? If the authorities had answered that John's baptism was a divine act, Jesus would have asked why, in that case, did they not believe the teaching of John. Had they responded that the baptism was a human invention, the followers of John amongst the crowd would have immediately retaliated in his defence. The authorities had to admit defeat. 'We can't answer that question', they said. Jesus retorted, 'Then nor will I answer your question about *my* authority!'

Jesus did not ultimately avoid the issue of the source of his authority. On many other occasions he made its basis very clear, claiming a direct relationship to God. By this he implied not only that he was God's instrument on earth, a direct exploitation of the messianic elements in the dominant ideology, but that there was no longer any need for there to be human intermediaries between the divine and human realms. He thus subverted both the claims of the priesthood to have responsibility for determining and establishing individual and national purity, and the role of mediating 'truth' which the scribes had appropriated. Jesus asserted that each person could have direct and personal access to the truth, and each become in effect his or her own authority. The liberating power of this claim to people under the yoke of oppression is not to be underestimated. The dominant ideology claimed that there were eternally established laws which needed to be discerned and applied by humanity and that responsibility for discernment lay in the hands of a specially designated class of people. Jesus subverted that process by turning everyone into a potential authority! It was, however, the ideology itself which had created that possibility, for it opened the way for Jesus to claim that he possessed 'the real truth' while the priests and scribes had latched on to only a pale imitation of truth.

We have noted in another context the way in which Jesus' enemies devoted a great deal of energy and imagination to setting him up in impossible situations, and that Jesus had to employ all his skills to extricate himself from those situations. He was particularly good at seeing through the opposition's tactics and of remaining one step ahead of them. The Gospels never record him in the position of being caught unawares. He had especially developed to a high degree the art of recognizing the hidden dimensions, whether economic, political or ideological, to his opponents' tactics. Earlier we saw how quick Jesus was to perceive the political implications of the question he was posed about the appropriateness of paying Roman taxes. Had he pronounced that people should pay the tax, he would have lost the ear of the Jerusalem crowd who were opposed to it. Had he supported the popular move to withhold payment, he could have been immediately arraigned on a criminal charge. It was this ability to recognize *all* the facets of even the most innocent-looking encounters with the opposition which gave him the advantage over them. Far from being a naive do-gooder, he was a skilled political, social and economic analyst.

In approaching the dominant ideology, Jesus' strategy was to seize upon those elements which could be re-worked in such a way as to challenge the ideology itself. Some might argue that he exploited its contradictions very successfully. He certainly manipulated some of its most powerful symbols in favour of his own cause. The most impressive example of this is the manner in which he applied the symbolism of the messiah, at that time in popular vogue, to himself.

Jesus noted the details of a promise referred to in the book of the prophet Zechariah:

> Rejoice heart and soul, daughter of Zion!
> Shout with gladness, daughter of Jerusalem!
> See now, your king comes to you;
> he is victorious, he is triumphant,
> humble and riding on a donkey,
> on a colt, the foal of a donkey.
> He will banish chariots from Ephraim
> and horses from Jerusalem;
> the bow of war will be banished.
> He will proclaim peace for the nations.
> His empire will stretch from sea to sea,
> from the River to the ends of the earth (Zech. 9.9–10).

He takes this symbol of the universal ruler, who will establish the rule of peace, and physically enacts it precisely as the passage predicts, riding into Jerusalem on the back of a donkey. The ideological implications are clear to all who witness this great spectacle. Jesus is claiming for himself the mantle of the peace-bringing messiah. Through the deliberate manipulation of this rich imagery he both makes public his intentions and captures the imagination of the crowd.

Another ideological strategy he employed was to stress the opposite value to those inherent in and being promoted by the dominant ideology's code of meaning and behaviour. Thus when the code alludes to the maturity of adults, Jesus talks about the wisdom of children. When the code reinforces the proper role of the master, Jesus focusses on the nature of the servant. When it gives pre-eminence in society to the rich, he elevates the poor.

Where it indicates correct orders of precedence in society, Jesus reverses them declaring that the first shall be last. This tactic of inverting the ideology's values enables the oppressed to understand the dynamic of oppression.

As well as confronting the ideological oppression of the scribes, Jesus also attacks the conservative stance of the priesthood. He fundamentally questioned their role of determining issues of pollution and purity for everyday life. By so doing he was directly challenging the ideology's conception of what was pure and impure. In many cases he does this by direct action which breaches the code. He dines with prostitutes and tax collectors, he consorts with lepers, he touches a woman with a menstrual disorder, he talks to a woman beside a well, he allows a woman to anoint his body with oil.

When the authorities, as they are bound to do when faced with such deliberate breaches of the code, publicly reprimand him for this behaviour, Jesus once again begins reworking the ideological categories. Where the code demands elaborate ceremonial washings to prevent internal contamination through the eating of impure foods, Jesus points out that people are not made impure by food which passes through the digestive system, but by unclean thoughts which have an internal origin and then become manifested in external actions (Mark 7.14–23). This once again, is a reversal of the dominant ideology.

In the end, Jesus attacks the most powerful ideological symbol of all, that of the Temple in Jerusalem. We have already alluded to the way in which the ideology depicted the Temple as the axis at the centre of the world, the pillar supporting the heavens in their place. In St Mark's Gospel we find Jesus proclaiming that the Temple, the world's axis, is going to be so totally destroyed that not one stone will remain upon another (13.24–32). Clearly, if the Temple were to fall, everything else will fall with it. The heavens would no longer be supported and would collapse upon the earth. Jesus speaks of the sun being darkened, the moon losing its brightness, the stars tumbling down, and the powers of heaven being shaken. He is foreshadowing the destruction of the entire Judaic universe.

Those who had heard Jesus on this occasion would have instantly comprehended his message. He is here using the rich language of the apocalyptic literature, so attractive in his day, to attack the most destructive features of the ideology. Don't put your trust in the Temple and its ceremonies, Jesus is saying. Don't believe what the religious establishment foists on you. Don't be bound by the ideological rigidity of the present order. Don't compromise with the enemies of the human spirit. The whole of the old order is about to change.

Finally, we should note as a strategy the teaching methodology which Jesus used to great effect. He employed parables, stories drawn from popular sources and in many cases referring to events which would be quite fresh in people's memories, as vehicles for both questioning the dominant ideology and reinforcing counter-values. Jesus explained his choice of this methodology by suggesting of the marginalized groups he was concerned about that 'they look without seeing and listen without hearing or understanding' (Matt. 13.13). In other words, these groups have not yet developed a critical awareness of what is happening around them. They see events without being able to interpret their implications, they hear what the powerful are telling them, unable to discern how they are being manipulated. The purpose of Jesus' teaching, on the other hand, is to help people unmask the reality of their situations. Through parables he teaches the art of critical awareness so that reality stands in the bright light of day to be seen for what it is, rather than as what the powerful wish to interpret it. When we look at the ministry of Jesus in its total context, we cannot but be struck by the emphasis he laid on educational strategies. We would have to admit that education was his primary strategy.

We cannot leave the issue of ideology without noting the principle which Jesus espoused for himself and demanded of his followers: that they witness to the power of the counter-ideology by living it out in the community. There can be no more powerful strategy than that of people who dare to be different. In the face of ideological deathliness, the liveliness of a counter culture or what is sometimes called an alternative life-style is enormously persuasive.

Strategies for building and maintaining an organization

In contrast to the biblical tradition of the prophet – a 'man alone' bringing the word of the Lord to his people – Jesus deliberately set about creating an organization. This organization or movement was integral to his overall strategy.

That the establishment of an organization was a matter of deliberate intent is indicated by the fact that Jesus began laying down its foundations before he had even developed a popular following. The calling of the first four disciples at the beginning of his ministry ensured that his work was given an embryonic framework. All the Gospels confirm that this structure was loosely in place before Jesus began attracting large crowds. It becomes a formal structure when, following an occasion on which Jesus has to ask the disciples to secure a boat for his escape as he is in danger of being crushed by the crowd (Mark 3.9), Jesus appoints the twelve to positions of responsibility.

The terms of the disciples' appointment are that they are to serve as Jesus' companions and they are to be sent out as front-line workers for the mission (Mark 3.13). The first function, in addition to providing a support group for Jesus, required the disciples to exercise skills of crowd control. These skills are best demonstrated in the case of the feeding of the five thousand (Luke 9.10–17), where Jesus specifically delegates the task of organizing the vast crowd to the disciples and they seat people in groups of fifty. At other times, the disciples act as bodyguards, keeping people at bay when Jesus is seeking solitude. That they occasionally overdid this is suggested by the account of Jesus taking his disciples to task for overly protecting him, when they had turned away people who had brought their children to be blessed by him (Mark 10.14).

The Gospels indicate that while the twelve disciples formed an inner circle of the organization, Jesus singled out three of these people: Peter, James, and John were his particular confidants. It was with them that he shared the experience of transfiguration which opened their eyes to the real nature of his life and mission (Matt. 17.1–8). Yet Jesus makes it clear that these special relationships of trust and confidence are not the establishment of precedence or hierarchy. For when the mother of James and John approaches him asking that he give her two sons pride of place in his Kingdom, Jesus quickly rejects the request as inappropriate (Matt. 20.20–28). He goes on to explain to the rest of the disciples who are angered by what has occurred that the request mirrors the worst of the secular world, where people like to exert authority and lord it over other people. Jesus rejects this model out of hand, and stresses the counter-value of serving others rather than ordering them about! The emphasis for him is not on a structured hierarchy but on a community of equals.

In terms of the front-line work that the disciples were expected to perform, the Gospels of Matthew and Luke elaborate on how it is to be carried out. The basic requirement is that the disciples travel light without haversack, food, money or even a change of clothes. They are not to establish any peramanent bases, but are to seek out temporary accommodation with a trustworthy person in each area they visit (Matt. 10.1–16; Luke 9.1–6). There is a double sense of urgency and mobility about their task. Whether this is due to the need to cover a wide area as quickly as possible, or whether it is an indication of the need to constantly remain one step ahead of the authorities, is hard to say. Furthermore, while travelling light may have been a simple precaution for escaping from the mob, it could also have been a strategy of identification with the poor. As one writer has pointed out, the work of preaching and healing is not diminished by a large wardrobe, but it is difficult for the person who has a change of clothes for each occasion to identify with the poor![3]

We find the disciples embarking upon their first front-line mission in verse six of the ninth chapter of St Luke's Gospel. By verse ten they have returned to offer Jesus their report, which must make it one of the shortest campaigns in history! And from this point on, the Twelve appear constantly in the company of Jesus. There are no more front-line missions until after his death when they take on the responsibility of extending the organization throughout the Gentile world. This may well mean that this initial mission was something of a training event in which the Twelve tested out the strategies that Jesus had recommended: travelling light, proclaiming the Kingdom, healing the sick and casting out demons. The Twelve reflect with Jesus on the success of the approach but subsequently devote their energies to the tasks of personal support for Jesus and managing the crowds.

Jesus then develops an alternative front-line strategy. He appoints thirty-six teams, each comprised of two people, and gives them the task of going ahead into the towns and rural areas which he is proposing to visit in order to prepare the ground for him (Luke 10.1–20). Working in pairs suggests that the Twelve had encountered difficulties in working on their own: personal loneliness, the hostility of the mob, and lack of confidence. Working in pairs would help overcome these problems. The teams are given the same instructions as the Twelve about travelling unencumbered and seeking temporary board. They return very enthusiastic about the success of the strategy. They've been able to fulfil the task, even to the extent of casting out demons, a skill which seems to have taken them by surprise. They have obviously tapped new resources while testing out the strategy.

The shape of the new organization is now becoming clearer. Jesus is its leader. There is a core group of three who have a very clear perception of the direction and purpose of the organization. The three are members of the Twelve whose responsibility it is to serve as a support group and to manage the on-the-spot arrangements of public events. And there are the thirty-six front line teams to undertake the preparatory work.

As Jesus' concept of a structure was the precise opposite of that which was a feature of the religious establishment, so was his policy of recruitment. Where the priesthood was open to a powerful hereditary class, and the scribes drawn predominantly from the middle strata of society, Jesus recruited from the lowest strata. He directed his message to those without power in the community, to those who were being victimized by the economic, political and ideological structures of the day, and these people gathered around him in vast numbers. He promised status to the marginalized, power to the powerless, freedom to the imprisoned. In his day-to-day life he publicly identified himself with these groups and took it upon himself to confront the rich and the powerful in the community on their behalf. It was natural, therefore, for him to plan in terms of building an organization of the oppressed, and to recruit from the ranks of workers, tax collectors and prostitutes.

The organization or movement was not some free-wheeling, happy-go-lucky social club. Membership required that people abandon all ambition, all family ties and, in the case of those who stood to inherit wealth, all claims to property, in favour of absolute loyalty. As Jesus put it: 'Anyone who prefers father or mother to me is not worthy of me. Anyone who prefers son or daughter to me is not worthy of me. Anyone who does not take his cross and follow in my footsteps is not worthy of me. Anyone who finds his life will lose it; anyone who loses his life for my sake will find it' (Matt. 10.37–39).

Commitment to the death is the bottom line of membership of this movement! Those who, like the rich young man are incapable of letting go, exclude themselves from the outset (Mark 10.17–22). Other disciples desert the movement in large numbers when the going gets tough (John 6.66). Only the totally committed survive, and that was the secret of the strength and the effectiveness of the movement. Its solidarity was such that even in its most vulnerable hour following the execution of Jesus, it proved impossible to crush and to the contrary, developed from a purely local struggle into an international one.

In addition to calling for total commitment to enhance the solidarity of the movement, Jesus prepared his followers for the hostility, intimidation and violence which they would encounter. His personal experience had alerted him to those realities. When he had stood up in his home synagogue to offer a commentary on the scriptural reading, the enraged audience hustled him to the edge of town where they made to throw him over the cliff, forcing Jesus to engineer a hasty escape (Luke 4.16–30). Had he not done so the mission would have ended there and then! So he is determined to warn his followers about the personal costs involved. He wishes to prepare them for every possible ordeal. 'I am sending you out like lambs among wolves,' he tells them, alerting them to the probability of being torn apart (Luke 10.3). He later becomes even more explicit about the strategies which their opponents will adopt: 'They will hand you over to sanhedrins and scourge you in their synagogues. You will be dragged before governors and kings . . . Brother will betray brother to death; children will rise against their parents and have them put to death . . . You will be hated by everyone on account of my name, but the one who stands firm to the end will be saved. If they persecute you in one town, take refuge in the next; and if they persecute you in that, take refuge in another' (Matt. 10.17–23).

Jesus never paints a rosy picture for the immediate future of the movement. On the contrary, he describes the worst possible scenario, and by doing so fosters the disciples' resolve to resist.

In addition to his public education programme, Jesus paid great attention to education within the organization. We have already commented on the manner in which Jesus employed parables in order to encourage an elementary analysis amongst the crowds. In St Mark's Gospel we read that while Jesus spoke to the crowds in parables 'so far as they were capable of understanding', he 'explained everything to his disciples when they were alone' (Mark 4.33f.). Similarly we read in St Luke of Jesus explaining the deeper meaning of a parable to the disciples (8.1–15) again in private, and alerting them to the special position they are in by virtue of being able to discern what others are unable to see (10.23f.). This programme of deepening awareness and analysis within the group itself both increased trust and built a common thrust.

In creating his community of equals, while individuals may have been given particular responsibilities with Judas, for example, acting as treasurer, Jesus took care to ensure that nobody was delegated to undertake menial tasks while others were left to get on with 'the real work'. All shared in the essential tasks of proclaiming and healing. There was not a single power that Jesus possessed which he refrained from sharing with members of the organization. A re-organization along the lines of particular and specialist functions within ministry, some preaching, others teaching, others healing, and some interpreting was, along with the establishment of a special group – the deacons – to attend to housekeeping duties, a development which was promoted within the Gentile church. There was no room for such distinctions in the thought of Jesus. He had created a genuinely participative organization.

There are three general comments to be made about the organization which Jesus set up as a framework for his mission.

The first is that even to speak of it as an organization can be misleading, if by that term people think of it as a structure similar to some of our contemporary and specifically political organizations. Jesus was not establishing a counter-political apparatus which would inherit power in the vacuum created by the collapse of the present order. Rather he established a critical movement or counter-culture, grounded amongst the marginalized of the community, which publicly voiced its critique of the dominant structures and urged people to explore a particular alternative. Those who wish to interpret Jesus' role as that of a political organizer are therefore on very flimsy ground. If we are to identify a political component to Jesus' work it is that of being a political educator, opening people's eyes to the nature of the powers and processes at work in society, and offering them an alternative vision to work towards. His organization was very much a movement within society, rather than a political party.

Secondly, there is obscurity surrounding the role of women within the new movement. The conservative view is that Jesus chose to work only with men as the most appropriate strategy, the liberal view that he chose to work with men because only that approach was culturally acceptable and the mission was more important than the question of the gender of those who promoted it. But in view of the fact that Jesus offered such radical challenges to the dominant ideology in almost every other aspect of its dominance, and promoted alternative cultural values, these explanations are totally inadequate. Modern scholarship, acknowledging that the scriptures were written by males from within the patriarchal perspective of the Gentile church which significantly modified the ground rules which Jesus established, argues that the role of women was deliberately misrepresented. The establishment of feminist critical methodologies and historical reconstructions alerts us to the essentially inclusive emphasis Jesus laid on the nature of the Kingdom. In contrast to the alienating institutions of the day, the Kingdom was open to all who were on the margins of society, which naturally included women. The fact that women are mentioned at all within the new movement hints at the importance of the role they played. Indeed, when its male members all fled Jerusalem after Jesus' execution, it was the women who stayed on and saved it from extinction![4] Suffice it to say that the radical way, given the cultural norms of his society, in which Jesus related to women, is the best indicator of the value he placed upon them in the Kingdom.

Thirdly, we have stressed that the movement which Jesus established in Palestine was quite different in character from the structure which developed into the Gentile church after his death. The internationalization of the movement fundamentally altered its character. Where the liberating message of Jesus had been addressed to the poor and the marginalized in the community, the international organization addressed it to sinners in general, which gave it more general appeal. And while Jesus' movement could accurately be described as encompassing the rejects of society, the international movement quickly took root amongst the middle classes of the Roman empire and worked out its compromises with the new dominant ideology. That ideology successfully married the institutional church to the governmental structures of Rome, and facilitated the 'spiritualizing' of the hard sayings of Jesus so that the wealth and power of the elites would not be too threatened. The organization we today call 'church' as a consequence bears little resemblance to the Jesus Movement, and indeed, in its dogmatism and hierarchical patterns, runs directly counter to it. We earlier discussed the manner in which the contemporary church accommodates itself to the Western world's dominant ideology, and we suggested that although this has occurred, there are ways of recovering the essence of Jesus' message and methodology. This book is just one signpost in that direction.

Direct action strategies

The majority of Christians do not take easily to the suggestion that Jesus was concerned with issues of power in the community. They prefer to think of him as a person who avoided questions of power in order to concentrate only upon an interior reconstruction of the human personality. We have attempted to show that Christians who think like this have been socialized into their views by the dominant ideology. In this section we turn our attention to the issue of power and to the strategies Jesus employed against the power centres and the power wielders.

There was no confusion in Jesus' mind as to who the real enemies were. Whereas some of the resistance groups operating within Palestine at that time – the Zealots for example – saw the Roman occupying power as the enemy to be defeated, Jesus had concluded that the real enemy was internal and not external to the nation. Where the Zealots were essentially a nationalistic and reformist group with the aim of replacing a Roman administration with a distinctively Jewish one, the option Jesus offered called for the liberation of all marginalized and oppressed people. That meant removing rather than reforming the oppressive structures. The Kingdom he kept alluding to, with its emphasis on co-operation and community, was the only radical option to the existing divisive and authoritarian model.

So, as we have already seen, Jesus nominated as enemy those who controlled the dominant ideology. He was explicit in his personal identification of them. By far the great majority of priests and scribes belonged to the Pharisaic party which promoted the strict observance of the Law's prescriptions about food, clothing, almsgiving, prayer, ritual washing and Sabbath. In the first three Gospels, we discover Jesus frequently declaring the Pharisees to be the obstacles to a genuinely free humanity.

St Luke records the details of an occasion on which Jesus was having dinner at the home of a Pharisee (11.37–54). The host must have remarked on Jesus' failure to wash before eating and Jesus, ignoring the cultural conventions about not insulting one's host, subjects the man to a blistering attack. He says the Pharisees are fools and like unmarked graves which people walk over without knowing it! A scribe in the party takes exception to Jesus' remarks, pointing out that they insult lawyers as well. So Jesus turns his attack on the scribe. 'Alas for you lawyers also,' he says, 'because you load people with unendurable burdens, and do not lift a finger to move them. . . Alas for you lawyers who have taken away the key of knowledge.'

This passage in Luke directly parallels the much more detailed indictment of the scribes and Pharisees in Matthew 23. There Jesus uses the strongest possible condemnatory language against them, referring to them as hypocrites, blind guides, fools, and a brood of vipers. It is their hypocrisy which really offends him, because they are hiding behind masks of authority and respectability in order to mislead people. He says they are 'like whitewashed tombs which look handsome on the outside, but inside are full of dead bones and every kind of corruption' (23.27).

Having identified the enemy, Jesus never underestimates the power which they exercise within the ideological and the political apparatus of the state. They control both the tools of persuasion, and those of coercion. So what tactics can people employ against such naked and manipulative power? What kind of resistance can people offer, other than combating power with power in armed resistance? It is at this point that Jesus suggests a strategy which marks a quite radical break with the norms of his society, not to speak of ours! Jesus says: 'You have learnt "eye for eye and tooth for tooth". But I say, offer the wicked no resistance. On the contrary, if anyone hits you on the right cheek, offer him the other as well. If anyone takes you to court in order to gain your tunic, let him have your cloak as well. And if anyone orders you to go one mile, go two miles with him' (Matt. 5.38–41).

Jesus rejects the strategy of meeting violence with violence. But what exactly is he offering us in its place? Many Christians have come to interpret this passage as indicating that the appropriate Christian response to evil, corruption and brutal assault is an attitude of submission and acceptance. They take it to mean that Christians should accept whatever is handed out to them, no matter what the provocation. They conveniently ignore the fact that while Jesus may give the appearance of submissiveness at the time of his legal arraignments, he remained the person with real power in that situation. Furthermore he displayed no submissiveness when he confronted the religious authorities of his day. So obviously Jesus means something other than meek submission. To understand what he was getting at we need to employ the scriptural methodology we have constructed and place the sayings within their precise cultural contexts.

'If anyone hits you on the right cheek, offer him the other as well.' Hitting someone in the face, particularly in front of witnesses, was in those times, just as it is today, a humiliation and loss of dignity for the victim in Middle-East society. It demands retaliation. Readers may well be familiar with the character of inter-family feuding in the culture, with successive acts of retaliation becoming ever more violent until they result in serious injury, and often in death. Honour, dignity and justice demand that a positive response be made to even the smallest insult. Yet we here find Jesus calling for precisely the opposite response to that sanctioned by the tradition. He says, 'Don't retaliate. Don't behave in the way your enemy expects you to behave. Do what your attacker least expects: behave in the opposite way.' In these circumstances, the cycle of violence is unexpectedly interrupted. The enemy, formerly in the position of knowing precisely what to expect by way of retaliation, is now confused. He is suddenly at an immense disadvantage and no longer in control of the process he initiated. He is, in a very real sense, disarmed!

Similarly Jesus suggests that if somebody takes you to court in order to gain your tunic, you should hand over your cloak as well. The tunic was the long inner garment, which provided basic covering for the body. The cloak is a heavier and more expensive garment worn over the tunic as a protection against the extremes of the weather, as well as serving as a covering during the night. Nakedness is offensive in traditional Eastern communities, as I quickly discovered on the occasion when I appeared dressed in my New Zealand summer shorts. Even bared legs constituted an offence! So if through a lawsuit an enemy claims a person's inner garment, and the victim responds by handing over in addition his only other covering, his public nakedness would be utterly offensive. In such instances, the community's anger is far more likely to be directed against the enemy who brought about this state of affairs than against the victim. The enemy would be made an object of the community's censure. And the victim would reap the sympathy. Once again, the anticipated result has been reversed.

Jesus poses a third example. 'If anyone orders you to go one mile, travel two miles with him.' The context of this saying has become obscured in translation, but it refers to a system developed during the Persian empire through which subjects could be impressed into service in order to carry important mail and messages throughout its borders. The precedent once established, it had later been extended as a method for forcing people into collaboration with governmental and military authorities. The example Jesus offers therefore has an explicitly political dimension. At a time when many Jews were advocating open defiance of Roman rule and authority, and collaborators often worked with the oppressor at the risk of their lives, Jesus implies that people should not only do what the military authorities demand of them, but twice as much. This strategy, however, far from being a recommendation that people co-operate with the authorities, is a way of subverting authority. When, in the face of excessive demands, people insist on doing twice as much as required, the balance of power begins to alter. Rather than the authority dictating the terms to which the victim must submit, the victim is claiming the power to determine for himself the lengths to which he is prepared to go.

This passage provides the key to Jesus' direct action strategies. He has identified the strategies which the enemy is most likely to employ against members of the Jesus Movement: physical intimidation, manipulation of the legal system, and military co-option. Jesus was not simply plucking these examples out of the air. He was naming the tactics which the powerful were already employing to good effect against the poor and the marginalized. And each of them involves a form of violence, a violation of the individual.

The strategy which Jesus designs in response is a genuinely radical one. It is sometimes referred to as the Surrender Tactic. It dictates that whenever a group or an individual is confronted by overwhelming power, the deliberate choice to offer no resistance on the one hand, and to insist on doing more than is being demanded on the other, incapacitates the enemy and gives the victim control of the situation.

We cannot claim that Jesus invented this tactic, because there are examples of other groups having previously used it as a spontaneous gesture.[5] But the contribution of Jesus is to codify it and to recommend its intentional use to his followers. It is a tactic which naturalists like Konrad Lorenz have identified as a survival tool amongst certain groups in the animal kingdom. Particularly when animals are operating within a hierarchical structure, with young males challenging dominant males for positions of power, the tactic comes into its own. The animal on the verge of defeat will suddenly adopt a defenceless posture and even bare its throat to its opponent. For as long as the posture is maintained, the stronger animal is unable to kill. Lorenz comments:

> I have extracted from (this behaviour) a new and deeper understanding of a wonderful and often misunderstood saying from the Gospel which hitherto had only awakened in me the feelings of strong opposition. 'And unto him that smiteth thee on the one cheek offer also the other.' A wolf has enlightened me: not so your enemy may strike you again do you turn the other cheek toward him, but to make him unable to do it.[6]

Thus Jesus delivers to his followers a strategy which does not only ensure their survival against impossible odds, but which commands power. The question is, of course, the degree to which Jesus and his followers successfully employed it. In Jesus' case we can certainly see him pursuing the tactic of non-resistance through the drama of his arrest, trials and crucifixion, and reprimanding those amongst his followers, like Peter, who abandon the tactic to physically retaliate against the Temple police. Likewise we can interpret the personal and community empowerment created through Jesus' death and resurrection as a complete vindication of the tactic. The pity of it was that, as Tolstoy points out, the newly-empowered church quickly flexed its muscles and abandoned the tactic, eventually producing the theology of the Just War as a way of condoning all manner of violence against people and property. The irony of it all is that today we find the institutional church employing in its day-to-day activities not the strategy that Jesus affirmed, but those used by his enemies: intimidation, the use of the judicial system to maintain and reinforce its power, and the blessing of military establishments!

In choosing the surrender tactic, Jesus was not avoiding the issue of conflict. It is salutary to remember that the major exponents of this tactic, Jesus, Gandhi and Martin Luther King, all died violent deaths. It might even be argued by some that turning the other cheek, handing over one's cloak and insisting on the second mile, may be regarded as provocations which themselves engender violence. It can certainly be argued that they expose the violence of particular structures. We have already seen how Jesus skilfully employs a conflict model against the ideological agents, the scribes. So it cannot be argued that Jesus either in his own action or in his teaching, eschewed conflict. He revelled in it! What he did reject were forms of institutional violence which coerce people into conforming to the wishes of the powerful.

I believe we also have to see Jesus' attitude towards the Law as a direct action conflict strategy. The principle which he articulated in his teaching was that laws – like those of the Sabbath – should serve human interests. It is perverse for people to be enslaved to the Law (Mark 2.27). It is one thing to make this kind of declaration, another to demonstrate it in action. Jesus would have been only too well aware of the anger he would generate if he deliberately contravened the Law. Yet he persisted with flagrant breaches like healing on the Sabbath. He could not have been taken by surprise by the vehemence of his enemies' response. He was neither naive about their tactics, nor the lengths to which they would pursue them. He had continually warned members of the Movement about the likelihood of death in the cause. He could hardly have been sentimental about the possibility of his own death. It is almost certain then, that Jesus deliberately broke the Law as a conflict engendering tactic.

The same would have to be said about his decision to manipulate the messianic symbolism and ride into Jerusalem to the popular acclaim of the crowd. By so doing, he was setting up a situation in which there could be no compromise. There can be no king but Caesar, yet here is a Jew being proclaimed king! His trials subsequently hinge on the charge that he was setting himself up, or being set up as a king, and the description 'King of the Jews' is nailed to his gallows. The entry into Jerusalem at the head of a mob is not a polite request to enter into meaningful negotiations with the authorities! It is a direct challenge to the authorities to shape up or shut up. Jesus delivers them enough hard evidence for them to arrest him. Yet throughout the events, we get the impression of Jesus always being in command of the situation, and of the authorities being continually forced to adapt to the plan that Jesus has declared to his followers in advance (Luke 18.31–34).

Even more dramatic however, is the direct action Jesus takes against the Temple after he has entered the city. We saw previously that one of Jesus' ideological strategies was to proclaim the collapse of the present world order with the collapse of the Temple. While the Gospel accounts of his attack on the Temple (particularly that in John 2.13–22) allude to the ideological implications of Jesus rebuilding the Temple in three days, there are even more important issues at stake. When he enters the Temple, Jesus avoids taking symbolic action against either the altar or the Holy of Holies. He begins to systematically sack the offices of the moneychangers.

A conservative reading of scripture at this point, while admitting the violence of Jesus' action, explains it in terms of his 'righteous anger' over the sullying of a religious shrine with commercial activities: the dealings in foreign exchange and the sale of animals for sacrifice. But we need to press the analysis further in terms of the way in which the Temple functioned as the political and economic apparatus of the state.[7]

In Jesus' day, not even the most religious of Jews could have claimed that the Temple was the focus of exclusively religious activities. The religio-ideological, political and economic aspects of the state had become so enmeshed that it was extremely difficult to tell where one ended and another began! The Sanhedrin, for example, the Council of seventy-one chief priests, elders and scribes, which met in the Temple under the chairmanship of the current High Priest, had become the final arbiter in all criminal, political and religious matters. And its power extended not just through Judaea and the Galilee, but to the Jews of the Diaspora.

Some of the chief priests had specially delegated functions within this apparatus. One was made Commander of the Temple and exercised the role of chief of the police. It was his staff who finally arrested Jesus. Then there were seven Temple Supervisors, overseeing various aspects of its life. Finally, one of the chief priests acted as Treasurer, overseeing the three Temple treasuries, revenues, stores and wealth.

The Temple treasury was to all intents and purposes the state treasury. It had become the centre of all economic activity with local taxes, the revenues from the great estates and the contributions from Jews overseas all flowing into its coffers. It can be argued that it fulfilled all the functions of the State Treasury, the Stock Exchange and the National Bank.[8]

To the Jew in the street then, the Temple represented an immense concentration of power. All that was repressive and debilitating in terms of crippling taxation, the domination of the aristocratic families, the domesticating ideology, and police brutality could be located in one form or another there. If one were asked to choose a single symbol to describe all that was destructive of human freedom and dignity, it would have to be the Temple.

And that is precisely what Jesus perceived. His 'cleansing of the Temple' was direct action against the seat of oppression. His violent disruption of the Temple's activities struck far deeper than an argument for the separation of commercial and religious activities. If he was, in fact, making that point, the institutional church seems to consider that it was not intended to be taken too seriously! No, in the Temple Jesus is making a clear stand. Inflicting damage upon property but not against persons, he embodies the frustrations and the aspirations of all the world's oppressed. His actions signal his intentions clearly to both the popular crowd awaiting the moment of liberation, and the Temple authorities seeking to prevent it. There can be no turning back now from this symbolic action, carefully conceived and brilliantly staged. The Gospels record that while the authorities redouble their efforts to eliminate Jesus, they are now afraid of him, because he has captured the imagination of the people (Mark 11.18). The Movement is gathering force, the final showdown with the authorities has been set up, the downtrodden will soon be free.

We have now identified all the major elements of Jesus' strategy. Let us summarize them:

Jesus developed a clear analysis of the dynamics of oppression. He identified those in command of the process, and their strategies, and publicly confronted them.

He established a closely-knit organization, a community of equals, in which responsibility for overall mission was shared even though some exercised specific functions. The life-style of the organization itself demonstrated the alternative Jesus was offering people.

Jesus made use of a particular educational technique, that of parable-posing, to help people develop an awareness of the political, economic and ideological realities of their situation.

He perceived that the most important area to address was that of the dominant ideology. He subverted the power of the ideological agents, and manipulated the most important symbols of the dominant ideology both to highlight its contradictions and to strengthen the counter-ideology of the Kingdom.

He urged people to reject the authority of the ideological and political establishments on the grounds that each person was his or her own authority under God. He did not hesitate to breach the Law, particularly when it was seen to be preventing human wholeness and dignity.

He formulated the surrender tactic as a way of immobilizing opponents, effecting subtle shifts of power in situations of conflict, and maintaining control over the course of events.

When the moment was right, he marched on Jerusalem at the head of a political demonstration, and took direct action against the Treasury.

Obviously we need to ask how effective were these strategies as a whole? Those who have come to regard the historical significance of Jesus purely in terms of political strategy may well claim that he miscalculated his power base and the strength of the opposition, and was executed by the state. They might argue that while Jesus' strategies are superb in their formulation, and have inspired almost all the world's subsequent political radicals, they need to be employed with considerably more caution than Jesus used.

Christians, however, regard Jesus' death on the cross not as defeat, but as his ultimate victory over the powers he confronted. At the moment of death the curtain of the Holy of Holies was torn apart, and the secret centre of the old order lay exposed to common gaze. It can at last be recognized for the sham that it is. Nor does Jesus' death halt the Movement. In total disarray in the days preceding his death, in tatters following his death, it comes to power and its members travel to the four corners of the known world to proclaim the possibility of liberation for all humankind.

In the end, even those who will have no truck with the divinity of Jesus are left to marvel at the way in which he singlehandedly created an organization of oppressed people which persists, albeit in a form he would not recognize, to this day. That Movement became so powerful that it overtook the Roman empire itself, and held unchallenged authority over vast areas of the world for more than sixteen hundred years. It is only within this century, and within the lifetimes of many of us, that it has been divested of its power through numerous revolutions and liberation struggles. And wherever those struggles have succeeded, their leaders have generally adapted in one form or another Jesus' strategies. That's how effective they are!

CHAPTER SEVEN

The Wisdom of Serpents
The Practice of Counter-Culture

Jesus embodies a model of counter-cultural practice. At one and
the same time he offers a radical critique of the dominant
consciousness and a dynamic alternative to it. Let us examine
some of the steps we can take in our situations today to develop and
practise counter-culture.

We have made frequent reference to the importance of the
eighth-century prophets. Their understanding of the root causes
of problems within their societies, their vision of a personality,
community and nation with a renewed heart, and their passion for
social justice have moved people down the ages. They still have a
very contemporary ring to them and are a source of inspiration and
energy for today's Christian activists. In deciding how we as
Christians should build a counter-culture, the fundamental approach of the prophets both illuminates the practice of Jesus and
has some profound lessons for us. It is possible to identify the process by looking at the witness of any of the prophets. Hosea is a
particularly good example.

Four elements in prophetic witness

Like all of us, Hosea interpreted his world on the basis of his
history, his personal experiences and the values he had espoused.
It could even be argued that these determine the way in which he
approaches society. They provide the foundation for the analysis
he makes, for the vision he is possessed by, and for the strategies he
recommends for the wellbeing of the nation.

Hosea is a rural man who is most at home with the things of the
natural world and the cycles of nature. He comes to the city as a

person unused to its ways and horrified by the ruthless competition, the affluence and the corruption he encounters there. The contrast between city and rural life is very stark, and in trying to describe what he sees, he often falls back on the rural imagery with which he is familiar. He addresses urban questions from an essentially rural perspective.

Furthermore, the prophet has suffered a devastating personal experience, so painful that it colours all his thinking and becomes the dominant image he employs. His wife had been unfaithful to him, had turned to temple prostitution, and seems to have ended up in slavery. Faithlessness, prostitution and slavery in consequence become themes through which he explains the history of the nation of Israel. Perhaps contemporary psychoanalysts would conclude that Hosea was suffering from a very deep obsession. If that were to be proved the case, it would seem that Hosea had discovered a useful therapy: redirecting obsession and grief as a motivation for personal and community renewal.

The fact that his marriage was ruined by the claims of a corrupt cult casts Hosea as himself a victim. His perspective is that of one who personally suffers the effects that victims of other structures in society also suffer. He locates himself firmly on the side of victims of all kinds against the powerful of his day.

The values he feels to be most important for humanity are those embodied in the Covenant relationship. Supreme amongst these is the value of faithfulness, demanded by God of his people, but singularly missing from his wife's relationship with him! But he holds other Covenant values equally dear including that of justice manifested in the principle of jubilee and in caring for the vulnerable in the community. These values align him politically with the Covenanters rather than the Monarchists; with the Samuel party as opposed to the Saul party.[1] This alignment has two effects: it persuades him that the point at which things began to go wrong for the nation was when, contrary to God's will, monarchy was adopted as the system of government. And it leads to the conclusion that the nation can only flourish when there is a return to the Covenant relationship and to the values and behaviours demanded by it.

On the basis of this history and experience and these values, Hosea makes judgments about the nation's life. In his lifetime the prosperity which had been such a feature of Jeroboam's reign had eroded. There was little common purpose remaining within society which was being torn apart by internal squabbles. The political scene was just as chaotic with different groups vying for power and foreign alliances creating additional strains. To all intents and purposes the nation was on the verge of collapse. Hosea described what he saw in the following terms.

Corruption had permeated all aspects of life, leading to the complete collapse of law and order. Hosea complains of there being no tenderness, fidelity or knowledge of God in the country, 'only perjury and lies, slaughter, theft, adultery and violence; murder upon murder'. The effects of this disorder even spill over into the environment where the countryside itself is 'in mourning' with wild animals, birds and fish all perishing (Hos. 4.2f.).

A major cause of the nation's loss of heart is that religion has become debased. Priests are no longer speaking the truth and have given up teaching people about God's demands. The suggestion is that they too, have fallen victim to the dominant corrupting consciousness. Hosea describes the clergy as 'greedy for iniquity', a reference to the fact that because priests got a considerable personal share of offerings made for sin, it was to their economic advantage to encourage sin rather than dissuade people from it. There has been a large-scale desertion of true religion to the Baal cult in which drunkenness, debauchery and sexual licence were rife under the guise of religion. Hosea of course, had personal knowledge of the effects of this pseudo-religion, for the cult had claimed his wife's affections and ruined his marriage. He describes the situation as 'everyone wandering off with whores and offering sacrifice with sacred prostitutes' (4.4–14).

The political situation is just as confused with what amounts to a civil war raging (Hos. 5.10f.). The failure of the monarchy to dispense justice has been the major contributor to this. Plots and counter-plots abound as different factions 'addle the king and leaders with wine fumes as he mixes with these scoundrels' (Hos. 7.3–7). The population is having to make frantic adjustments as first one side, then another, gains power. All this, along with the air of conspiracy which flourishes in such circumstances, made for extreme political instability.

The scene was even more disquieting when Hosea examined international politics. King Manahem had foolishly entered into an alliance with Tiglath-pileser III of Assyria which had committed him to the payment of massive sums by way of tribute. The King was only able to meet these debts by imposing a penalizing land tax upon the population. The prophet regards the King's attempts to find a way out of the nation's difficulties by establishing alliances with Assyria and Egypt as folly in the extreme. He likens the nation to a half-baked cake and to a silly, witless dove (Hos. 5.13f.; 7.8–12).

Hosea goes on to examine what is happening within the economy. In addition to the crippling tax burden which has been imposed, the government has embarked upon extravagant building projects including royal palaces and a whole string of fortified towns (8.14). To add to these economic burdens, the use of fraudulent weights and measures in the market place means that consumers are being ripped off, while the merchants are able to congratulate themselves on how wealthy they have become (12.7–9).

So in building his analysis, Hosea documents what he sees happening in the fabric of society at large; in the local and international political arenas, in the economy and in the religio-cultural area. He then makes a judgment about the facts he has identified. The crisis in the nation is due to the fact that people have forsaken their own culture, religion and values for foreign culture, religion and alliances. Economic and political corruption have proliferated as a consequence. The 'punishments' of exile and slavery are not to be regarded as accidental or capricious, but flow directly from the course the nation has deliberately chosen.

The third element in Hosea's prophetic witness is that he possesses, or perhaps in his case it is better to say that he is possessed by, a clear vision of what society ought to be like. Indeed, it his vision of what ought to be which very often fuels his analysis of what is wrong with the existing situation! The Covenant relationship embodies his vision, but he prefers to describe it in terms of the countryside he loves. The entire earth will be renewed with Israel blooming like a lily and thrusting out roots like a poplar; possessing the beauty of olives and the fragrance of Lebanon; a land in which cornfields and vineyards flourish once more (14.6–8).

Finally, Hosea suggests some practical steps or strategies which will have to be implemented if the nation is to progress from crisis to recovery. There must be a basic change of heart, of perception.

The nation must 'provide itself with words' – with the appropriate vehicles to facilitate a return to Jahweh God and to the values of his Covenant. Reliance on the great powers must be ended. People must be convinced that security and salvation will not spring from either Egypt or Assyria. The present economic system will have to be dethroned so that the people no longer worship materialism: no longer 'say "our God" to what our hands have made'. And justice must flow to the outsider and the vulnerable: orphans must once more find compassion in Jahweh God (14.1–4).

In our own age, as the power of the state becomes more centralized and ever more people experience the burden of its oppression, the call goes out for the church to exercise a prophetic ministry. Some people demean prophetic ministry by wanting to reduce it to the offering of predictions about the end of the world, the return of Christ and the last judgment. Others speak vaguely about an ability to discern the signs of the times. For a prophet like Hosea, however, it was much more a case of being able to explain why they were so angry, what they saw going on, where they wanted to go and how they intended getting there. It is these four interlocking strands of prophecy which provide a good model for us.

Understanding where we have come from

Our personal history informs our social action. My commitment to working for justice did not develop in a vacuum. My forbears emigrated from nineteenth-century conditions of abject poverty in Britain to the promise of a new life in the colonies. They travelled halfway around the globe to an unknown land, uncertain of the future but convinced that it had to be better than the one they were leaving behind. In New Zealand they became soldiers, traders and pioneer farmers, playing their part in the creation of what would become known as one of the great social laboratories of the world. They tried to build a more just and egalitarian society than the one they had left behind. They introduced universal, free and secular education; they invented the welfare state, and were the first nation to give women the vote. I was raised on stories of my grandparents' struggles both to survive in hostile and isolated environments and to participate in building a bright future for succeeding generations.

Their struggles are inevitably part of my history. Whereas they for the most part arrived in the country as working-class people, I, two generations later, was born into the middle class. Whereas they always regretted their lack of educational opportunities, I was offered education to an advanced level, paid for by the state, as a matter of course. Not all my legacies were positive ones. One of my great-grandfathers came to the country as a member of the imperial army sent to quell what I was taught in school to be the 'Maori wars' but which should more accurately be described as the 'European wars'. For his efforts he was rewarded with a plot of land, part of a tract confiscated from the Maoris. One of his sons was to become a pioneer educator, responsible for extending the education system into some of the more remote Maori areas. Although he was hailed as a good man in his day, and idolized by his family, there are those who would regard my grandfather as nothing more than a lackey of British imperialism who, by advocating European language, customs and values, helped destroy the indigenous culture.

So my history is one of ambiguity. Being in touch with one's history and culture can be a powerful motivation to action. My own cultural history, a history of oppression in Europe, became part of the settler culture imposed on the young colony. The history of having suffered oppression enables me to identify with the struggles of the indigenous culture to reassert itself in New Zealand; yet as a middle-class European, I am seen by many as an agent of the dominant culture. This is but one of the contradictions I have to reckon with.

I also inherited an interesting mix of religious attitudes from my forbears. Some were Anglicans of an evangelical and somewhat puritanical bent; some became Methodists when their vicar unwisely permitted dancing in the church hall! Some emigrated as members of the Free Church of Scotland. This, despite its rigidity in belief and practice, is something of a libertarian tradition, being adamantly opposed to state religion, or to the interference of government in religious matters. My grandfather, who was raised in this tradition, profoundly influenced my life with a mixture of Calvinist austerity and exotic mythological tales from the Western Isles. Politically, he identified with progressive elements in the colony's governments, rather than with the new landowners, old lairds. Tales of struggles back home in Scotland, in the Highlands in his case, and in the Borders in the case of the other side of my family, are in my blood.

So the answer to the question 'What makes you tick?' is that I experience anger over social injustice and wish to contribute as much as I can in my lifetime towards building a world free of oppression. Some of my motivation obviously comes from particular instances of injustice in my own experience: when institutions, bureaucracies and state agencies have acted without sensitivity. But at a far deeper level, I inherit cultural and family traditions in which suffering exploitation and oppression were commonplace. On the other side of the coin, it behoves me to remember that my history also demonstrates how people seeking to escape exploitation in one context may become instruments of injustice in another.

There are many exercises and techniques which can help people tell their stories and clarify their values. One simple framework I often use in training programmes is to ask each member of a small group to spend up to an hour recounting their journey to other members of the group. They begin with their family's story; then go on to talk about their own upbringing and education; then about the work, the roles or the profession they have engaged in. Three further elements can be added: the involvements and commitments people have beyond home and work; the sources of information which they regard as reliable; and the vision for society which they embrace. In the telling of stories within this framework a number of things become clear: the values people espouse, the things which motivate them, the contradictions in their lives, and the classes to which they belong or wish to be identified with.

While it is vital for us to clarify the values we hold, to know where they have come from and how they shape the way we interpret social reality, we also have to avoid the temptation to impose our values on other people. This is an unhappy tendency amongst some Christians who feel so certain of their position that they must win the world over to a predetermined set of values. The process of social change may then become simply an exercise in modifying social reality so that it accords with our values. But such values should not be the starting point; rather we need to begin with our engagement in an unjust social reality, to which we then bring our values to bear in a dialectic in which both social reality and our values are challenged and transformed.

Our spirituality is obviously an important factor in understanding who we are. Spirituality in its widest sense is that which nourishes and sustains us in our struggle to be divinely human. For Christians the model of divine humanity is Jesus. Our spirituality also has to be grounded in social reality, not something external to us, or separated from our life and activity in the world, even though some traditional approaches to spirituality would suggest otherwise. It is whatever turns us on, and certainly embraces our sensuality and our sexuality. Indeed, in workshops on spirituality which I have facilitated, sexuality and patriarchy are often identified as crucial elements. Most Christian activists have had to struggle to affirm the former and to overcome the latter in order to establish an authentic spirituality for themselves.

Much of what is promoted as traditional spirituality is both domesticating and disempowering. Bishop John Robinson pointed out that we latter day Christians have inherited forms of spirituality which evolved amongst professionally religious people who were committed to celibacy, poverty and obedience and the monastic life. This spirituality was subsequently held out to lay people as an ideal which was always impossible for them to emulate. Robinson angered some people, but liberated many when he declared that he had never felt himself to be on that particular merry-go-round. Those of us who live beyond the cloister, and who fail to achieve the high goals established by monastic religion, are made to feel failures: second-class citizens of the Kingdom. Failure and guilt are both debilitating and dampen enthusiasm for action. Furthermore, encouraging Christians to embark upon a wild goose chase for an elusive and frankly unattainable spirituality is a ploy which the dominant ideology exploits to good effect. There's not much energy left to tackle anything else! Similarly, the search to establish the equivalents of monastic virginity and celibacy in a lay context ensures that spirituality becomes a way of denying rather than affirming that which is authentically human.

Authentic spirituality will always nourish us, never impoverish us. Grounded in life, it springs from all those moments of wonder, exhilaration, longing, tenderness and sensuality which meet us. It appreciates moments of anguish, ambiguity and alienation not as negative and destructive, but as growing points of the spirit. It takes some of the strongest feelings we experience: anger, distrust, betrayal, and fashions them into motivations for changing our world. Nor is it in the nature of a distant goal we are striving towards; it is as immediate as the sustenance we receive from friends and lovers. It cannot remain something academic which we discern in the writings of the great mystics, although we are able to make the connections and to say of them 'I know what you're talking about.' It is not something we seek to identify within the pages of scripture and then impose upon our lives; yet it is always illuminated by the way that scripture sets our lives in the contexts of Jesus' actions and words.

Our spirituality and our personal history are also deeply related. One revealing exercise is to produce a time-line of our lives on a sheet of paper, noting at the appropriate dates along it the major influences on our lives. These will include people who have increased our understanding, books we have read, music we have heard, plays and films we have seen, movements we have joined, particular events which have challenged and changed us. Looking at a list of this kind we can see not just the story of our own development, but something of the power and the persistence of liberating ideas. It can sustain us to know that we are never working on our own as activists, but are part of a movement for justice and liberation which continues to shape our world.

There will be moments of dispiritedness aplenty, days of outright despair. There will be occasions when we question whether the time hasn't come to give up on the action and to take a comfortable job in the city! Yet these, too, become energizing moments, as we see them linking us in a real sense to the suffering of the outsider; or as Hosea and Jesus did, as embodying in oneself the powerlessness and despair of those on the margins of life.

Analysing what we see

The task of interpreting social reality for the most part has been left to experts; that army of sociologists, political scientists, demographers, planners, historians, educators and economists who earn their living from it. Explanations are professional and scientific and as a result, mystified. In many instances the process is turned into yet another tool through which the dominant class maintains its control. The myth of scientific objectivity plays an important role in this, persuading people that the fields of economics, planning, education and politics are better left to those experts who understand their complexity and the scientific principles which govern them. The idea that economics and politics may be common sense is resisted.

It is of great advantage to the dominant class if scientific knowledge can be broken up and repackaged in a manner so that it is of the least possible use to people who wish to employ it as a basis for challenging the *status quo*. The more confusion that can be created in this domain, the better the chances of ensuring that social and political action are abortive. Consider the following examples. If we were wanting to develop a class analysis of British society, it would be useful to know within each industry the proportion of people who are owners, or earn their living in management, or as workers. For two years I tried to get such a breakdown of statistics from the Department of Employment without success. All they could provide me with were the official employment figures which lump all employees within an industry together. Again, when working in New Zealand I discovered that government statistics on unemployment were not provided on the basis of racial groups, whereas the figures on crime were. Why the difference? One explanation is that it is to the disadvantage of the dominant class to reveal the fact that an excessively high proportion of the unemployed are from racial minorities, but to its advantage to suggest that the majority of criminals are!

The effect of this kind of mystification is to conceal the precise nature of the links which exist between various systems in our society, as well as the logic which binds them together. Systems can then be treated as if they were totally independent of one another. When we looked earlier at the way in which the dominant ideology functions, we saw how important it was for its existence to maintain this degree of separation. On the other hand, it is vital that those wishing to promote change should fashion tools with which this logic and these links can be exposed.

Science itself is now assisting in this task by breaking down the old hegemony. One of the side effects of quantum mechanics has been to demonstrate that the results of a scientific experiment, far from being the product of an immutable scientific principle, may in fact be determined by the person carrying out the experiment. The human agent is no longer a detached observer of a process, but an integral factor within it. This understanding leads to holistic approaches to the sciences which enables them to be located within what we would call a spiritual dimension. A number of popular books which set science within an Eastern spiritual tradition have recently appeared.[2] Sociology has not remained unaffected, and it can be argued that in struggles for justice, as in the scientific laboratory, there can be no such thing as a detached observer. Because the values, the beliefs and the commitments of a person undertaking a sociological survey or evaluation can determine its outcome, it is important that one declares one's perspective from the outset. In these contexts the sociologist or the community worker can be said to be acting as a militant observer.

Paulo Freire argues that it is only the oppressed themselves who can unmask the reality of their oppression. It is not possible for the powerful to unmask their own reality and remain in power. Nor is it likely that those of us who are beneficiaries of the present ordering of society, and who are financially dependent upon it, will come up with an analysis which will run counter to our own class interests. If we are to gain an accurate picture of the society we live in, like Hosea we must pursue that analysis from the underside of history, from the perspective of those who are the victims of the present order. This means that our analysis has to be developed within the context of our commitment to the poor and marginalized, not simply in a notional manner, but through working alongside them and in their interests to create a new social reality. And if through some circumstances it is not possible for us to work with oppressed groups, our analysis must at least be subjected to the corrective criticism of their analysis.

In solidarity with the marginalized, we can build an analysis on the basis of the knowledge which people already have about their situation. This is usually referred to as 'popular knowledge' or 'social knowledge'. People are already in possession of an enormous amount of information about what is happening in their lives and going on in their community. This is generally not expressed in abstract ways like 'inflation is rising' but in the fact that 'I can no longer afford to buy meat'. The process of social and structural analysis must begin at this point, listing all the 'facts' that people know about their situation in terms of their economic, political, social and cultural existence.

Social or popular knowledge on its own is not sufficient, however, to determine the root causes of the problems a society experiences. To do that, we have to be able to test or verify social knowledge against scientific knowledge. At this point that wealth of data which a society like ours delights to produce becomes invaluable. It is frequently complained that people can take statistical data and make what they want of it, manipulating figures in the cause of a particular argument or ideological perspective. That is why some element of proof or verification is important. I have heard it argued, for example, that what is happening within a local economy is entirely directed by the global economy. This may express itself in a piece of popular knowledge like 'our industry is owned by a multinational company which takes its orders from overseas and sends its profits overseas'. Such a hypothesis has to be tested by looking at the share holdings, board structures and financial statements of both the local and multinational company. Only by calling on this kind of data are we able to determine the reality of the situation.

In using statistics for verification we have to assume that none of them are neutral and that the vast majority have been produced by the dominant ideology in support of its case. Because we are locating our analysis in the underside of history, we will always try to interpret statistics from the perspective of the poor, the marginalized and the dispossessed in society. We do this in either of two ways. We can make use of the counter-information produced by research groups biased in favour of the poor and in some circumstances by the poor themselves from the midst of their struggle. Or we can take the statistics produced by the dominant ideology and by breaking them down and rearranging them, use them to indicate something other than was intended. Thus in the case of the New Zealand statistics on crime and unemployment referred to earlier, we are able to use counter-information material to assess the racial component of the employment figures and juxtapose these with the statistics on crime which the dominant ideology likes to present on a racial basis, in order to expose the links between classes, the economy, unemployment, survival and 'crime'.

The interaction between social knowledge and scientific knowledge produces transformative knowledge which, put simply, is that form of knowledge which enables people, having understood their situation, to change or transform it. Freire has described this process as people becoming subjects rather than objects of history.

There are several strands of social analysis around today which Christian activists can adapt to their own situations. In our work, we have found the most helpful of these to be that which combines elements of structural and conjunctural analysis. The former, as its name suggests, is concerned with the structural relationship between the various systems in society. It tends to focus on the base economy and its system of production, and the superstructure built upon that base. Conjunctural analysis is more concerned with the particular forces, trends or movements operating in society at a given time and the relationship between them. It tends to focus more on ideological and political factors.[3]

In selecting an appropriate methodology, it is important to ensure that the analysis presses beyond the mere presentation of data to an examination of the links between systems, and the root causes of oppression. It is also much better, as this book has been at pains to emphasize, if the analysis becomes a group exercise built around the social knowledge which people already possess. There are some analytical approaches which in effect undertake the analysis for people, presenting them with conclusions rather than encouraging them to discover their own solutions. There are others in which, although a group process, the facilitator takes responsibility for categorizing people's social knowledge, and so directs the process in what amounts to a predetermined way. Some of the more effective methodologies are those which have been developed in particular struggles in Africa and Asia and which can be regarded as a gift from the Third World to the First World. A good example is the Delta Programme from Kenya which can be easily adapted to industrialized contexts.[4] Aspects of this particular methodology have been utilized throughout this book and can be specifically identified, for example, in the section in the first chapter examining the way in which the dominant class controls the state apparatus.

The main steps of this form of analysis are:

1. *Observation* What do we see happening? We begin by making an accurate description of the reality we wish to understand.

2. *Classification* We classify whether our descriptions relate primarily to questions of (a) survival or economics; (b) decision making or politics; or (c) values and meaning, or culture.

3. *Inter-Relation* We ask how these facts are related to one another. What are the links between them? We note the patterns which emerge.

4. *Insight* Having seen the inter-relationships we ask what is cause and what is effect? What is important and what is relatively unimportant?

5. *Causes* We examine why things inter-relate: systems, causes and situations, bearing in mind that persons and situations can alter structures.

6. *Hypothesis* We draw up an hypothesis which explains why things happen and how to bring about change. The verification of our hypothesis is the extent to which it works in practice. For example, does moderating the cause moderate the effect?

Analysis should be neither an academic nor a tedious process. It will become both if it is undertaken as an exercise divorced from engagement in concrete situations of change. Undertaken by a group which has already embarked on action, it clarifies and energizes. Nor is it a methodology which has to be slavishly followed. Any Christian confronted by a critical issue can immediately begin an analysis by asking three questions: Who decides? Who benefits? Who is disadvantaged?

Determining where we want to go

Our analysis will very often begin from strong feelings we have about what is wrong with society. Paulo Freire speaks in terms of generative words or generative themes and suggests that the feelings these elicit become powerful motivations for initiating and sustaining social change. The fact that we are possessed by such negative feelings is an indication that locked away somewhere inside us is a positive idea of what society ought to look like. We have to try to identify these positive elements and build them into a detailed vision.

This vision building is an essential step in working for effective social change. Like other parts of the process, it doesn't take place in a vacuum, but is very much related to who we are as persons and to our experience of the world. In our third chapter we looked at the way that both Old Testament teaching and the witness of Jesus provide us with elements of a vision for a just society which Christians would probably wish to incorporate in constructing a contemporary vision.

We have already noted the common characteristic of people talking in vague generalities and saying that they are committed to a 'more just' or a 'more loving' or a 'more Christian' society. These claims are meaningless until we spell out in precise detail how a more Christian political system would operate or how a more just society would be structured. Exactly what would a Christian economy look like? Would it use money, or barter, or something else as the basis of exchange? Would it allow workers the ownership and control of the industry they work in, or would there be community ownership? Would it be committed to pay differentials or to a concept of a social wage? Would it legitimate profit making and if it did, how would profits be distributed? Who would undertake the unpleasant jobs in the community? What degree of technology would be employed? The list of specific questions is endless.

The process of vision building also reveals whether or not there is a common thrust within a group, and the degree to which people's interests are working against one another. In one seminar I facilitated, thirty activists were invited to list the projects and programmes in which they were investing their energies. The range was enormous: anti-racism work, rape crisis counselling, unemployment unions, political education programmes, battered wives' refuges, housing action groups, gay and lesbian rights, Maori language and culture organizations, land grievances, and work with street gangs. There was a feeling of solidarity within the group, reinforced by the conviction that all were responding to injustices caused by a fundamentally unjust society. But solidarity on this basis can be quite illusory. It is claimed of the Gadarene swine that they kept congratulating each other that they were at least all heading in the same direction![5]

Once participants began to spell out the details of their vision for society, however, their differences became patently clear. In reality they were working towards quite diverse kinds of societies. Some even began to discern that their projects were in fact reinforcing the present unjust system. Others discovered that basic elements of their vision were in contradiction to those of other groups and that they were actually working against each other's interests. Simply to become engaged in action for justice is not enough. We need to enunciate our vision for society and discover who our enemies and allies are, before our action stands a chance of succeeding.

There are, of course, pitfalls in this process. A danger for Christians is to seek perfection in all things and to produce a utopian vision which tries to replicate the Garden of Eden and return the world to a pristine state in which no problems exist and everyone loves one another. The attempts of certain alternative life-style groups to reinvent paradise are doomed to failure because they are quite unrealistic visions. Our visions certainly need to be painted on a broad canvas, but we must also be concerned with detail. We have to work on forms of social, political and economic organization which are not only possible but also achievable. Our vision must be earthed.

If it is to be convincing to other people, our vision must be incorporated into our own lives. That is a very simple test of its achievability. The potential of my vision is best judged by the degree to which others discover it in my personal relationships, my economic practice and my political activity. If I can't manage to embody it, it would seem to stand little chance of succeeding on a wider scale. What we particularly have to avoid is the contradiction that many organizations find themselves in, where their lofty intentional language is totally betrayed by their institutional behaviour. It is precisely at this point that the church's vision often founders. Consider this statement.

The Church takes the following stand:
She denounces the unjust lack of worldly goods and the sin that engenders it.
She preaches and lives spiritual poverty, adopting an attitude of spiritual childlikeness and openness to the Lord.
She commits herself to a state of material poverty. The poverty of the Church is, in effect, a constant in salvation history.[6]

In practice, the only one of these intentions which the church is actually able to implement in its own life is the preaching of spiritual poverty. It acknowledges no contradiction in denouncing the injustice and sin of worldly goods which it possesses to abundance. Its denunciation is further tempered by its outstanding success as a transnational corporation. What recent significant moves have there been towards exemplifying material poverty by divesting itself of its vast landholdings, its banks, its commercial enterprises, or its stocks and shares? Its intentions may be wholly admirable but they are totally contradicted by its behaviour. If the institution is incapable of living out its vision in the world, what expectations should it have of its members doing so?

In constructing an authentic vision, the process itself is crucial. There are some forms of community intervention which advocate that the community must build a vision on the basis of its own knowledge and experience alone. Outsiders like community workers or animators should be excluded from that process. But vision building is a dynamic and educative counter-cultural process which in order to be critical, needs to draw on as wide a range of experience as possible. It is important that communities are made aware of what others have managed to achieve. There needs to be a free exchange of ideas both from within and beyond the community or group. Of course we must avoid the imposition of a ready-made vision, be it Christian or anything else, upon the community. But the animator's declared vision, values and ideology can contribute towards rather than hinder the process.

Articulating its vision usually turns out to be the most difficult step in a group's programme of change. If blocks are experienced at this point we need to ask why they are occurring. We also need to remind ourselves that the dominant ideology has a vested interest in preventing the creation of alternative visions and in demonstrating their impracticality. People have often been socialized into believing that we require experts to assist us in this task; that we can't talk sensibly about an alternative economic order unless we have economists to help us. There may well be occasions on which we do require specific assistance of that kind in understanding how systems work, but for the most part, communities are perfectly capable of embarking upon the process on the basis of their own knowledge and experience.

The following example of principles of vision building gives the sense of what we mean.

1. Our vision, firstly, is a human one. It expresses the social character of human beings, stressing therefore co-operation rather than domination.

2. The vision is also universal. Human beings exist in relation with their wider environment. This relationship must also be based on co-operation, hence our vision has an ecological perspective.

3. Co-operation cannot be built on unequal relations, but only on social justice. We work from the perspective of redistributing wealth and power in favour of the poor and powerless.

4. Social change entails not just a change of leaders or rulers, but a change in the structures and attitudes within society.

5. Structures must be built which promote the fullest possible participation of people in solving their common problems.

6. The means chosen to promote social change affect the ends. Our organizations must reflect in their structures and methods the vision we are aiming for.

7. We cannot sacrifice a generation now to build the future. Our vision must speak to the present reality.

8. Motivations of envy, hate and greed are self-defeating.

9. An authentic vision reflects people's deepest concerns, hopes and aspirations. It comes from among the people and is not imposed upon them.

10. Our vision must be not simply a future hope but a present reality: we must live now as far as possible the future we hope for.[7]

Deciding how to get there

There is very little by way of advice or comment which can be made about specific strategies and tactics. The whole tenor of this book has been to suggest that it is for groups struggling to right injustices to select and test those strategies which are appropriate to their particular circumstances. We have looked at the broad strategic approaches which Jesus adopted; contesting the dominant consciousness, building an organization, and taking direct action; as well as at the specific tactic of surrender. These obviously provide guidelines which Christians will consider as they devise, modify and refine their strategies.

But we can certainly make some general points about strategies. The first is to express caution about strategies which move from issue to issue without seriously addressing their underlying causes. Some current approaches to community action and community organization repeat the errors of the 1960s. They rely on a constant flow of new issues. When the spectacular issues run out, so does the ability to mobilize people. When this began to happen in one community programme in which I was involved, a consultant recommended that an issue be artificially created just so that momentum would not be lost. There are ethical questions to be asked of such a strategy as well as the criticism that it fails to exploit the fundamental economic, political and ideological contradictions which remain constant in our kind of society.

Our action is likely to be more effective, be more directed and produce greater long-term results if, in addition to working at the level of issues in the community, we are also working at the political level; working, in other words, on constructing a counter-political and counter-ideological apparatus. In some cases this will demand that the activist join a political party or movement. Some may find that the vision they have worked on already exists within, and may well have been informed by a transformative or revolutionary political movement. For example, anarcha-feminism, stressing as it does both individuality and collectivity, organization and spontaneity, and committed to ending authority, hierarchy and state government, may perfectly encapsulate the kind of world some are striving towards. In such cases people will identify with the movement's strategies, adapting them to local needs and conditions.

Other Christians may feel that it is not necessary for every detail of their vision to be embraced by a particular political option, but that it is sufficient if the option carries them a fair distance in the direction of that vision. A pragmatic approach may lead Christians to support democratic socialist parties because the vision these ultimately aspire to is shared, even although the strategies for getting there may not be shared in their entirety. Still others will choose to work in the interest of whatever opposition party stands the best chance of unseating the party of the dominant ideology. They feel that the opposition at least creates the space within which alternatives may develop and where it is possible to talk freely about them. It is of interest that a strategy advocated by the Communist Party of Great Britain is to create an alliance of parties of the Left in order to defeat Thatcherism. Given that the Conservative party commands considerably less than fifty per cent of the popular vote, that would seem a sensible strategy.

The identification and formation of alliances is vitally important in strategies for change. Christian groups and organizations which seek to establish strategic alliances may find themselves in the company of some fairly strange bedfellows. But to be in alliance with another group is not to imply that one totally accepts its vision or approves of its strategies. When we talk about *strategic* alliances, we are talking about working together in some common action which will enormously speed the rate of change. To do this, our group would look at the cultural level to see which groups are working to establish or to reinforce the counter-ideology. We would look to the political arena to determine which groups were trying to establish people's participation over against centralized decision-making. And in the economic sector we would try to identify organizations supporting workers rights or building an alternative economy. We would then be in a position to decide which group or groups we could ally with in an action which would meet both our objectives and theirs.

The major area of strategy for Christians has to be that of the counter-consciousness or counter-ideology. At the beginning of the book we examined the way in which the church generally functions as one of the dominant consciousness's instruments of persuasion, and we suggested that, by deliberate choice as an institution or through the choice of some of its members, it can begin to promote values of the counter-consciousness consistent with Christian truth. Brueggemann suggests that this process is at the same time critical and energizing: it helps dismantle the dominant ideology and it provides the impetus for doing it.

The fact that the institutional church is located within the state's ideological apparatus means that it can work from within the system to challenge or subvert it, as well as supporting the emerging counter-ideology established by groups outside this structure. It can commence the task of internal challenge or subversion very easily through its preaching, its liturgies, its witness, its life-style and its educational programmes.

It can begin with any one of the dominant ideology's basic concepts. We can take the idea of stability as an example. The dominant ideology takes this to mean that everything should remain in its proper place in relation to the natural order. Change is threatening, therefore undesirable and not to be encouraged. If change does become necessary, it should be only that minimum which will enable the system to keep functioning and to maintain its power. The institutional church itself became captive to this kind of thinking, particularly since the 1848 revolutions which gave birth to groups wishing to expropriate church property! The church in its preaching and its popular hymns began to affirm the value of changelessness. Its children sang that the explanation for 'the rich man in his castle, the poor man at his gate', was that 'God made them high and lowly, and ordered their estate.' Its adults enthusiastically intoned 'Change and decay in all around I see; O Thou who changest not, abide with me.'

On the other hand, the church can begin to emphasize the value that runs counter to stability, that of change. It can preach and teach that repentance demands a radical change of direction from that in which we were heading; that change is of the essence of God's creative and redemptive work in the world; that gospel values turn the world's values on their head; that resurrection is a process of continual renewal of persons and institutions; and that Christians should welcome God's promise of fundamental change. When the church acts in this way, three things are happening. The dominant ideology is being directly challenged; the mood is being generated for reception of the ideas of change which the counter-ideology is calling for; and people are being motivated and energized for the struggle. The battle has been carried into the heart of the dominant ideology itself.

Similarly, whenever the church promotes a holistic view of life and emphasizes the need for humans to integrate their health, spirituality, sexuality, politics and so on, it undermines the capitalist strategy of keeping these things compartmentalized and functionally separated from one another. When it emphasizes the idea of the *people* of God and the salvation of the believing *community*, it subverts the capitalist cult of the individual. When it insists that the gospel is not impartial, but that God has a bias towards the poor and powerless, it destroys the dominant ideology's claim that both gospel and Christ are neutral in character. Where it employs contextual theology to demonstrate that God's word and truth are revealed in our engagement in concrete political, economic and social struggles, it is contesting the capitalist contention that theology is truth revealed and transmitted by a male hierarchy.

The analysis we did in the opening chapter indicated that because auxiliary-class people staff both the ideological and political apparatus of the state, they are in a good position to assist the struggles of oppressed people by exploiting the contradictions which exist within the apparatus. But there are also many other actions that auxiliary-class people – who make up the bulk of our church congregations and who possess a wide range of skills – can take to express solidarity with oppressed people. The following list, complied by New Zealand activists, suggests some possibilities.

Counteract community distrust of action for change.

Emphasize the rightness of the cause.

Build up the good name of the organization undertaking the action.

Drum up support from auxiliary class organizations.

Act as a buffer against harassment.

Offer an auxiliary-class group as an umbrella under which an oppressed group can act.

Mediate between oppressed groups and the authorities.

Find financial support for actions and projects.

Provide professional legal and financial services.

Create access to the media.

Facilitate links nationally and internationally to groups with similar aims.

Support mass actions like demonstrations and strikes.

Document the history of popular struggles. Those at the grassroots often don't have time for this.

Issue supporting statements and position papers from one's own group.

Provide base groups with information and data which can assist their struggle.

Provide training in specific skills.

Introduce base groups to key sympathizers in the state apparatus.

It is to be understood, of course, that such actions would normally follow specific requests from popular movements for assistance and solidarity, and are not to be initiated without reference to the base group.

We have been stressing throughout the value of the action-reflection-action model of social transformation developed by Paulo Freire. This implies that the most effective strategies will be discovered in the midst of our action and that we need to take time to assess their impact. If our strategies aren't working effectively we need to ask why, analyse their strengths and weaknesses, and modify them accordingly. If the strategy ultimately doesn't work, it may be that we have got our analysis of the problem wrong and we need to do some more work in that area.

The reader probably does not need to be reminded that in talking about strategies, we are not assuming that we will move in one gigantic leap forward from the present injustices to the new society we have envisioned. Change does not happen like that. We will in all likelihood continue to move as history has moved in the past, from one form of social reality in which there are contradictions to a liberating form in which new contradictions may appear which will have to be addressed. But we are all the time advancing in the direction of our vision.

All the elements we have been discussing in this chapter, solidarity with the poor and marginalized, the identification of our personal perspective and values, the continuous cycle of socio-economic analysis, the building of a new vision and consciousness, the channelling of energy into creative strategies, make up what we call transformative practice. Transformation is a word at once sociological and theological in content. It suggests the reworking of that which already exists so that it liberates from injustice. It reminds us of the manner in which the Hebrews borrowed elements from the surrounding pagan cultures, transforming them into vehicles for the worship of Jahweh God and the organization of social, political and economic life. It also has links with Christian understandings of conversion and salvation; with the change of heart, of behaviour and of relationships that is demanded of the believer; with the switching of loyalties from the conformist values of this world to the transforming values of the Kingdom.

Transformation is about relationships. It implies that we are able to move from a state of injustice to one of justice, from a state of oppression to one of liberation, by changing the nature of the relationships which create and maintain these conditions. It does not require a violent revolution against state oppression to initiate such changes. That is the point of difference anarchists have historically had with Marxist strategies. The German anarchist Gustav Landauer put it very simply. 'The state is not something which can be destroyed by a revolution, but is a condition, a certain relationship between human beings, a mode of human behaviour; we destroy it by contracting other relationships, by behaving differently.'[8] We have seen that it is precisely this strategy, changing the character of relationships and behaviours, that Jesus followed in his ministry.

That it is also a very effective contemporary strategy was illustrated towards the end of 1989 when in East Germany and Czechoslovakia, thousands of people behaving differently and seeking to establish new political relationships took to the streets in non-violent demonstrations. In the face of the claims of popular power, the power of the powerless as it has been called, totalitarian regimes collapsed. Oppressive institutions and authoritarian systems were swept away. This happened neither through force of arms, nor by magic, but because through years of oppression, groups of people had been discussing and establishing new relationships with one another and those relationships eventually constituted what Vaclav Havel has called a parallel political system. Springing from the human condition and based upon ethical values of trust, openness, responsibility, solidarity and love, rather than upon ideology, it simply grew too powerful to be resisted.

Writing in 1978, Havel described what he called 'post-democratic' society in terms of the radical renewal of human relationships amongst people and within communities. These new relationships transform existing political structures, whether socialist or capitalist, giving rise to new non-bureaucratic, dynamic and open communities, small and human in scale, dispersing rather than accumulating power. They derive their energy from a living dialogue with the genuine needs from which they arise, and disappear to make way for new dynamically appearing and disappearing organizations.

Paulo Freire suggests that when people rediscover their suppressed culture, they are energized for transformative action. This too, runs counter to the bulk of Marxist strategic thinking which often appears to assume that it is sufficient to alter the economic base of a society for the superstructure to be necessarily changed as a direct result. It also explains why Ceausescu's Romania went to such extraordinary lengths to impose a 'socialist culture' and to obliterate minority cultures which it regarded as seedbeds of dissidence. That cultural renaissance can become the stimulus if not the base for profound social change is attested to in situations as diverse as the Cuban and Nicaraguan revolutions and the Maori movement in New Zealand.

One counter-cultural strategy each one of us can adopt is that of claiming more and more areas of human life for freedom. We can claim this in our personal lives, in our spirituality, in our intimate relationships, in our dealings with other people. We can claim it for our families. We can claim it in our work situation, and for the community in which we live. It is simply, as Camus pointed out in his book *The Rebel*, and as Jesus demonstrated on the cross, a case of saying 'No'. We take a stand and proclaim 'No further!' To say no is to say yes to an important part of oneself and to refuse to compromise our integrity. We can say it to anyone who would exploit, manipulate or coerce us. We can say it to any instrument of oppression. We can say it to any unjust law. We can say it to any relationship which is dehumanizing.

I recently read in a London newspaper an article about a man whose family was kept awake for nights on end by a faulty burglar alarm on the next door house which was at the time unoccupied. He spent days complaining to the police, complaining to the local authority, complaining to the firm which had installed the alarm. ,The bureaucracy was such that no one was willing to transgress on another's territory, and nobody was willing to authorize action. In the end, so that his children could get some sleep, the man took a ladder and dismantled the alarm. He became an instant hero, applauded by other residents in the street who had done nothing presumably because, like him, they had been socialized by the state into accepting that one must put up with inconvenience, call in a specialist, and never act beyond the law. But what this man had done was simplicity itself. In the face of oppression, however minor, he said 'no further' and claimed freedom for himself, his family and his neighbourhood. Anyone can do it.

On being as wise as serpents

The practice of counter-culture suggests that our major strategies, in solidarity with the marginalized will be directed towards contesting the dominant ideology and building liberating alternatives to it. How much energy should Christian activists therefore put into reshaping the institutional church? Can it be reclaimed so that it can serve as a counter-cultural movement in the manner that Jesus intended it to?

The Libertarian poet Shelley took a totally pessimistic view of the situation.

> Christianity was intended to reform the world: had an all-wise Being planned it, nothing is more improbable than that it should have failed; omniscience would have foreseen the inutility of a scheme which experience demonstrates, to this age, to have been utterly unsuccessful.[9]

We may share Shelley's disappointment over the failure of Christianity to deliver freedom on the scale that it promised. But the fact that it hasn't been able to do so is not because the ideas upon which early Christianity organized itself were mistaken, or the teachings of Jesus false, but because, as Tolstoy points out, the message was emasculated and the structure subverted by the agents of the Roman empire and its successors.

This book suggests that in the light of this, Christian activists need to return to square one to discover what Christ's teaching demanded in the first century. Having done that we can ask, if it meant that in his culture, what does it say to our culture? The immediate problem for Christians who are grasped by Christ's message in a new and empowering way is that they face a great deal of criticism and often outright hostility from the church itself. Many Christians today speak of the dilemma of staying with what they regard as a dying institution, or identifying with the new church they see emerging on its margins.

There can be no simple answer to that dilemma. Things are no easier for those who regard themselves as part of the emerging church. Some of the Anglican communion's women priests who felt it was their vocation to establish a new Christian witness on the margins of the institution in order to call it towards a liberating life-style, profess dismay over the fact that the institution appears to have budged little. Even if the church were to radically alter its structure along feminist lines and reshape itself as a community of equals in the way Christ intended, would novelty once again be institutionalized? Francis of Assisi's radical espousal of the Gospels' values and communitarian life indeed set the mediaeval church alight. But even within his own lifetime the fire had begun to peter out as members of the community argued about internal orders of precedence and their structural relationship to the institutional church. Little wonder that we find the Franciscan

Order today cast in the role of caretakers of history, guardians of the holy places in Palestine.

The question is one about the domesticating role of institutions. Furthermore, there is a frustrating sense in which people who consider themselves the emerging church are only able to do so because the traditional church exists and offers them space, protection and encouragement. A case in point are the Base Christian Communities and their objective of deinstitutionalizing the church which survive because of rather than despite of the church.

On the other hand, those who remain inside the church and see their role as challenging and changing it from within, face equally daunting problems. The church acts as an enormous clobbering machine. Activists can become truly marginalized and ineffective to the point of being heartbroken. They suffer at the hands of hierarchies and bureaucracies which, exhibiting little of the freedom and the joy Christ entrusted to his apostles, secure the *status quo* and along with it, their own survival. I have heard some Christians say that they remain with the church despite the difficulties because their beliefs, their values and their political vision all spring from their Christian formation. The church has made them what they are, and it is for the church to own what it has created. That strikes me as a very persuasive argument for staying!

Others insist that to expend energy on changing the church as institution is a mistake, especially if people perceive the church as being in the vanguard of change. The history of the church is that, except for a few instances, it has been overtaken by change and forced to adapt itself to altered social, economic and political realities. We have looked at numerous examples of the unfortunate consequences which flow from the church believing that it possesses the gospel. It is when the world draws the gospel out of the church that its transforming nature lies revealed. It is when the church is possessed by the gospel that it will be itself transformed.

The reality is that there is no safe or comfortable place for the activist to be. The church is not a monolith but a body of many parts, many movements. There is always a pioneering part of the church, trying to extend the frontiers of theology and action. Sometimes its voice becomes muted. At others, like at the time of the campaign against slavery, it drives the church into new forms of social and political action. It could well be that today's Christian radicals are called to stand both at the heart of the institution to challenge its ideological captivity, and at its margins, establishing new centres of resistance and liberation.

What advice did Jesus offer those who have to work in situations of ambiguity and hostility? When he sent the Twelve out on their first mission, he warned them that persecution would issue from a number of sources: the state, the religious establishment, and the family. Calling on the imagery of the natural world which he was fond of using, he urged them to be as wise as serpents and yet as harmless as doves (Matt. 10.16), a combination of subtlety and non-violence. His choice of the image of the serpent is unusual, given that in the book of Genesis it is depicted as the most cunning of animals, blamed for tempting Eve into the first sin, and then accursed by God for all time. Jesus redeems this most despised of symbols and incidentally, by doing so suggests another strategy of counter-cultural practice! Dominant ideology commentators typically have difficulty with Jesus' words at this point and would have us read 'prudent' for 'cunning'. They cannot comprehend how cunning can possibly be regarded as a virtue.

But the cunning of the serpent is not something underhand, malicious or manipulative. Rather it is a tactic which an animal, vulnerable and lacking the advantages of many others, has developed for its own protection. It has no eyelids, and unable to close its eyes, has to be eternally vigilant. It is also superb in the art of camouflage, adapting itself to its surroundings and moving unnoticed whether in tangled forest or open desert. Jesus suggests that this degree of subtlety, combined with the practice of non-violence, are basic survival skills in a hostile environment.

Finally, let it be said yet again that the practice of counter-culture is not a new option for Christians. It appears time and time again in Christian history. We see it at work in the way the first Christian commune in Jerusalem was organized. We see it in Wycliffe's Poor Preachers who dispensed with private property and hierarchical organization; in the Hussites and Taborites whose communities rejected all solemn oaths and legal systems; in the Amalricians who proclaimed that those who live in God's love cannot sin; in the Followers of the Free Spirit who resisted all earthly authority; in the Levellers who tried to give practical form to the idea of a genuinely communitarian society; in the Anabaptists who lived under the New Covenant requiring no human laws or government; in the Mennonites who rejected law and organized themselves into non-hierarchical communities of non-resistance. In these and numerous contemporary expressions, it persists as a genuine and liberating expression of the Christian gospel.

Such initiatives have in general been declared heretical or written off as impractical utopianism, for they stand not only over against statist perceptions, but also against the church's understanding of itself as a property-owning political power affirming law and order. The *Oxford Dictionary of the Christian Church* reinforces this view when it describes almost all the communitarian experiments I've listed as 'extremist'. The liberationist-anarchist tradition has proved more than just an irritant to the church. It has demonstrated the fact that the gospel is good news to the poor by living it out in a way that has proved quite impossible for the institutional church to match, encumbered as it is with too much power, too much authority, too much property, and too much wealth. The institution's reaction has always been to attempt to grind this exquisite flower of the gospel into the dust.

That for almost two thousand years such attempts to stifle the spirit of the gospel have singularly failed gives us enormous hope for the future. Liberationist anarchism continues to offer Christians a way of embodying the Kingdom of God in our lives, in our relationships, in our political and economic practice, and in our communities. Perhaps we should leave the final word to Tolstoy, who liked to proclaim that he had become such an anarchist as Jesus and the Sermon on the Mount had made him.

NOTES

Chapter One   Looking Through Scripture

1. *Churches Among Ideologies*, WCC, Geneva 1982, p. 3.

2. The Cuban Revolution is generally considered to be a movement of national liberation in the first instance, which only came to be regarded as Marxist–Leninist retrospectively, following the United States' embargo.

3. *The Confession of Faith*, Editorial Orbe, Havana 1978, pp. 17, 20f., 21f.

4. Ibid., p. 8.

5. This was in an article 'Christianity for Capitalists' in the Face to Faith column of *The Guardian*, 19 June 1989. Leech points out that Anglican bishops once argued that, although Graham's gospel is inadequate, it at least provides the basis to which other corrective elements may be added. Michael Ramsey, at the time Bishop of Durham, responded that elements like social responsibility could not be added at a later stage because this form of evangelism cuts at the root of both rational faith and Christian social criticism.

6. Robert Schuller, *Tough Times Never Last, But Tough People Do!*, Garden Grove 1982, p. 9.

7. Edward Norman, *Christianity and the World Order*, Oxford University Press, 1979.

8. Edward Norman, 'The Denigration of Capitalism: Current Education and the Moral Subversion of Capitalist Society', May 1977.

9. Brian Griffiths, *Morality and the Market Place*, Hodder and Stoughton, London 1982 (new edition 1989).

10. Methodist theologian John Vincent has argued that while Wesley was indeed a High Tory, he was also committed to the improvement of conditions for the working class. This extended to arguing for 'primitive communism' as 'the highest concept of economic organization', a far cry from Thatcherite policies. See Vincent's article in the Face to Faith column of *The Guardian*, 19 October 1987.

11. See Jonathan Raban's pamphlet *God, Man and Mrs Thatcher*, Chatto and Windus, London 1989, a commentary on the Prime Minister's 1988 sermon delivered to the Church of Scotland.

12. Press Release by Mr Alan Sim, Executive Vice-President of the New Zealand Chambers of Commerce, 3 October 1978.

13. Letter from the Minister of Labour, the Hon. J. B. Bolger, to the Ecumenical Secretariat on Development, 28 May 1981.

14. Letter from the Under-Secretary of National Development, Mr B. E. Brill, to *Zealandia* newspaper, 26 May 1981.

15. Press Release by Winston Peters, MP.

16. Speech by Mr Talbot (Government – Ashburton) reported in Hansard, 1981, No. 16, 2137–38.

Chapter Two   Back to Basics

1. Walter Brueggemann, *The Prophetic Imagination*, Fortress Press, Philadelphia 1978.
2. Francois Houtart, 'An Application of Structural Analysis to the Palestinian Milieu in the First Century of Our Era', in ICMS Asia Document Reprint Service, Hong Kong, April 1979; Fernando Belo, *A Materialist Reading of the Gospel of Mark*, Orbis Books, Maryknoll 1981, ch. 2, 'Politics in the First Century AD'; Joachim Jeremias, *Jerusalem in the Time of Jesus*, SCM Press, London and Fortress Press, Philadelphia 1969; George Pixley, *God's Kingdom*, Orbis Books, Maryknoll and SCM Press, London 1981.
3. Houtart, op. cit., p. 13.
4. Kenneth Bailey, *Poet and Peasant* and *Through Peasant Eyes* (combined edition), William B. Eerdmans, Grand Rapids 1983.
5. Bailey, op. cit., page 203.
6. Ernesto Cardenal, *The Gospel in Solentiname*, (four volumes), Orbis Books, Maryknoll 1979.
7. See Paulo Freire, *Cultural Action for Freedom*, Penguin Books 1972.
8. Manuka Henare, 'The Option for the Maori' in John Ker and Kevin Sharpe (eds), *Towards An Authentic New Zealand Theology*, Auckland University Chaplaincy, Auckland 1984.
9. See Cardenal, op. cit., vol. 3, pp. 280–290.
10. Elisabeth Schüssler Fiorenza's book, *In Memory of Her: A Feminist Theological Reconstruction of Christian Origins*, Crossroad, New York and SCM Press, London 1983, takes its title from this event.
11. Cardenal, op. cit. vol. 3, pp. 45–47.
12. Evelyn Waugh, *Brideshead Revisited*, Penguin Books 1945, p. 122.

Chapter Three   Sightings of a New Earth

1. Neville Chamberlain, Eric Forshaw and Malcolm Goldsmith, *Understanding Inequality*, British Council of Churches, London 1977.
2. Luke 6.20–26. The blessings and curses are separated in the original. I have put them together to demonstrate the contrast.
3. Joseph Fletcher, *Situation Ethics: The New Morality*, Westminster Press, Philadelphia and SCM Press, London 1966.
4. See Rev. 19.11 to 20.6 in particular.
5. See for example *Gathered for Life* (*The Official Report of the Sixth Assembly of the World Council of Churches*) ed. David Gill, WCC, Geneva 1983, p. 88, paragraph 14.3.
6. José Porfiro Miranda, *Communism in the Bible*, Orbis Books, Maryknoll and SCM Press, London 1982, p. 8.
7. See Charles Avila, *Ownership: Early Christian Teaching*, Orbis Books, Maryknoll 1983.

Chapter Four   Old Wine in New Bottles

1. J. Philip Wogaman, *Christians and The Great Economic Debate*, SCM Press, London and Westminster Press, Philadelphia 1977.

2. The description 'Fundamentalist' dates only from 1909 and was a movement in reaction to the material, educational and social demands of an increasingly technological world.

3. Andre Gunder Frank, *Capitalism and Underdevelopment in Latin America*, Penguin Books 1971.

4. Sergio Arce Martinez, 'Development, People's Participation and Theology' in *The Ecumenical Review*, vol. 30, no. 3, WCC, Geneva 1978.

5. Presbyterian Reformed Church of Cuba, op. cit., p. 18.

6. Charles Elliott, *Inflation and the Compromised Church*, Christian Journals, Belfast 1975, p. 133.

7. *Gaudium et Spes*, Catholic Truth Society, London 1966, p. 73.

8. Ibid., p. 74.

9. *Rerum Novarum*, Catholic Truth Society, London, 1983 edition.

10. See Milton Friedman, *Capitalism and Freedom*, University of Chicago Press, Chicago 1962.

11. This is the argument of Herbert Marcuse in *One Dimensional Man: The Ideology of Industrial Society*, Sphere Books, London 1968.

12. See Richard J. Barnet, *Intervention and Revolution: The United States in the Third World*, Paladin, London 1972.

13. These quotations from the Santa Fe Document come from an article in French: 'Where is Reagan's America Heading?', privately circulated.

14. *New Zealand Times*, 1 September 1985.

15. *Rerum Novarum*, op. cit.

16. *Quadragesimo Anno*, Catholic Truth Society, London, 1962 edition.

17. *Mater et Magistra* in Joseph Gremillion (ed), *The Gospel of Peace and Justice*, Orbis Books, Maryknoll 1976.

18. *Populorum Progressio* in Joseph Gremillion, op cit.

19. Ibid.

20. *Octogesima Adveniens* in Gremillion, op. cit.

21. José Porfiro Miranda, *Marx and the Bible: A Critique of the Philosophy of Oppression*, Orbis Books, Maryknoll and SCM Press, London 1974. See particularly the introduction.

22. Quoted in Alain Gheerbrant, *The Rebel Church in Latin America*, Penguin Books 1974, p. 267–68.

23. That is the conclusion drawn by David A. Yallop's book, *In God's Name: An Investigation into the Murder of Pope John Paul I*, Bantam Books, New York 1985.

24. See John Cornwell, *A Thief in the Night*, Viking, London 1989.

25. Joel Kovel, 'The Theocracy of John Paul II' in *Socialist Register 1987*, Merlin Press, London 1987.

26. See Tony Benn, *Arguments For Socialism*, Penguin Books 1980, ch. 1.

27. *The Report of the Lambeth Conference, 1978*, CIO Publishing, London 1978, p. 69.

28. Ibid., p. 70.

29. *Churches Among Ideologies*, WCC, Geneva 1982, p. 44.

30. See *The Humanum Studies 1969–1975*, WCC, Geneva 1982, p. 44.

31. See, for example, Charles Elliott, *Patterns of Poverty in the Third World*, Praeger, New York 1975.

32. See Michael Bakunin, 'Critique of the Marxist Theory of the State' in Sam Dolgoff (ed), *Bakunin on Anarchy*, Alfred Knopf, New York 1972.

33. Julio de Santa Ana (ed) *Towards a Church of the Poor*, WCC, Geneva 1979, p. xxiii.

34. *Octogesima Adveniens*, op. cit., 37.

35. *Octogesima Adveniens*, ibid.

Chapter Five   Like a River in Flood

1. See Gaston Leval, *Collectives in the Spanish Revolution*, Freedom Press, London 1975.

2. Walter Map, *The Waldenses* (1179); quoted in Sheila Delaney (ed), *Counter-Tradition: The Literature of Dissent and Alternatives*, Basic Books, New York 1971.

3. See Norman Cohn, *The Pursuit of the Millenium: Revolutionary Millen-arians and Mystical Anarchists of the Middle Ages*, Paladin, London 1970.

4. Peter Marshall, *William Blake; Visionary Anarchist*, Freedom Press, London 1988, p. 18.

5. Herbert Read, *Anarchy and Order*, Souvenir Press, London 1974.

6. Giovanni Baldelli, *Social Anarchism*, Penguin Books 1972.

7. Luigi Fabbri, 'Anarchy and "Scientific" Communism' in Albert Meltzer (ed), *The Poverty of Statism*, Cienfuegos Press, Sanday 1981; pp. 22–23.

8. Michael Bakunin; quoted in E. H. Carr, *Michael Bakunin*, The Macmillan Press, London, 1975 edition.

9. Michael Bakunin, *Revolutionary Catechism* (1866) in Sam Dolgoff (ed), *Bakunin on Anarchy*, Alfred Knopf, New York 1972.

10. Paul van Buren, *The Secular Meaning of the Gospel*, Macmillan, New York and SCM Press, London 1963; Penguin Books 1968, pp. 138–39.

11. Peter Kropotkin, *Mutual Aid: A Factor of Evolution*, Heinemann, London 1919.

12. *Populorum Progressio*, Paragraph 22; in Joseph Gremillion (ed), *The Gospel of Peace and Justice*, Orbis Books, Maryknoll 1976.

13. See Colin Ward, *Anarchy in Action*, George Allen and Unwin, London 1973, especially ch. 5, 'Topless Federations'.

14. For a full exposition of his ideas, see Alexander Berkman, *The ABC of Anarchism*; Freedom Press, London, 1987 edition.

15. See Giovanni Baldelli, op. cit.

16. Michael Bakunin, in Dolgoff, op. cit., p. 76.

17. William Godwin, *An Inquiry Concerning Political Justice*, 2 vols, Alfred Knopf, New York, 1926 edition.

18. Errico Malatesta, *Anarchy*, Freedom Press, London 1974.

19. Godwin, op. cit.

20. Paul Goodman, *Compulsory Miseducation*, Penguin Books 1975.

21. Read, op. cit.

22. Emma Goldman, 'The Psychology of Political Violence' in *Anarchism and Other Essays*, Dover Press, New York, 1969 edition, p. 107.

23. Richard and Val Routley, 'The Irrefutability of Anarchism' in *Social Alternatives*, vol. 2, no. 3, February 1982.

24. For a discussion of anti-power see Baldelli, op. cit., pp. 169–172.

25. Michael Bakunin, quoted in Carr, op. cit., p. 110.

26. Luigi Galleani, *The End of Anarchism?*, Cienfuegos Press, Sanday 1982, pp. 60–61. A useful discussion of Propaganda of the Deed anarchism.

27. Quoted by Vernon Richards in his introduction to Malatesta's *Anarchy*, op. cit.

28. Leo Tolstoy, *The Kingdom of God is Within You*, University of Nebraska Press 1984.

29. We would have to modify this view today to take cognisance, for example, of the spiritual basis of Gandhi's non-violent practice. Deeply influenced by the teaching of Tolstoy and Kropotkin, his Sarvodaya movement is an example of anarchism in a non-Western context.

30. Leo Tolstoy, *The Inevitable Revolution*, Housmans, London 1975.

31. Nicolas Berdyaev, quoted in Fuad Nucho, *Berdyaev's Philosophy: The Existential Paradox of Freedom and Necessity*, Doubleday, New York 1966.

32. The church is generally reluctant to acknowledge anarchists in its midst. The Catholic Truth Society's pamphlet *Dorothy Day and the Catholic Worker Movement* (London 1986) glosses over the anarchism espoused by both Day and Maurin and presents Day as a saintly believer in orthodox Catholic dogma and church structure.

33. Nicolas Berdyaev, *Dream and Reality: An Essay in Autobiography*, Macmillan, London 1951. Note that the valuing of aristocratic culture is not necessarily a reactionary position. In a poem on revolution, D. H. Lawrence urges 'Don't do it for the working classes. Do it so that we can all of us be little aristocracies on our own . . .'

34. *In Search of the New (III): Documents of an Ecumenical Action/Reflection Process on New Life Styles*, WCC, Geneva 1981, p. 12.

35. *Quadragesimo Anno* 23, quoted in *Mater et Magistra* 53 in Gremillion, op. cit., p. 154.

36. *Economic Justice for All: Pastoral Letter on Catholic Social Teaching and the US Economy*, United States' Catholic Conference, Washington 1986, Section 124.

37. *The Truth Shall Make You Free: the Lambeth Conference 1988*, Church House Publishing, London 1988, p. 172.

38. Phillip Berryman, *Our Unfinished Business: The US Catholic Bishops Letters on Peace and the Economy*, Pantheon Books, New York 1989.

Chapter Six   Direct Action Against the Treasury

1. *Churches Among Ideologies*, WCC, Geneva 1982, p. 3.

2. Herbert McCabe OP, in lectures delivered to a conference of the Industrial Mission Association in 1985, contended that as Marxism is the critique of the ideology of capitalism, so theology is the critique of the ideology of Christianity.

3. Jay Haley, *The Power Tactics of Jesus Christ and Other Essays*, Avon Books, New York 1969. A number of ideas in this chapter are based upon Dr Haley's highly entertaining essay.

4. See Elisabeth Schüssler Fiorenza, *In Memory of Her: A Feminist Reconstruction of Christian Origins*, Crossroad, New York and SCM Press, London 1983; and Rosemary Radford Ruether, *Sexism and God-Talk: Towards a Feminist Theology*, Beacon Press, New York and SCM Press, London 1983.

5. Josephus, for example, records an occasion of which Jesus must have been aware in which a group of Jews use the tactic successfully against Pilate at Caesarea.

6. Konrad Lorenz, *King Solomon's Ring*, Methuen 1955; 1964 edition, p. 197.

7. This analysis is drawn from Fernando Belo, *A Materialist Reading of the Gospel of Mark*, Orbis Books, Maryknoll 1981.

8. This is the contention of Francois Houtart, op. cit.

Chapter Seven   The Wisdom of Serpents

1. See the description of the Samuel/Saul dispute over the establishment of the monarchy on pp. 73–75.

2. See, for example, Gary Zukav's *The Dancing Wu Li Masters*, Rider, London 1979.

3. This has been published in three volumes as *Training for Transformation: A Handbook for Community Workers*, ed. Anne Hope and Sally Timmel, Mambo Press, Gweru 1984. Books 1 and 3 contain frameworks for social analysis using models developed by INODEP, the Ecumenical Institute for the Development of Peoples, in Paris. The books can be purchased through CAFOD and similar agencies concerned with development and justice.

4. The Institute for Social Research and Education, which I co-founded, runs workshops on this form of analysis. Its address is: 20 The Glebe, Cumnor, Oxford OX2 9QA.

5. The reference is to the story in Luke 8.26–39 where Jesus cures a man possessed by many evil spirits which subsequently possess a herd of swine which rushes headlong over a cliff and is destroyed.

6. From 'The Poverty of the Church: Final Document from the Second Conference of the Latin American Episcopate', Medellin 1968; reproduced in *Confessing Our Faith Around the World*, vol. 3, WCC, Geneva 1984.

7. From *Community Transformation: A Resource Manual for Programme Leaders* compiled by John Lockhart for the Institute for Social Research and Education, Oxford 1989 (private circulation only).

8. Quoted by Colin Ward in *Anarchy in Action*, George Allen and Unwin, London 1973, p. 19.

9. Percy Bysshe Shelley; notes to the poem *Queen Mab*, 1812.

GENERAL INDEX

INDEX OF GOSPEL PASSAGES